ECONOMICS
AND
ALL
THAT

Library of Congress Control Number: 2022944592

ISBN (hardback): 978-1-956450-94-1
(paperback Volume I): 978-1-956450-40-8
(paperback Volume II): 978-1-956450-65-1
(eBook Volume I): 978-1-956450-41-5
(eBook Volume II): 978-1-956450-66-8

Armin Lear Press Inc
215 W Riverside Drive, #4362
Estes Park, CO 80517

ECONOMICS
AND
ALL
THAT

VOLUME I: *Markets, Money, and Finance*

VOLUME 2: *From Firms and Industries to Labor, Government and the International Economy*

JEFFERSON HANE WEAVER

This book is dedicated to my mother and father,
Helen and George Weaver, and to my wife, Shelley Weaver.

CONTENTS
VOLUME 1

PART 1: MARKETS 1

PART 2: MONEY AND FINANCE 77

CONTENTS
VOLUME 2

PART 3: INFLATION AND UNEMPLOYMENT   245

PART 4: THE GOVERNMENT AND
THE ECONOMY   259

PART 5: INTERNATIONAL ECONOMICS   307

ABOUT THE AUTHOR   **353**

INTRODUCTION

Economics and All That explains the most important concepts of economics (or at least those concepts that the author feels are important) to both students and members of the lay audience who want to learn more about such things as markets and money and banks and trade. The title of this book is borrowed from the classic tongue-in-cheek thousand-year history of England called *1066 and All That,* which has been a classic for almost a century. Sadly, *Economics and All That* offers very little in the way of information about the history of England and even fails to include any gossip about the Royal Family. But it does attempt to explain over the course of 100 or so pithy essays many topics that invariably crop up in conversations at dinner parties and at high-end dance clubs such as the elasticity of demand, fiat money, the paradox of value, the yield curve, frictional unemployment, and monetarism. After all, there is little that can compare with an exhilarating discussion of oligopolistic pricing while one is sashaying across the dance floor to the throbbing beat of techno-punk hits.

So, the hope is that this book can be true to the subject of economics and offer clear-headed explanations of its most important concepts while having a little fun—through the use of silly and, often, self-deprecating examples—if only to keep the reading audience from nodding off or leaving the room altogether. The subject matter is discussed at an introductory level so that no prior knowledge of economics is required. But the author is confident that all readers will recognize the many profound insights into the human condition that are scattered throughout this book and feel that their lives have been immeasurably improved as a result of it. Regardless of whether you believe *Economics and All That* is a modern classic of economic literature worthy of a Noble Prize or not, the primary purpose of this book is to make the basic concepts of economics accessible and easily digestible. In this way, perhaps we can show that economics is the social science that is closest in spirit to the physical sciences in its efforts to map the patterns of and predict the future behavior of those curious individuals who populate our modern economy.

Economics was once described as the "dismal science" by Thomas Carlyle, the dour Scottish philosopher who was not known to be one who bought much joy and laughter to those around him. But his pessimism was exceeded by the gloomy predictions of Thomas Malthus, the English economist, who had concluded that the human population would grow at an exponential rate and invariably overwhelm its ability to grow enough food to feed itself. This cataclysmic event would then result in widespread starvation and misery and put a damper on everyone's evening.

Carlyle, however, was not about to let the prospect of millions of deaths stop him from understanding the fundamental *raison d'etre* of economics—which is to reconcile humanity's infinite wants with the limited means it possesses to satisfy those wants. Although this may sound like a dry, abstract principle, it is a struggle that each one of us must engage in every day as we try to acquire as many goods and services as we can with whatever money we have on hand. Indeed, no less an economist than the English poet Robert Browning declared that "a man's reach should exceed his grasp." His poem had more of an aspirational theme, but we could mangle its interpretation to think of it as a metaphor for our infinite wants as being incapable of being satisfied by the puny material means that we have in our hands at any one time. Or maybe not.

Some dreamers and poets (other than Mr. Browning, of course, who was clearly homing in on the most fundamental tenet of economics) might decry the crass materialism of the world of economics in which everything has a price and everyone must work to survive. But the continuous reconciliation of our limited bank accounts with our desires to own private jets and luxurious penthouse condominiums and fancy limousines is a fact of life that we cannot escape. Yet economics is inherently quantitative and those who are willing to draw upon their grade school mathematics may be able to find a way around their limited means (at least for a limited period of time until the creditors catch on) so that they can purchase goods that they might not have otherwise thought possible to acquire.

Whether we like it or not, we all must deal with economics and decisions involving money and the allocation of scarce resources. One does not even have to attend a fancy school to learn about economics because we all engage in behavior that mirrors many assumptions underlying the basic principles of economics: If the local grocery store lowers the price of milk, for example, then many of us will probably buy more milk (unless we are lactose-intolerant). The point is that economics is a social science, and its validity is ultimately dependent upon our delineating the collective behavioral patterns of human beings who we assume will usually act in pursuit of their own self-interests. Although economics is often laden with mathematical equations, its basic principles are rooted in anecdotes and everyday observations that have not changed appreciably in many hundreds of years.

PART ONE:
MARKETS

SUPPLY

In many ways, supply is the flip side of demand. Here, we begin with the basic assumption that the suppliers of a good will offer greater quantities of that good for sale as the price paid by buyers of the good increases. In other words, there is a direct relationship between increased prices and the increased production of a specific good. But this is not the entire story because the fact that people are willing to pay higher prices for a good does not constitute the sole determinant as to whether a firm will devote the additional resources needed to increase its production of that good. No, any decision to increase production will naturally depend on the firm's determination that such a decision makes sense from a financial standpoint. More specifically, the firm may produce more goods as long as the price it receives from the sale of those additional goods is greater than the cost of actually producing those very same goods.

To illustrate this principle, suppose that you are the owner of a firm that manufactures ornamental stuffed chickens for use by politically-correct vegan cults that do not want to harm living animals during their ritual sacrifices. You might offer your deceased poultry products at a price of $50.00 per chicken and, with your crack poultry stuffing staff of Old World Masters, Sven and Hugo, be able to produce 5,000 stuffed chickens per year.

What if these stuffed chickens suddenly become all the rage with people having little interest in rituals but who decided to wear them in place of hats? Your firm would be overwhelmed by the public's demand for this hot product and you could respond to this new craze for stuffed chicken hats by increasing the price of the stuffed chickens hats to capitalize on this buying frenzy. You could also consider increasing your production capabilities to get more stuffed chicken hats on the market as quickly as possible before the general public came to its senses and moved on to the "next big thing." Raising the price would be simple enough but you might decide that you could sell ten times the amount of your current production at the higher price and so you would want to consider how best to increase your production in the quickest and most efficient manner possible.

Because stuffing dead chickens is a labor intensive process that can only be carried out by skilled artisans, you might have to hire more Old World Masters to ramp up production. Because Old World Masters are typically in short supply, however, you might have to offer higher wages to both your new hires as well as to your existing employees to keep them from defecting to your chicken stuffing rival—Stuffed Chickens, Inc. You could also consider upgrading your current factory—the unventilated windowless basement under your house. Your Old World Masters would undoubtedly appreciate your providing some flashlights and cutting open a window for fresh air in order to show both your concern for the welfare of your chicken stuffers and quell any thoughts of rebellion or mutiny by your more restless employees.

So, by adding additional Old World Masters to your staff and throwing in a few workplace perks such as allowing each of your employees to have one half hour of exercise in your backyard each day, you would be ready to increase production dramatically. If the demand for stuffed chicken hats continued to soar, you should be able to sell thousands of additional units and, assuming the market price continues to exceed the cost of production, earn a tidy profit.

But what if the consuming public suddenly began to take a hard look at how horrid they look wearing dead chickens on their heads? What if these people decided *en masse* that they would no longer don poultry carcasses to make bold fashion statements and returned to more traditional forms of headwear such as fedoras and berets? As the owner of an ornamental chicken stuffing company, you would be dumbstruck by the consuming public's poor sense of timing and lack of gratitude given your recent expansion in production capacity. However, if your orders were now being cancelled left and right (and in between) so that you could now only sell 100 ornamental stuffed chickens a year, then you would have to cut your production costs sharply. This would probably entail firing all of your Old World Masters and perhaps even taking over the chicken stuffing duties yourself so that you could bring your costs in line with your greatly diminished revenues. This sad example illustrates a feature of the market that all sellers must contend with which is the fact that the demand for any given product (no matter how desirable) can change at a moment's notice and must therefore be monitored constantly.

DEMAND

The demand side of any market is based on the assumption that a fall in the price of a product or service will, all things being equal, cause people to increase their purchases of it. Following that same line of reasoning, a fall in the price of a product or service should lead consumers to clamor for more of it—regardless of its desirability. Like all assumptions, however, this one may not hold true in all cases. If a nuclear power plant is seeking to sell its radioactive waste materials as stocking stuffers for holiday shoppers, for example, the owners might first pick an arbitrary price and advertise its radioactive wastes for $100.00 per ton in its "winter wonderland sale." However, the owners might find—much to their surprise even several days after the sale had commenced—that no one was showing up at the front gate of the plant to purchase a couple of tons of radioactive wastes for their home and garden needs. This lack of interest might prompt the owners to conclude that the waste matter was overpriced and thus to begin a new advertising campaign featuring the "buy one ton, get one ton" sale of radioactive wastes. If there was still no interest in the product, the owners might drastically reduce the price to $100.00 for 10 tons of radioactive waste.

Although they might receive some random inquiries from several tin-pot dictators seeking inexpensive nuclear materials, the plant owners might find, much to their disappointment, that there was still no visible sign of interest on the part of the general public in radioactive knick-knacks. This would be an obvious example of a situation in which the product being offered for sale was so undesirable in the eyes of prospective purchasers that no amount of reductions in price could jumpstart sales. In a fit of desperation, the owners might resort to certain gimmicks to try to make the waste products more appealing to consumers such as covering each pile of waste in rich milk chocolate or infusing them with various fruit flavors. However, the owners would probably have to conclude at some point that radioactive wastes are such a dangerous product that no rational consumer would want to purchase them at any price— no matter how low the price.

This is certainly an absurd example but there are many equally preposterous ones that were actually real products, one of the most famous of which was Premier smokeless cigarettes. Introduced with great fanfare by RJ Reynolds in 1988, these cigarettes had no burn, no smoke, and no ashes to flick but they certainly had bad taste–described by the handful of duped users as "burning plastic." The poor reception convinced the higher-ups at RJ Reynolds to pull the plug on this innovative but unappealing product in short order– thus costing the company an estimated $800 million in losses–monies that were presumably deducted from the bonuses of soon-to-be former company executives.

In most cases, it is reasonable to assume that a fall in price will lead to an increase in demand and, conversely, that a rise in price will result in a reduced demand for that product. Certainly, this would be the case for most goods sold to consumers. A lower price for a can of beans, for example, should result in more cans of beans being sold unless there was some undesirable side effect resulting from the consumption of the beans such as bloated bellies and hour-long bouts of flatulence; these symptoms might dampen the general public's ardor for beans and more than offset the beneficial sales effect that we would expect a lower price to bring.

You can also have situations where the decision by a seller to drop the price of a good drastically might cause the prospective consumer to question the quality of the good itself. A vendor selling oranges that had turned black might cut the price in half to try to sell them quickly before they completely rot. But a buyer would probably not be keen to purchase black oranges no matter how exotic they appeared to be. Significant price drops might cause people to question the quality of the goods even when there is no actual deterioration in the quality of those goods—such as a "going out of business sale" in which a pet store is offering dog bowties at a 50 percent discount. People might be wary about this new price, fearing that the bowties might be of an inferior quality or that they would not be able to return them to the store if their dogs did not like them or refused to wear them due to their own fashion sensitivities.

It does not follow that a dramatic increase in the price of a good will necessarily choke off demand for that good. If John Paul Giorgio, the noted fashion designer, raises the prices of his top line of ballroom gowns—which are favored by wealthy female socialites and male cross dressers — the price increase might actually lead to an increase in demand for the gowns due to the perception that they are luxury products. Fans of John Paul Giorgio might worry that there will be additional price increases in the future and purchase more gowns to "beat the crowd." Or the attendant publicity surrounding the price increases might reaffirm in the minds of consumers that the gowns were even more prestigious than before and thus cause them to race over to the boutiques and climb over the backs of other shoppers who were not as fortunate to make it to the sales desks before being trampled to death.

SUPPLY AND DEMAND

Every market for goods and services consists of two groups of individuals or entities—those who supply the goods and services and those who consume (demand) those goods and services. At first glance, the interests of these two groups would appear to be diametrically opposed to each other so much so that they would stick their tongues out at each other and call each other names instead of engaging in commerce with each other. After all, the suppliers of any product want to charge the highest possible price for their goods whereas the consumers of those same products wish to purchase them at the lowest possible price. This would seem to present us with something of a quandary. How can two such divergent interests be reconciled without virulent name-calling or bloodshed? Must some power from above dictate the price at which any good or service can be bought and sold or can prices be set through a more autonomous, perhaps even more efficient process?

We should look at the market for antique fruitcakes to understand better how the price for a specific good arises from the voluntary interactions of buyers and sellers— as opposed to an artificial price set by all-knowing government officials. Of course, antique fruitcakes are a specialty dessert in which a single fruitcake such as the one once owned Napoleon Bonaparte may trade for thousands of dollars. The seller of an antique fruitcake will extol the succulent flavors of the dusty ingredients including fruits, candies, twigs, rocks, nails and glass in trying to convince wary buyers to make top-price offers. The prospective buyers, for their part, want to acquire antique fruitcakes for the lowest possible price; their enthusiasm for paying top dollar may also be mitigated by fears of bacterial infection. The seller of the Napoleonic fruitcake, for example, may set a price of ten thousand dollars; the prospective buyer may only be willing to pay four thousand dollars, perhaps thinking he should set some money aside to have his stomach pumped should the fruitcake prove to be a bit "tart." Our seller and buyer may go back and forth with their discussions and the seller may lower his price once he notices a strange black mold growing across the top of the fruitcake. The buyer, for his part, may raise his offer, perhaps mistaking the mold for a coating of Caspian Sea caviar. At the end of the day, the two parties may come to an agreement and complete the transaction at a price somewhere in between their original positions.

When one considers the worldwide market for antique fruitcakes in which many sellers and many buyers are actively buying and selling fruitcakes from each other, the story becomes a little more complicated but still can be extrapolated from the interactions of a single buyer and seller. The market price for antique fruitcakes arises from the bargaining between the sellers and the buyers of antique fruitcakes. As the sellers lower their prices and the buyers raise their offers, the supply and demand for antique fruitcakes moves closer and closer to a price where both the sellers and buyers are willing to part with their ossified baked goods and cash, respectively—even though the sellers are selling at a lower price and the buyers are buying at a higher price than they might have originally planned. The point at which the price offered by the sellers equals the price paid by the buyers is a magical moment in economics when the market for antique fruitcakes is in equilibrium. A price has thus been set through the autonomous activities of the buyers and sellers which will result in all the offered antique fruitcakes being purchased.

But the equilibrium of any market may not last very long as any number of things can cause the supply of or the demand for antique fruitcakes to change and thereby alter the market price for these tasty, albeit cement-like, bakery treats. If the International Fruitcake Council publishes an independent study by nutritionists (that was fully funded by the Council) stating that a steady diet of fruitcakes will extend the average lifespan of an adult by at least ten years, then we would not be surprised to see a massive upsurge in the demand for fruitcakes. People would be breaking down the doors of bakeries across the country to grab as many fruitcakes as they could. This spike in demand would result not only in an increased price for fruitcakes but, soon afterwards, an increase in the production of fruitcakes by manufacturers anxious to cash in on the frenzied demand for their product. Conversely, the discovery that several basic ingredients in fruitcakes such as asphalt and marbles could be produced more inexpensively due to recent innovations in the manufacturing process might reduce the costs of the fruitcakes themselves—assuming that the fruitcake manufacturers pass the savings onto consumers. In any event, a reduction in the price of the fruitcakes should lead to an increase in demand for these baked treasures which should, in turn, result in a new price equilibrium.

ELASTICITY OF DEMAND

Suppose that you and I were both interested in purchasing the Flying Squirrel Furniture Company's newly released "catapult recliner," which features a spring-loaded seat that not only helps people to their feet but, if they are feeling particularly adventurous, tosses them up to thirty feet into the air, thereby greatly reducing the time needed to walk to the kitchen during commercial breaks on the television set. The catapult recliner features state of the art catapulting technology which incorporates significant advances over its medieval forbearers and comes in a variety of fabrics and colors—thus making it the sensible furnishing choice for anyone who likes to be launched through the air, regardless of nationality or political affiliation. However, you and I may not desire to own a catapult recliner with the same degree of fervor. In other words, I might have been dreaming about owning a catapult recliner for many years whereas you might have had only a casual interest in possessing such a unique piece of furniture. You might agree that my becoming a catapult recliner owner is more important to me than it is to you—even though we might both be willing to pay the same $1,000.00 price tag to purchase it.

But what if the Flying Squirrel Furniture Company decided to double the price of a single recliner to $2,000.00, after seeing news reports of people lining up and camping out for weeks in front of furniture retail stores across the country so that they could be the first to purchase a catapult recliner? Because of my obsession with all things catapult—extending to tattooing a catapult on my bottom—I might still be willing to pay the higher price for the recliner—even though I would not be able to purchase groceries for a month. However, you, having only been mildly tempted by the original $1,000.00 price tag, would probably decide that you did not need such a recliner at double the price and might instead invest your money in something more practical such as a home taxidermy kit. The fact that I am willing to pay the higher price and you are not illustrates the differing elasticities of demand that we have for the recliner. After all, I still want to purchase the recliner at double the original price (which shows that I have an eye for a bargain) whereas you are far less keen to acquire the recliner at the new price and would prefer to begin disemboweling wild animals in your living room with your newly acquired taxidermy tools. My ardor for the recliner illustrates that my demand for it is far more inelastic than your demand for the recliner because my desire to purchase it did not change despite a doubling of the price. Your demand for the recliner is far more elastic in that it became far less fervent with the increase in the price of the recliner.

Whether the catapult chair is considered a necessity with few alternatives like drinking water or a good for which alternative substitutes are available is also important in considering the concept of elasticity. Everyone needs to drink water or at least add some water to their vodka as a chaser. People who have studied medicine and think they know more than the rest of us about the needs of the human body (just because they have years of training and a medical degree and thousands of hours of clinical experience) say that we can only live for a few days without water. This means that water is essential for life and does not have any substitutes—not even very moist cupcakes. Because we have to drink water to live, our demand for water is inelastic. Our demand for water will not change very much regardless of whether the price of a glass of water doubles, triples or even quadruples. However, there are other items such as catapult recliners which, despite my beliefs to the contrary, are not critical to human life. Many people might be happy with an ordinary chair that has no launching capabilities whatsoever. For these people, a change in the price of the catapult recliner will cause them to look for other types of chairs to satisfy their seating needs. Their willingness to consider other types of chairs reflects a greater elasticity of demand on their part or, alternatively stated, a greater willingness to consider alternative furnishings in response to a significant increase in price.

CONSPICUOUS CONSUMPTION

Many of us would like to be the center of attention in a crowd of people. There is nothing more satisfying than to walk into a room and bring all the facile conversations to a halt accompanied by the swiveling of every head in your direction. For most of us, however, that will not happen unless we run into the room while naked or on fire. But there are some individuals who crave the attention of others and have the resources to buy expensive cars, clothes, and homes so that they can attract the jealous stares of their neighbors and colleagues. After all, what is the point of driving an expensive car or living in a mansion if you cannot cause everyone you know who cannot afford these luxuries to feel empty and inadequate?

Buying expensive luxury items to cause others to feel jealous of you is an example of what we call conspicuous consumption. It was a term coined by the economist Thorstein Veblen in his *Theory of the Leisure Class* which contrasted what he saw as the frugal individualism of his native Norway with the mindless, almost herd-like efforts by Americans to accumulate luxury items and thereby emulate the lifestyles of the upper class in the late 19th century. For Veblen, the desire of ordinary individuals to step into the shoes of their economic superiors—if only for a little while—was nothing new but the widespread adoption by ordinary citizens of the tastes embraced by the wealthy was facilitated by the mass marketing of comparatively inexpensive replicas ("knock-offs") of such things as clothing and jewelry.

But the term conspicuous consumption has a snarky connotation because it suggests that the purchase or acquisition of an item is motivated by something more than just the desire to use that item. Suppose that you have just purchased a lovely full-length, red-striped skunk fur coat imbued with authentic odor. Animal rights' activists have not bothered you because no one can come within twenty feet of you while you are wearing your coat. Indeed, it is this overwhelming stench and the difficulty of finding a red-striped skunk at all that makes this fur coat such a rare find. And as you have plenty of money due to a suspicious inheritance, you could have purchased any of a wide variety of fur coats. But you wanted to make a statement about your individuality and broadcast to the least fortunate of your neighbors that you are a trendsetter and a collector of luxurious and extremely rare things such as a coat fashioned from the pelts of the seldom-seen red-striped skunk. You also wanted to enter the dining room at your country club and see the looks of want and sadness in the eyes of your friends and acquaintances who know that they can never hope to have a red-striped skunk fur coat of their own. How wonderful to be able to trigger such feelings of jealousy and uselessness by merely wearing a simple garment!

So even though you have a rare coat that very few mortals can ever hope to wear, the fact that it becomes an iconic fashion statement will be recognized by many enterprising plagiarists. These copy-cats, always in search of a quick dollar, will start looking for pelts that can be dyed to look like those of red-striped skunks and then stitching them together into coats that (after being infused with horrible smells) can be sold to penny-pinching customers who want that *haute couture* look at bargain basement prices. Hundreds of thousands of consumers can purchase these *faux* red-striped skunk fur coats for a fraction of the amount you paid and revel in the fact that they (and most of their neighbors and colleagues at work) are wearing a garment that appears to be both very rare and very expensive.

This mass production of knock-off red striped skunk fur coats will thus enable individuals of modest means to enjoy at least some semblance of the good life every time they put on their coats and pinch their noses. So even though the term conspicuous consumption was originally applied to members of the *nouveau riche* upper class who purchased items such as red striped skunk fur coats to demonstrate their real or imagined social status, it was later used to refer to those member of the middle or working class who sought at least a fleeting taste of the prestige enjoyed by the wealthiest citizens as a result of their purchases of knock-off clothing and jewelry.

Sociologists later expanded and refined the concept of conspicuous consumption by coining two new terms—invidious consumption and conspicuous compassion. Invidious consumption is essentially a restatement of Veblen's original concept of people consuming luxury goods to provoke feelings of jealousy in their peers. However, conspicuous compassion refers to individuals who make charitable donations to demonstrate their financial heft as opposed to any real desire to help improve the lives of others. The fact that these individuals can also get their picture in the newspaper for making a tax-deductible charitable donation is an added bonus because no one ever gets their picture taken for paying their taxes.

THE INVISIBLE HAND

One could imagine a horror movie entitled *The Invisible Hand* featuring a ghostly hand that had been severed from the body of a dead king which had subsequently come back to life and begun exacting revenge on each of the decedent's murderers. Although such a movie would probably be very popular with monarchists, it would not have very much to do with the "invisible hand" that is discussed when considering the behavior of buyers and sellers in markets. The "invisible hand" of economics—which was first offered by the 18th century Scottish economist and social philosopher Adam Smith in his heavy book *The Wealth of Nations*—was considerably more benign than might otherwise be expected from its horror movie manifestations and, in any event, certainly did not go around running swords through evildoers. However, Smith's "invisible hand" was a conceptual breakthrough whereby Smith sought to explain why markets form spontaneously from the independent and self-interested actions of millions of vendors and their customers—without any guidance or dictates from a preening, self-indulgent central government.

Smith's analysis began with the question as to what prompts individuals to enter into markets—whether as sellers of meat, clothing or cat mittens or as buyers for those very same items. After all, no one orders these individuals to sell or buy these products but people nevertheless engage in numerous voluntary transactions with each other even though they may not know each other or even like each other.

So why do markets arise spontaneously almost like a phoenix from the chaos of a world in which everyone is supposedly trying to maximize their own economic self-interests? Why do any goods or services ever change hands at all if every buyer and every seller is looking out only for his or her own welfare? Smith's genius was to recognize that the apparently conflicting self-interests on the part of buyers and sellers of goods and services was also the reason that such transactions ultimately occurred. As an example, you could be the greediest fish-head vendor in the world but if you priced your fish heads at three times the going rate being charged by other vendors of these pungent but tasty treats, then you would probably find that no one would stop by your shop to purchase your products—despite their becoming more pungent with each passing day. After a week or so of watching your fish heads literally rot on your shop floor, you would have to consider if your pricing decision may have been a bit rash. Indeed, you might conclude that if you wanted to stay in the glamorous business of fish-head sales, you would have no choice but to lower your prices to be able to compete with those prices offered by your competitors unless you simply enjoyed stepping over rotting fish all day long and prized the autonomy of being your own boss.

The fish head peddler example underscores the way in which self-interest or, alternatively, financial survival, causes any vendor who is interested in making a living by selling his or her products to adjust the product prices until he or she can find enough buyers to purchase all the inventory. Of course, rotting fish heads may be an exception to this general principle as it may be impossible to sell out the supply at any price because very few people really have a desire to purchase them. But the invisible hand of the market ultimately comes into play because even though every seller wants to sell their product for as high a price as possible and every buyer wants to purchase those products for as low a price as possible, both parties must adjust their expectations if they wish to conclude a deal at all. If they do not come to an agreement, then the seller loses the sale and the buyer is unable to acquire the product. The invisible hand referred to by Smith may be thought of as the pricing adjustments that both sellers and buyers are required to make as they negotiate the terms of their agreement even though neither is compelled to do so.

PARADOX OF VALUE

Many philosophers—their keen intellects sharpened over time by vigorous debates over the number of angels that can dance of the head of a pin and the types of pins that might be used by the angels and the kind of music that would cause the angels to begin furiously strumming "air guitars"—have wondered about the "paradox of value." In a nutshell, the paradox of value raises the question as to why some things such as basic foodstuffs (for example, water, beef, vegetables), which are vital to our daily survival, are so much less expensive than other items such as gold coins or silver bullion or sparkling jewels, which have no nutritional value and contribute nothing to our physical well-being. So why would we place a higher value on a gold coin instead of a glass of water in terms of their relative prices?

One response might be that we are very stupid. However, economists and philosophers have devised an explanation for this paradox of value which causes goods such as gold coins (which are of no relevance to our satisfying our basic biological needs) to be prized a thousand times greater than a cup of water (which is of vital importance to life itself). The answer to this paradox lies in the concept of marginal utility and the relative scarcity of each of these items.

"Now we are getting somewhere!" you might say. "Marginal utility! Scarcity! Please tell me more!" Very well. You will recall that the concept of utility relates to the satisfaction experienced by an individual that results from the consumption of a particular good or service. In short, utility describes the amount of pleasure that you derive from the acquisition of that item. The so-called diamond-water paradox is explained by noting that it is not the total utility of the diamonds or the water that determines the price that you or I are willing to pay. Instead, it is the incremental or marginal utility that the consumption of a unit of either diamonds or water brings to the consumer that sets the relative values of the two commodities. Diamonds are extremely scarce, and water is quite plentiful in the world. Hence, the value of exchange of diamonds (to borrow from Adam Smith's argument in *The Wealth of Nations*) is going to be far greater than the value of exchange of water because diamonds are very hard to find and are sparkly whereas water is, well, water. However, the value of use of water is going to be greater than the value of use of diamonds because water is necessary for life whereas diamonds are worn to proclaim status and display wealth and can sit in a drawer when they are not needed. As a result, one has to consider both the value of exchange and the value of use of an item to understand the paradox of value: An object that has a very high value of exchange such as diamonds may have a very low value of use as diamonds are not really needed for us to carry out our daily business. Similarly, water has a very low value of exchange because the earth is covered by water, but it does have a very high value of use because people usually die if they are deprived of water for more than a few days.

The permutations of this paradox may be considered further if we consider the more obscure leather nightwear-water paradox that has been made up especially for this essay. Suppose that your purchase of an exotic leather outfit with a matching bullwhip brings you far more pleasure than drinking a glass of water. If that is true, then we can say that the dominatrix ensemble brings a greater degree of utility to you than the consumption of the water even though water is clearly more important than the leather outfit in sustaining life (as opposed to sustaining the life of a costume party where the leather outfit would clearly be more useful). There is nothing terribly exciting about water. Indeed, once you have drunk a glass of water and satisfied your thirst, the marginal utility that is experienced from consuming a second or third or fourth glass of water will probably decline precipitously as you become waterlogged and have to make trips to the bathroom.

The difficulty of finding such a fine example of leather craftsmanship along with a matching monogrammed whip that can cut through the air like a razor means that your acquisition of it will give you a great deal of pleasure—far in excess of that which could be obtained from drinking even the purest bottled water in the world. Water is very common and can be found in any part of the world; black leather outfits with the exposed buttock openings are comparatively difficult to locate and not even carried by most fine clothing retailers. As a result, this scarcity causes such outfits to command a correspondingly higher price. Of course this entire analysis may be worth less than the paper it is printed on if your plane (which has the outfit in your luggage) goes down in the middle of the Sahara Desert. After a few days without water, you may be willing to trade your entire collection of fine leatherwear for a single glass of water. But this does not get us away from the fact that we have to consider both the value of exchange (price) and the value of use (relevance to sustaining life) of both the leather outfit and the water to understand better the paradox of value.

THE EFFICIENCY OF THE MARKETS

Efficiency is generally viewed as a good thing. To be efficient with one's time is typically regarded as a virtue. Of course, the desirability of any virtue can have its limits. If you were a sloth in your habits who found even the prospect of climbing out of bed before noon each day to be absolutely daunting, you might find a highly-efficient partner who is a blur of motion and energy to be aggravating because you do not attach the same importance to putting your dirty underwear in the clothes hamper instead of leaving it on top of a lamp-shade. Whether life with an efficient person is a won-drous blessing or a living hell arguably depends on the perspective of the narrator.

For economists, the idea that markets are efficient is an assumption that underpins the field of economics. It is no less central to classical economics than Euclid's axioms are to geometry. As with every other social (and physical) science, it is necessary to make certain basic assumptions about the phenomena that you wish to study or else you will find yourself doomed to travel toward an ever-receding horizon in search ever-more fundamental principles with which to anchor your anal-ysis. As a result, one must devise certain arbitrary but foundational principles that can serve as the intellectual bedrock upon which the scaffolding of the field of eco-nomics may be erected. No doubt the concept of effi-ciency is a shining star in the firmament of the so-called dismal science because the allocations of scare resources to satisfy infinite wants in the most efficient way pos-sible is the reason for its very existence as a discipline.

An efficient market is one in which all the actors (buyers and sellers) are presumed to possess perfect information about the products and services being mar-keted. Therefore, if you decide one day that you would like to buy a purple wool overcoat lined with peacock feathers, you are presumed to know or be able to obtain fairly easily any information that might relate to purple wool overcoats lined with peacock feathers. This would include information about which company produces the highest quality overcoats and the prices charged by each of the leading manufacturers, and so forth. In a world in which the internet is available to provide the unvarnished truth about every conceivable matter possible, the efficient market hypothesis would suggest that I would be able to assemble all the information I needed in order to decide which purple wool overcoat with peacock feathers to purchase.

Indeed, you might be overjoyed to find on a random search of the term "purple clothing" that the Purple Threads Emporium does indeed have a purple wool overcoat lined with peacock *and* ostrich feathers—but less excited to learn that it was for sale for the princely sum of $500.00. Now you would be willing to wear a purple wool overcoat with peacock *and* ostrich feathers to a red-carpet premiere but you would not be willing to part with $500.00 for an overcoat. But at least you have been able to utilize information about the price of the overcoat to have some sort of vague idea as to what such a garment might cost.

But the real world is a little messier than the pristine abstractions underpinning the efficient market hypothesis. Because purple wool overcoats lined with peacock feathers are not widely sold, you might find it difficult for purposes of comparison shopping to locate other stores carrying this garment, even if you went so far to search on the internet for "purple wool overcoats lined with peacock feathers." And wandering around your favorite clothing stores might prove to be equally unsuccessful as you might find yourself turned away by hostile salesclerks indignant at the thought that they would stock such an *avant garde* garment.

But you could continue your efforts find a second-hand store that might carry the overcoat or even start asking your friends if they might know of a store that would have the keen fashion insight to stock such a product. You could even beg some of your colleagues at work to allow you to come to their homes and search through their closets to see if they might have anything resembling a purple wool overcoat with peacock feathers. Even though some might not appreciate the lengths you were willing to go to find your prized garment, they would have to admire your tenacity—even if they had to call the police to remove you from their homes.

Imagine that days pass into weeks and weeks into months and you are unable to find any other purple woolen overcoats with any type of ornithological decorations—whether it be peacock, ostrich, chicken or even feathery dogs. This would, of course, be very frustrating, because it would mean you might have to dig up $500.00 to purchase that very smart overcoat still sitting in the Purple Threads Emporium if you still wanted to acquire it. Your inability to find any similar type of overcoat with which you could compare prices might lead you to conclude that there simply are not many purple wool overcoats to be found, no matter where you happen to look. The market could be telling you that the absence of information merely reflects an absence of the desired product and perhaps some hope for the aesthetic tastes and fashion sensibilities of humanity. After all, a market can be perfectly efficient and provide the information to a prospective buyer but if the product is so unpopular or otherwise unavailable, all the information in the world is not going to change the fact that you may have but one purple woolen overcoat with peacock feathers to select from in the entire world.

PARETO EFFICIENCY

Economists are very concerned about the efficient allocation of resources in society as humanity's infinite wants must be reconciled with the limited means it has to satisfy those wants. The satisfaction of those desires on an individual basis necessarily leads us to the concept of utility, which is premised on the idea that each person will usually select the most desirable of the available options in order to maximize their pleasure or happiness. This makes intuitive sense as we would expect most people to act in their own self-interest because certain decisions will be beneficial whereas other decisions may be less beneficial or even harmful. Indeed, much of economics and the assumptions underpinning its most basic principles are necessarily dependent on the idea that people are rational individuals who will seek the best possible or, alternatively, the most rewarding outcome among all possible alternatives. The Italian engineer Vilfredo Pareto offered the notion that these choices by all individuals to maximize their welfare would give rise to a situation in which no other actions by any person would be possible without causing one or more individuals to be made worse off—the so-called state of Pareto efficiency or Pareto optimality.

Suppose that I have a head of lettuce and three pinecones in my lunchbox as part of my neo-vegetarian diet promising reduced cholesterol and a longer life—or at least one that seems longer. You, on the other hand, have recently begun the highly-popular chocolate frosted doughnut regimen which expressly prohibits the consumption of foods having any measurable nutritional value—a diet which is followed unknowingly in various forms by most consumers in our sophisticated modern society. Although I now have numerous stitches in my mouth due to the difficulty of chewing the pinecones, I have persisted in my quest to enjoy this crude cuisine. You, on the other hand, have steadfastly avoided anything even remotely beneficial to your health. Yet we both share a common opinion in that we both hate our diets. I detest "roughage" and dream of eating chocolate covered doughnuts whereas you are revolted at the idea of consuming another wad of sugary dough. Because we have both stockpiled enormous quantities of our respective dietary delights due to our both having originally overestimated the zeal with which we were going to pursue our respective diets, it seems that we are destined either to force ourselves to finish them up (however violently) or simply throw them away.

But there is a third alternative that would enable us to avoid having our stomachs pumped and that is for each of us to exchange some of our dietary treats with each other so that I can enjoy the sugary smoothness of your doughnuts and you can savor the spikey delightfulness of my pinecones. Because we are both eager to try each other's goodies, we both realize a greater degree of satisfaction by adding a little variety to our respective diets. You are happier grinding pinecone chips between your teeth, and I am thrilled to sink my teeth into your soft sensuous chocolate doughnuts. We have both increased our satisfaction and so we are both better off than before we were before—at least in a culinary sense. Professor Pareto, who may have spent a great deal of time thinking about pinecones and doughnuts, would say that this new situation of shared diets was a Pareto improvement or, alternatively stated, represented a more efficient allocation of resources between the two of us.

Our original dietary selections would be characterized as being inefficient from Pareto's perspective because both you and I were made better off in terms of our personal satisfaction by our exchange of pinecones and doughnuts. This exchange resulted in an overall improvement in efficiency from Pareto's standpoint. This would be true even if one of us was indifferent to whether we ate pinecones or doughnuts. As long as the trade of one for the other provided greater satisfaction to at least one of us, then the new allocation of pinecones and doughnuts would represent an overall improvement in satisfaction and bring a smile to Pareto's face. Unless, of course, he had been eating too many pinecones.

RISK AND REWARD

Anyone who has ever gone on a blind date has some familiarity with the concept of risk and reward. In the brutal search for a mate, the prize is the perfect match but the would-be Romeo (or Juliet) must also put aside their fears of rejection or bodily injury in order to spend some time with their would-be partner and find out if he or she is truly the "one" (or at least a solid "two" or "three"). But investors and economists are also cognizant of the trade-off between higher rates of return and higher degrees of risk. The safest investments such as cash earn very little interest when they are deposited in savings accounts at banks. Other types of investments such as stocks and real estate are inherently riskier but may provide greater rates of return to investors. Unlike cash in a savings account, the values of stocks can fluctuate wildly. Fortunes can be made or lost in the blink of an eye in the stock market. The pile of cash sitting comfortably in the bank vault, however, will continue earning a steady, albeit miniscule, rate of interest. Of course, if safety is your concern, there is no better place to keep your cash than in your undergarments. The rate of interest earned by that cash will drop to zero but you will never have to lie awake in bed at night staring at the ceiling wondering if your cash is being removed from the bank vault under cover of darkness by unscrupulous bankers.

The point: Investors expect to receive greater returns from those investments having correspond-ingly greater risks of failure. But the greater risk poses a greater likelihood that an individual could lose their entire investment. The possibility of receiving an extraordinary return on an investment prompts most individuals to assume that risk.

Suppose that you are a budding venture capital-ist who wishes to invest $100,000 of your hard-earned funds in a device that converts cow dung into fine choc-olate candies. Fancying yourself as one who can spot the next big thing, you imagine the possibilities of convert-ing millions of tons of bovine waste into tasty bon-bons with no discernable material costs other than those incurred in collecting the manure from the pastures and transporting the manure to the factory for processing. But you also realize that the finished product poses cer-tain problems in terms of potentially negative public perceptions. After all, it does give new meaning to the phrase "Eat Sh*t!" Indeed, very few people who are not avowed scatologists relish the idea of consuming animal wastes even that which is produced by pure-bred cows. The device, which you believe can be mass-produced, does pose certain risks that people might not wish to use it at all—let alone consume its products. Most people probably would not even embrace the idea of carrying a shovel out to a pasture to seek fresh ingredients for their confectionary activities. Therefore, the potentially vast rewards of being able to manufacture practically limitless amounts of chocolate treats for very little cost carries great allure even though it may pose a public relations problem.

Whether you press forward with your confectionary gamble will probably depend on a variety of factors such as test-marketing the chocolates with select focus groups so that you can identify potential marketing issues with these products. The other determinant may be the willingness or unwillingness of your lenders to fund your venture due to their concerns about the public's willingness to embrace this product. The cost of the venture may also require you to enlist the support of various investors who will also have to be convinced of both the worthiness of the product itself and the potential size of the marketplace for what your advertising agency calls "pasture confectionary." All these factors will enter into the calculus of risk that necessarily must be considered before the product can be launched. And because of the uniqueness of the product, there is really no way to quantify fully the risk of failure beforehand. In short, you may have no choice but to walk the plank and take a flying leap of faith to see if the risk of this product is ultimately justified by the reward.

RISK AND UNCERTAINTY

Every decision we make in life has elements of risk or uncertainty. This truth carries over to the world of economics where we are constantly besieged with choices as to what items we should purchase or which investments we should make or even which numbers we should select on a roulette wheel. Although risk and uncertainty might appear to be synonymous with each other, they are really very different concepts because risk may be calculated mathematically whereas uncertainty is, well, uncertain. What do we mean by this academic blather? Risk may be calculated using probability theory whereas uncertainty—that is, the occurrence or non-occurrence of a certain event—cannot be mathematically determined. This idea may be better illustrated by turning to the actuarial studies of an Englishman named John Gant, who discovered that the births and deaths of his fellow English countrymen could be systematically catalogued. This grouping and organizing of seemingly random events enabled Gant to discern certain patterns in these births and deaths that could make it possible to predict some of the demographic trends of the population as a whole; this achievement thus gave birth to the field of statistics.

Probability theory enables us to examine the masses of demographic data and thereby predict with some degree of accuracy when a particular individual of a specific age and background can be expected to die. This does not mean that you can predict with any certainty when any given individual, such as your mortal enemy, will draw his last breath unless, of course, you expedite the process by by putting a pillow over his face. But Gant's prescient observations gave rise to a trillion-dollar life insurance industry in which exacting calculations could be made as to the expected lifespans of individuals wishing to purchase life insurance policies and the premiums that needed to be collected for such coverages so that the insurers themselves could remain in business. The added benefit of getting people to pay hefty premiums for death benefit policies is that the redemption of these policies greatly assist the decedent's grief-stricken relatives and very young trophy wives in getting over the tragedy of their loss—in about ten minutes.

Unlike risk, uncertainty involves events in which there is no mathematical method for calculating the probability that an event may or may not occur. You can put this theory to the test by standing in the middle of a department store and then leaping out from behind a rack of clothes and proposing marriage to every woman who happens to wander into view. Although the question "Will you marry me?" typically invites two distinct responses ("Oh, yes!" or "Not if you were the last man on earth!"), there is really no way to calculate beforehand whether your inquiry will be favorably received or not. Of course, the student who has taken a course in statistics and wishes to curry favor with the instructor by pointing out that there are only two possible outcomes—"Yes!" and "No!"—would be assuming that a decision to marry is akin to a coin flip. But one cannot say with any certainty that a marriage proposal offered to a stranger in a department store would have a 50 percent chance of success and a 50 percent chance of failure—even though you could try to sweeten the pot and, hence, secure an affirmative response, by proffering fake tax returns to your prospective bride which purport to show that you are the wealthiest person in the United States. But affairs of the heart are not precise undertakings as compared to the odds of whether a coin lands on head or tails. Indeed, your repeated marriage proposals to dozens of passing women might result in an extremely messy situation with three women spraying you with mace and four women promising to mull over your proposal and six women slapping your face and seven women saying that they actually prefer the company of other women and twelve women advising you that they had suddenly decided to join a convent and would thus be unable to consider you as a future mate. The net result from this admittedly dangerous exercise is that you would have no clear idea as to what you could expect because the response would not be limited to a simple "yes" or "no" but could range from the wildly enthusiastic to the deeply negative with all variants in between. No matter how skillful your statistical skills might be, however, you would not be able to predict the likelihood of any woman's response to your proposal.

MORAL HAZARD

Imagine that you liked to drive your car very fast through hospital zones and bus stops and knew that you could smash into as many cars as you wished but that you would never be required to pay for any damages nor prosecuted for any of your crimes by the authorities. In short, you would never face any consequences for damages and injuries caused by your careless actions. You would be free to act out your most nihilistic fantasies while using your car as a battering ram without a thought that you might be spending the rest of your life in a cramped cell with a homicidal roommate.

This freedom from having to worry about any adverse results that might arise from your blatantly anti-social behavior reflects the absence of moral hazard in the calculus of your decision-making process. The concept of moral hazard arises from a shared desire by society to tie together undesirable actions with the unpalatable consequences that will be suffered by the perpetrators of these acts and, hopefully, deter such conduct in the future.

Moral hazard is a key element of life insurance policies. When an insurance company issues a policy to a person, the policy premiums are based upon several factors including the age and gender of the individual as well as the extent to which the insured indulges in smoking or drinking as well as hazardous physical activities such as skydiving. Insurance companies always want to assess the risks posed by insuring an individual and, as a result, they will want to gather as much information as possible about the applicant. If they discover that the applicant likes to juggle live hand grenades at the company holiday party or sneaks into the serpent pit at the local zoo so he can become a better snake charmer and avoid being bitten so often by cobras, then the insurance company is going to be very concerned about the wisdom of insuring the applicant at all. People who appear to have a death wish are the last type of customer that any insurance company wants to have because these individuals do not seem to care about their own physical well-being. They are not motivated to avoid the consequences of their dangerous hobbies. As a result, they are considered to be a greater risk because they do not think about what could go wrong and thus subject themselves and their insurance carrier to excessive risks.

The rest of us who are not enthusiastic about learning to juggle hand grenades or charm cobras want insurance companies to price the risks of these dangerous hobbies into the policies that they ultimately issue to these individuals who walk to the beat of a different drummer. For one thing, the incorporation of an analysis of the risks that dangerous behavior will result in undesirable (and costly outcomes), will mean that these individuals will pay a lot more for their insurance policies. If all goes well, those of us who do not go near hand grenades or cobras, should see much lower policy premiums; a recognition by the insurance company that our comparatively sedate lifestyles will mean a far lower probability of having to pay out a death benefit prematurely. If insurance companies simply charged the same premium to everyone—regardless of any extenuating factors such as age, gender, medical history—then those of us who behaved ourselves would find ourselves paying higher prices for our insurance policies and, in effect, subsidizing the policies being issued to the high-risk individuals. This effort to rate the risks posed by everyone's personal circumstances and thus calculate an appropriate premium in effect adopts the concept of moral hazard by imposing higher insurance costs on those who insist on engaging in nitwit behavior.

RISK AVOIDANCE AND INSURANCE

Suppose that you lived in the magical town of Happy Valley where everyone was clean and honest, and no one ever locked their doors because theft was almost unknown. As the possibility of property loss would be perceived to be very low by the townspeople, you might find that your career as a property insurance salesperson would be on the skids. After all, insurance is a product that is designed to enable people who are risk adverse to protect themselves financially in the event of a loss—regardless of whether it results from theft or a casualty event (for example, fire or flood) or some other form of covered loss. If you are the enterprising sort, you might devise a clever scheme to increase the demand for property insurance by donning a black mask and cape and breaking into homes in the middle of the night to demonstrate first-hand the need for theft insurance. As news got out about the rash of home burglaries by the bandit popularly dubbed "the guy with the mask," you might find the demand for property insurance coverage would increase dramatically and your sale of policies would skyrocket. But after a while the surge in sales would subside because there are only so many people who will act responsibly to insure their possessions from theft.

After the initial excitement died down and the sale of theft insurance policies flattened out, you might seek a new line of business by donning a red mask and cape and setting bonfires in front of private homes. After all, there is nothing that stokes the popular interest in casualty insurance more than the specter of one's home sweet home going up in flames. The broadcast on the local evening news of repeated stories of flames rising just a few feet away from extremely combustible wooden houses throughout Happy Valley would make all but the most thickheaded of the remaining homeowners seek casualty policies to protect their homes. Your responsibility would be to collect premium checks and issue as many policies as possible, all the while avoiding detection or capture by the police.

People do not like to buy insurance because it is not a tangible asset. It is a contract that will be triggered only if the policyholder suffers some sort of loss—which could range from the loss of one's home to the loss of one's life. At least with homeowner's insurance, the policyholder may get to rebuild his or her home and perhaps do a better job the second time around in picking the furnishings and selecting color schemes that did not go out of fashion in the 18th century. Life insurance is not such a great thing for the insured because he or she must die for the policy to pay out. However, it can be a cause for celebration for the beneficiary of the policy, particularly if he or she was not very fond of the decedent even though the beneficiary will doubtless have a fleeting thought or two about the decedent when racing around town in a newly purchased automobile or taking a cruise around the world. If you have a hefty life insurance policy in place when you die, then you should take some comfort in knowing that a person who is largely indifferent to whether you live or die has seen his or her lot in life greatly improved by your demise.

Insurance policies must also address actual conditions that cause individuals to be concerned about their well-being. If people do not perceive there to be any risk of loss from a certain type of event, then they will not purchase an insurance policy to protect themselves from that event. A person who daydreams of having a yacht but who cannot even afford a kayak will not be very interested in purchasing boat insurance.

Not surprisingly, insurance appeals more to those responsible individuals who want to protect their families and their assets than it does to those devil-may-care free spirits who live life on the edge and refuse to wash their hands in public restrooms. The more concerned you are about the uncertainties of the world, the more appealing you will find the comforting blanket of insurance coverage. But your desire for homeowner's insurance, for example, will also depend on whether you own much in the way of actual property and, if so, whether it is of any real value. If you live in a grass hut and own only a few scraps of clothing and a table and a bed, you might not be very interested in purchasing insurance because the replacement cost of your possessions is virtually nil. The fact that your grass hut burns to the ground might not trouble you very much because there is a lot of grass around your hut and you can, if you so choose, gather more grass and build an even bigger grass hut (perhaps even a split-level or two-story grass hut) in a day or two.

The policies offered by the insurance company itself as well as the premiums it charges for various levels of coverage are all dependent on its statistical analysis of the expected frequency of the insured event (for example, fire or death) over time and the expected amount of losses resulting from that event. The insurance company is not driven by altruistic concerns about lessening the suffering of people who have been devastated by fire or theft but instead by the profits to be earned by collecting enough premiums from enough customers to more than cover the costs of any payouts over a given period of time. The greater the number of policies sold, the more the insurance company can mitigate its own risks because it clearly has no way of determining ahead of time which house will burn down when.

AUCTIONS

Few things are more exciting than a high-stakes auction in which wealthy collectors and investors alike bid on items ranging from timeless masterpieces by Renaissance painters to extraordinarily ugly objects prized by the most esteemed tastemakers in high society. The purpose of an auction from the viewpoint of the seller is to get as much money as possible from the sale of the item. The buyer, by contrast, wants to submit the lowest winning bid and not engage in a needlessly costly battle with another bidder for the final say as to who will win the prize. The fun and, some would say, the peril of an auction is that the bidders can get carried away in the heat of a bidding war for a historically unique item such as a preserved dropping from Napoleon's horse and pay far more than they might if the event were held in a neighbor's basement. The overpayment by a bidder for an item is always welcome by the seller of that item because the seller naturally wants to see a furious bidding war. The back and forth of an auction, like the bright lights and sounds of a casino, encourage emotional, even reckless, decisions to overpay for items one might not otherwise even consider.

Getting caught up in a titanic battle to win a prize at auction can give rise to the so-called winner's curse—which occurs when the winning bidder submits a higher bid than would have otherwise been needed to win the auction. Suppose that a highly fashionable Tulie, a designer shawl woven from tarantula hair still attached to live tarantulas, is offered for bid. The bidding begins and, after a frenzied twenty-minute contest of bids and counterbids, the current bid for the Tulie (whose placement in the main room of the auction house has caused the first eight rows of seats to empty out) stands at $100,000. The bidding is down to two parties as all the other participants have dropped out, finding the bids to be too rich for their blood. You are one of the two remaining bidders, the other being your childhood nemesis, Richard "Icky Dickey" Walden, who pushed you off a slide when you were six years old. It is with a burning desire to embarrass Dickey that you have eyed his $100,000 bid and readied a crushing response to deprive him of the glory of winning this magnum opus of haute couture. But you want to do more than just win; you want to rub his nose in the proverbial playground dirt. You ready your bid. It is not $110,000 or $120,000 or even $150,000. No, you take a deep breath and proclaim your winning bid of $200,000, basking in the triumph of having finally vanquished Dickey. The auctioneer's gavel drops and you raise your arms in victory. But the room is silent—except for some chirping crickets and Dickey's guffaws of laughter. And then you realize that you have just been a victim of the winner's curse. Your bid was not just enough to win but it was so far above what would have likely ensured a victory at the auction house that you probably threw away tens of thousands of dollars you did not need to spend. A better strategy would have been to employ a more incremental approach by submitting bids that were just a little bit greater than those submitted by Dickey. Hindsight is everything and you will never know for sure if Dickey would have thrown in the towel at $120,000 or persisted in trying to win the Tulie and driven the price up. After all, one can never predict what people will do during a heated battle on the auction floor. However, the specter of the winner's curse (assuming we care about such things) should be enough to make us try to keep our composure when we go to auction so that we do not leave it realizing we just paid $200,000 for a garment made of live, angry tarantulas.

ADVERSE SELECTION

Everyone loves a bargain until they discover that their purchase was not such a good deal as they first believed. Who has not experienced the disappointment of learning that the lizard skin boots they thought they purchased for half price were actually pale imitations constructed from newsprint and glue? It is difficult to imagine how one could suffer a greater indignity than having to trudge through mud puddles in the rain with soggy bits of pulp stuck to one's feet. Unfortunately, the old adage "You get what you pay for" is as true in the search for fashionable footwear as it is in all other walks of life.

Sometimes the search for a "good deal" involves trying to decide whether it is better to settle for an older version of an object or spend a few extra dollars to get the latest model. Suppose that you are in search of a high-powered hand mixer and discover that many people have purchased the so-called "hypersonic hand mixer" which utilizes a fission reactor to obtain blazing mixer speeds that can blend baking ingredients effortlessly but also bore through bank vault doors. This sounds very promising to you until you discover that "hypersonic hand mixers" are yesterday's fad and that those who are trendsetters and "in the know" now stock their kitchens with the new and improved fusion-powered thermonuclear mixers that can not only mix cement but also drill through miles of solid rock. Aside from some minor engineering issues which have resulted in the leveling of a city block, this new mixer offers the power that even the most exacting of today's gourmet chefs require for their culinary creations. For that reason, these thermonuclear hand mixers are snapped up as soon as they come to market and, as a result, command a hefty premium in price as compared to the somewhat dowdy fission models. Not surprisingly, some vendors, who are anxious to cash in on the craze for thermonuclear hand mixers, try to foist the less desirable fission-powered hand mixers on the gullible public by advertising them as the newer, sexier fusion models.

The concept of adverse selection comes into play when we start to consider how many people who thought they were purchasing fusion-powered hand mixers discover instead that they have been sold deliberately mislabeled antiquated fission-powered hand mixers. The confusion is further magnified by unscrupulous vendors who have packaged the older models to resemble the newer models and taken a magic marker to the word "fission" to change it to "fusion," thus causing many buyers to think mistakenly that they had bought the new models. Over time, many purchasers would become disillusioned with these deceptive practices and conclude that they would invariably end up with the fission-powered models no matter how hard they tried to purchase their sleek fusion-powered counterparts. This belief would cause many customers to assume (quite naturally) that they would always end up stuck with the older model regardless of what was on the packaging. As a result, they would be suspicious and less willing to pay the enormous price tag for the fusion-powered hand mixer; they would instead lower their offering price accordingly.

Because so many fission-powered hand mixers would have been packaged as fusion-powered hand mixers, few people would be willing to pay the fair market price for a perfectly good fusion-powered hand mixer capable of radiating everything within a half-mile of the kitchen. In essence, there would be a breakdown in the market for these products because most purchasers would be unable to trust the vendors selling those products. That would cause the price they are willing to pay for the fusion-powered hand mixers to drop, perhaps until the prices approach those being charged for the fission-powered hand mixers, many of which have been recalled due to troublesome radiation leaks. So the antics of the merchants anxious to capitalize on the frenzied demand for fusion-powered hand mixers by mislabeling their cheaper fission models would ultimately (but metaphorically—at least most of the time) blow up in their faces: Consumers would come to believe that they would likely be purchasing the older models regardless of the name on the packaging and be unwilling to offer the full purchase price for the newer model under most circumstances. In short, the demand of most consumers for the newer model would ultimately be dampened by the suspicion that any package labelled as such would contain the older model. So even the most honest sellers of fusion-powered models (who never even considered passing off the older models for the newer ones) would find it more difficult to clear their out their inventories due to the deceptive business practices previously engaged in by their less honorable colleagues.

GAME THEORY AND THE PRISONER'S DILEMMA

When different economists are not predicting that dramatically opposite results will arise from a given economic policy, they may choose to engage in game theory which is a methodology used to help predict the behavior of actors in specific situations. Game theory can be applied to hypothetical problems to try to predict the decisions made by two or more actors facing a common dilemma with varying costs and benefits. The most famous example of game theory is the prisoner's dilemma in which two prisoners are being interrogated separately about a crime with which they are both charged. Although some students of game theory are vitally interested in whether the prisoners are charged with a crime that involves lewd and lascivious behavior, the particular crime is really not important. More significant is the analysis of the ways in which two or more people can be expected to select among an array of possible courses of conduct.

In the prisoner's dilemma, the prisoners are unable to communicate with each other so the interrogator presents them both with the following alternatives: If one prisoner testifies against the other, the testifying prisoner will be set free and the other (silent) prisoner will be sent to jail for ten years (where he or she can presumably commit more crimes involving lewd and lascivious conduct). If both prisoners testify against each other, they will both serve sentences of five years. However, if both prisoners stay silent, they know that they will each receive comparatively lighter sentences of two years. The authorities will tell each prisoner that the other is about to testify in order to elicit incriminating evidence. Because the prisoners cannot speak with each other, each will be strongly tempted to betray the other as quickly as possible. The best decision for both, however, would be to remain silent and receive the lightest sentence so that they would both be free to return to their carefree lives of plundering and looting in a very short two years. The question, of course, is whether they will be able to resist the temptation to betray each other; if they fail, both will serve longer (five years) prison sentences.

Game theory is also useful for studying the actions of states in the international arena because it can help us better predict the behavior of those states. One area in which game theory has proven to be useful is in the understanding of commodity cartels. These are organizations set up by countries that produce a particular commodity such as oil, copper, or coffee to try to control output so that higher prices can be maintained. In most cases, output is restricted by imposing specific production limits or quotas on each country. Most commodity cartels try to enlist the cooperation of all the major producers of that particular commodity. In this way, they can prevent outside suppliers from flooding the market with their products and thus depressing the price of the commodity itself.

Keeping a cartel together is an on-going challenge, however, as the higher price can be maintained only so long as all major suppliers cooperate to limit production. Each country will thus be naturally tempted to try to increase its revenue by cheating and producing more than its allotted amount for sale. Many of these countries are heavily dependent on the sales of a single commodity so they are very aware of the gains in revenue to be had by increasing production. The ideal solution for any single cartel member occurs when it (and no one else) can increase its production (and, hence, its revenue) to take advantage of the higher prices that have resulted from the actions of the cartel in restricting output. If everyone follows suit, however, then prices will fall and the purpose for setting up the cartel in the first place will be frustrated. Certainly, when other countries learn that one of their members is violating the production restrictions, they may decide to follow suit, particularly if they cannot convince the rogue producer to fall back in line. The result, however, is that the greater output of the commodity by the cartel members will ultimately cause the price to fall, sometimes dramatically.

Game theory tells us that the best result for these cartel members is for everyone to cooperate and thereby maintain price supports for the commodity. If all the members decide to increase production, it is similar to the decision of both prisoners to testify against each other because the outcome is worse for all of them than it would be if the cartel members and the prisoners had not betrayed each other in the first place. Even though it is better for these countries (and these prisoners) to stick together when confronted with a set of choices and courses of action that will lead to vastly different results, the self-interest of any single country (or prisoner) will often run roughshod over more calculated determinations as to the best path to follow so that less than optimal outcomes result: countries experience dramatic falls in revenue from the sale of their exports and prisoners receive longer prison terms due to the incentive to cheat and throw the other prisoner under the bus.

SUBSTITUTE AND COMPLEMENTARY GOODS

What if you had a sudden desire to eat a chocolate bar? You might rush over to the local Snack Shack and examine the shelves laden with tasty treats, trying to decide whether you should buy a milk chocolate bar or a dark chocolate bar or one with peanuts or something more exotic like fire ants. Although you might prefer the plain milk chocolate bar, you might be tempted by the crunchy peanut bar or even the tangy fire ants. Because you would probably be content with any one of these chocolate bars, though varying in flavors and ingredients, you could eat any one of these delicious treats and be perfectly content and hopefully not dead. These chocolate bars are substitute goods because one chocolate bar can be substituted for another and you would still experience a similar level of enjoyment. The point is that you can wander throughout the glittering aisles of the Snack Shack and find any number of chocolate sweets that you will enjoy.

What if your wanderings through the Snack Shack lead you to the aisle that features crackers and pungent cheeses which may have been sitting on the shelves ripening for too many years? For many people, crackers and cheese go together like cheap wine and phosphorescent prophylactics. They can be purchased separately but they are often consumed or used together and the demand for one is often directly related to the demand for the other. Such goods are known as complementary goods. For aficionados of peanut butter and jelly sandwiches, this notion that two items such as cheese and crackers are inseparable ingredients in a glorious meal is not unfamiliar. This is not to say that you cannot consume peanut butter without jelly because you are certainly free to smear a tablespoon of peanut butter on a filet mignon or a lightly grilled sea bass. Similarly, jelly can be spread on lettuce or cat food (if you are running out of ideas for creative party mixes) or even the body of your exhibitionistic next-door neighbor. But peanut butter and jelly are most typically associated with each other and it is reasonable to view them as complementary goods even though they are not invariably consumed together.

An economist might tell us that this complementarity suggests that an increase in the price of peanut butter could cause a drop in the sales of jelly, or vice versa. Indeed, one could say that the demand for complementary goods may have varying degrees of dependency in that two goods may be extremely complementary such that increases in the price for one will almost always cause a drop in demand for the other. Or the degree of complementarity may be less pronounced because we know that products such as peanut butter and jelly do not have to be consumed together to be enjoyed. I can use peanut butter as a bargain-priced skin care product while you can rub jelly on your head to style your hair. However, we may learn that I am severely allergic to peanuts and that our picnic in the country will be suddenly interrupted by my having a severe reaction resulting in anaphylactic shock. At least your use of the jelly as a hair dressing would not pose a risk of death unless, of course, it draws a hive of killer bees over to our blanket.

Even though the terms for substitute and complementary goods can be confusing, it helps to remember that a substitute good such as the chocolate bars that we might have slipped into our pants at the Snack Shack when the clerk turned his back are typically consumed separately. In other words, you might choose to eat a milk chocolate bar or a dark chocolate bar but you would not usually eat both of them together because it does not really augment the chocolate consuming experience. With arguably complementary goods such as peanut butter and jelly, however, the consumption of both is essential to the enjoyment of the peanut butter and jelly sandwich even though either the peanut butter or the jelly could be consumed separately. The lack of precision in the concept of complementary goods is evident in that some goods such as peanut butter and jelly may be eaten together. However, there are many people who like one and detest the other so that the complementary concept would no longer apply. Indeed, it can become something of a sliding scale of complementarity because people have differing degrees of desire to consume both peanut butter and jelly together.

NORMAL AND INFERIOR GOODS

When economists study the consumption patterns of people to construct behavioral models that have some basis in reality, they will consider the popular demand for both normal and inferior goods. Normal goods are those products that consumers will demand in greater quantities as their incomes increase. Economists go one step further and break normal goods up into necessity goods and luxury goods: Necessity goods are those in which an increase in the income of the consuming public by, say, 10 percent, results in a percentage increase in demand that is less (say, 7 percent) than the percentage increase in income. Luxury goods, by contrast, will see an increase in demand (say, 20 percent) that is greater than the increase (say, 10 percent) in the incomes of the consuming public. Inferior goods, on the other hand, are those products that will be in less demand as the incomes of consumers increase. Inferior goods may be very well made and have positive self-esteem; the term merely refers to goods in which there is an inverse relationship between the incomes of consumers and their demand for these goods.

Imagine that you were able to pick the winning numbers in the Gambling Addiction Sweepstakes. You might now find yourself flush with cash and eager to sample the tempting pleasures of the gilded class. And there would be no better way to begin your new life as a member of the *nouveau riche* club complete with a new powdered wig, bright green silk breeches and silver buckle shoes than to brush up on your ballroom dance techniques and take a serious look at your dietary habits. Up to now, your meager finances and lack of knowledge about the perils of alcohol poisoning have led you to consume large quantities of the locally-distilled but popular Pancreatic Vodka. It is an organic product that boasts both an extremely high proof and trace elements of various heavy metals found in breeder reactors. It is also very inexpensive and is sold in "family-size" 55-gallon drums. Now that you have an enormous bank account, however, you may no longer wish to consume so much of the beverage that has nearly burned a hole in your trachea. Instead, you might be ready for something smoother and more refined, something that does not melt crystal stemware upon contact. One possibility would be the famous French champagne *Snobbe*, which is produced by the Robespierre Vineyard in France (motto: "Don't lose your head over flat champagne!"); this champagne boasts an effervescence that is prized by both high society elites and corporate backstabbers alike.

For the first time in your life, you can now afford to purchase a case of the *Snobbe* champagne and could uncork a bottle of the gold foil-wrapped bottle at the tailgate party for the local high school football game and pour it into your cleanest clear plastic glass. You could mutter a phrase from a plotless French film ("Je t'aime le stylo!") as you swirl the pale bubbly contents around, ignoring the black bug floating on the top. You might sniff the fumes and offer unsolicited comments about the "cuteness" of the bouquet and the lack of lumps in the pale amber goodness.

In any event, the fact that your new-found riches now enable you to enjoy the pleasures of *Snobbe* champagne—coupled with your reduced interest in the searing burn of Pancreatic Vodka—underscore the fact that the *Snobbe* champagne is a normal good and the Pancreatic Vodka is, at least in your case, an inferior good. But because the changes in demand are personal to each consumer as their incomes change, a normal good can also be an inferior good. In other words, Pancreatic Vodka could see falling demand among existing consumers as their incomes increase. However, those consumers who have comparatively little money and who have always had to make due with fermented grass and leaves, would consider Pancreatic Vodka to be a normal good because their rising incomes would enable them to drop their horrid grass and leaf concoctions in favor of the pseudo-luxurious flavor of Pancreatic Vodka.

GIFFEN GOODS

Imagine that you were living in Ireland in the 1840s. You would not be swept up in the beauty of the emerald green landscape or the charming architecture of the rural villages because you would, more than likely, be dead. If you were alive, you would be little more than skin and bones, trying to scrounge enough food to stay alive. This was the time of the Great Famine in Ireland which was caused by the failure of the potato crop. Potatoes were the basic staple of the Irish diet but the disastrous harvest resulted in massive starvation. The failure of this vitally important crop also precipitated an unprecedented exodus from the island to many other countries, particularly the United States and Canada.

The widespread shortage of a vital staple food as potatoes would offer a very real test of our assumptions about the pricing of goods when the supply is reduced. An economist versed in the writings of Adam Smith carrying out research on how markets function would gingerly step over the rotting corpses strewn along the cobblestone streets of Dublin and confidently predict that the reduced supplies of potatoes would lead to higher prices and, therefore, less consumption of potatoes by the public. In other words, the higher price of potatoes should cause people to switch to other, less expensive substitute goods in response to those higher prices.

However, we would be surprised to find that the higher prices for potatoes did not dampen the enthusiasm of the Irish population for potatoes but, paradoxically, caused people to buy even more potatoes. We might scratch our proverbial heads in search of an explanation for this odd, seemingly illogical, behavior but it would be a better use of our time to consult the works of the Scottish philosopher Robert Giffen for a coherent explanation of this paradox. Giffen, who studied the consumption habits of the poor in Victorian England, saw that the increase in the price of cheap foods such as potatoes, which were a basic stable of the Irish diet, reduced the purchasing power of Irish households. Well, you might reason, the failure of the potato crop really only affected the supply of potatoes so our basic assumptions that prices will invariably fall when supply is reduced should still hold true. Indeed, we would expect Irish consumers to cut back on their purchases of potatoes and buy other goods to make up the shortfall.

This is where we would expect Irish consumers to fill their cupboards with readily available alternatives such as beef or fish. The problem with this idea of switching from potatoes to some other foodstuff is that there really are no other readily available cheap food substitutes that can take the place of a staple such as potatoes. Indeed, these substitute foods are more expensive than potatoes—even at the new, higher prices at which the potatoes are now being sold. The absence of any real substitutes for potatoes forces the consumer to grit his teeth and pay higher prices for more potatoes because the costs of other items such as beef or fish are already too dear for most consumers and, due to the shortages caused by the failure of the potato crop, may also become even more unaffordable for poor consumers.

Because his income has not increased, however,

our consumer has even less money left for buying other arguably essential goods likes tea or sugar. The apparent paradox is resolved because the consumer is, in effect, precluded from reducing his consumption of potatoes because he cannot afford to purchase anything else to replace those potatoes. At the same time, his purchasing power has fallen due to the price increases resulting from the food shortages so that he has even less ability and, perhaps, inclination to purchase the same quantities of those more expensive non-essential items that he formerly consumed.

UTILITY

The scarcity of resources in the real world and the assumption that people act, for the most part, in a rational manner to maximize their own material well-being leads us to the concept of utility. When we speak of utility in an economics sense, we are not talking about rapacious monopolistic suppliers of electricity and water. No, economists speak of utility in terms of the satisfaction expressed by an individual when he or she is choosing between two alternative purchases. If I am an aficionado of very expensive fine chocolates, for example, I might find myself torn between using my hard-earned dollars to buy a slice of bat fudge or a squirrel-flavored truffle at the Exotic Chocolate Shop. Because the proprietor of the shop refuses to split either piece in half so that I could purchase one half piece of each and presumably experience a confectionary nirvana, I must make the difficult choice between fudge filled with bat ears or a truffle featuring *l'essence de* rodent. My choice will ultimately depend on which of these two luscious treats is more appealing to me or—to use the economist's jargon—offers greater utility. My choice of the truffle would be regarded as my conscious selection of the item offering the greatest satisfaction to me. A consumer of more traditional types of chocolate might gag at the thought of such edibles but would probably conclude that I selected the truffle because I thought it would be the tastier *bon bon* of the two. There would be no real scale akin to a bathroom scale that can quantitatively measure my preference for one candy over the other. My saying that "I love bat fudge" as compared to "I *really* love squirrel-flavored truffles" is not a particularly precise measurement of my preference for one delicacy over the other. The fact that the concept of utility in economics may not be easily reduced to a numerical scale does not detract from its considerable value in helping to predict the choices made by people.

Utility is really a fancy, albeit mushy, way to describe the preferences an individual may have for one item over another. If I choose squirrel-flavored truffles over bat fudge, then an observer might conclude that I prefer it. Of course, this is not a foolproof method because our observer might not know that I had previously selected the bat fudge over the squirrel-flavored truffle ninety consecutive times and that this was the first occasion that I had wandered into the sweet world of squirrel confectionary—perhaps on a lark. Another explanation might be that I had had a severe addiction to bat-flavored confectionary and was only after years of psychiatric counseling that I was finally able to venture out into the sunlight and try something more squirrel-like. The analysis of an individual's preferences at any given time, therefore, may not provide us with a definite guide as to which choice we prefer at all times but merely show which choice is preferred at a particular moment in time. But if the observer knew of my previous 90 instances of consuming bat fudge as opposed to squirrel-flavored truffles, then the observer would be on much more solid ground in drawing a conclusion about my preference for the fudge.

OPPORTUNITY COSTS

For many of its more pessimistic scholars, the dreary drumbeat of scarcity and limited resources and Malthusian desperation runs through the field of economics. However, these themes do force us to consider the concept of opportunity costs—which is an academic way to say, "You can't always get what you want." Economists go one step further and say the following: Not only will you not be able to get what you want but your choice of one thing will invariably require you to give up another thing.

The notion that there are trade-offs in most decisions will confront every high school graduate who is contemplating whether to attend college or instead take up the electric guitar and become a rock superstar. On the one hand, the decision to go to college involves a number of costs including tuition, room and board, books, classes involving unrelenting political indoctrinations masquerading as social science prerequisites and the consumption of copious amounts of carbohydrates. All of these things will require the payment of hard-earned dollars—regardless of whether they come from generous parents anxious to reclaim their child's bedroom for use as a home movie theater or gym or kind-hearted banks hoping to lend out hundreds of thousands of dollars in student loans that may one day be fully repaid. At the same time, there is the foregone income that would otherwise be earned if the prospective student decided to enter to workforce right away and begin a storied career as a server in one of America's leading casual dining restaurant chains.

If the student decides to pursue a music career and purchases a guitar and a copy of *Becoming a Guitar God in Ten Easy Lessons,* the one immediate advantage will be the avoidance of all of the previously mentioned costs associated with a high-quality education. Plus, one would get to wear fabulous clothes and outrageous hairstyles and offer weighty political opinions to the daytime talk show hosts and, possibly, even sing on-key. Along with the lifestyle changes associated with being a rock guitarist would also be the income that would come from such upbeat compositions as *I Cut My Wrists With Your Kiss.*

The point is that your choice to go to college and learn about the syntax of ancient Babylonian dialects or the political views of the early Egyptian Pharaohs would probably mean that you would have to give up your dreams of musical superstardom. Similarly, your desire to become the singer for the heavy metal band Happy Apocalypse would mean that you could not devote enough time to earn a degree in *pseudo*-studies that might just get you an entry level sales position at the local telemarketing firm. As such, you would find yourself standing at the proverbial fork-in-the-road of life having to consider which path to follow while an oncoming 18-wheeler bears down upon you.

Opportunity costs can be thought of as a decision between two competing, often mutually exclusive alternatives. Of course, there may be that rare individual who is able to master every guitar chord and obtain an online education in fine art while traveling across the country in a pink neon tour bus. But most of us do not have such a broad array of talents and will find ourselves having to choose between career and college. The ugly specter of scarcity thus underpins any discussion of opportunity costs because most of us have no choice but to pursue one course of action to the exclusion of another because the resources we can devote to such pursuits are limited and necessarily force us to choose—in this case—between the search for knowledge and the pursuit of a multi-platinum recording career and groupies.

PERFECT COMPETITION

In a perfect world in which everyone rode unicorns and ate lollipops and candy canes at every meal without fear of dying an early death from diabetes, these lucky individuals would also presumably enjoy that most perfect of economic markets—that of perfect competition. In such a world, the economic power of buyers and sellers alike is widely diffused so that no entity has the economic clout to affect the supply of a good or the price paid for that good.

We can look at the market for a glamorous product such as crowbars to see how buyers and seller of this product would interact in a market of perfect competition. Suppose that there are numerous manufacturers of crowbars because there is little to prevent a would-be manufacturer from jumping into the fray of this market. All you really need to make crowbars is some steel, some molds, and a furnace. Oh, and gloves. Gloves are very important when handling superheated, newly-formed steel crowbars. As a result, there is a plentiful supply of crowbar manufacturers. The ease with which they can be produced is further enhanced by the fungibility of the crowbars themselves. Most crowbars look very similar to one another and are fashioned out of some type of carbon steel and painted black or grey (even though you can produce them in designer primary colors and vary the sizes as needed). There is also an untapped novelty market that might welcome a 12-foot tall 900-pound crowbar that could be advertised as "The Big Crowbar for the Big Man!" or some other subtle pseudo-phallic message. Nevertheless, crowbars are not going to vary much from one manufacturer to another. With hundreds of crowbar manufacturers in this market of perfect competition, an attempt by a single seller to increase the price of its crowbars significantly will result in that seller suffering an immediate loss of sales as prospective crowbar buyers quickly switch to lower-priced alternatives. This particular seller might try to justify the higher price by saying that its crowbars are more aerodynamic than others. Or it could advertise some other feature such as its crowbar's sensuous steel handle to forestall the possible loss of sales. But crowbars do not readily allow for much in the way of product differentiation so such sales "puffery" will probably not boost sales so long as the seller's products continue to be priced appreciably above those of its competitors. The inevitable result in such a market is that falling sales will force the company to drop the price of its crowbars back in line with the other manufacturers. Even an imaginative marketing programs such as offering the crowbar as an innovative marital aid will probably not stem the tide of negative sales.

Similarly, no buyer in a perfectly competitive market has enough clout to force sellers to drop their prices significantly below those prices being paid by other buyers. If the Slugg Hardware Store, a regional

chain, announces that it is willing to pay crowbar manufacturers only half the going price for crowbars, it will
likely find that very few manufacturers, if any, will be
willing to sell any crowbars to Slugg. Not wanting to
be left out in the cold and miss the expected holiday
shopping frenzy for blunt steel objects, Slugg would
likely drop its demand for preferential pricing so it
could restock its shelves just in time for the first night
of Hanukkah.

We spoke of the absence of significant barriers to
entry to would-be crowbar manufacturers in terms of
the physical assets needed to produce a crowbar for sale.
It is also true that crowbars are not typically subject to
extensive legal restrictions that might otherwise stymie
new entrants such as a massive crowbar licensing fee or a
set of onerous safety inspections replete with enormous
documentation requirements and lengthy delays prior
to approval. Moreover, few cities have tried to impose
a law requiring that the owner of a crowbar company
be named "Bob" or "Ted" or some other specific name;
a restriction that which would certainly prune the ranks
of eligible companies in short order. Needless to say, the
imposition of any licensing or permit fees would slow
down the entry of newer companies into the crowbar
market. Given the undifferentiated nature of crowbars, however, it would appear that there would be few
actual barriers to entry and that prospective manufacturers would be able to freely enter the market as they
so decided.

TRAGEDY OF THE COMMONS

Imagine that you have a flock of sheep that you allow to graze in the beautiful green pastures surrounding your village. These pastures offer succulent grass that provide all the nutrients that your fluffy white gentle lambs could desire before they are trucked off to town and butchered in the slaughterhouses. But the availability of this essentially free food supply is not lost upon your neighbors—many of whom also have their own flocks of sheep which they send out to frolic in the pastures each day. As word has gotten around about the lushness of the pastoral landscape, however, more and more farmers have brought their sheep to the pastures so that it has almost become impossible lately to walk in any direction without tripping over a sheep or stepping in a pile of sheep dung. Now there are hundreds and hundreds of baaing sheep roaming around the grasslands, eating every blade of grass in sight so that the green fields are now mainly brown mud. This destruction of the pasture due to overgrazing highlights the "tragedy of the commons": the fate that will often befall a communal resource in which there are no restrictions or limitations on use or consumption.

One solution might be to try to cut back on the number of cuddly lambs wandering around the pastures by encouraging everyone in the village to eat lamb— lamb chops, lamb shank, rack of lamb, lamb stew, lamb ice cream, lamb-flavored birthday cake—to thin the herds and relieve the stress on their food supply. But even the most fanatical fan of lamb and lamb by-products will eventually tire of such fare. Unfortunately, this culinary carnage will not really solve the underlying problem that all community-owned assets face—the lack of a regulatory authority to control the amount of consumption of that communal asset. This regulation is necessary because the self-interest of each of the owners of the sheep will drive them to breed as many sheep as possible which will, of course, require that those sheep be allowed to graze in the pastures.

Regulating the number of sheep being allowed to wander around the pastures is also necessary to permit the grasslands to recover from the feeding frenzy. Indeed, if the pasture has been stripped bare by the marauding sheep, then it may be extremely difficult for the grasslands to regenerate, particularly if the roots have been dug up. Instead of the lush succulent grass, the new growth of green in the pasture may be a patchy quilt of clumps of grass and weeds and perhaps a wildflower or two. There is no guarantee that the pastures can once again become a green blanket of grass because the roots and seeds of the pasture may be irrevocably damaged. Furthermore, the disappearance of the grass may have resulted in the topsoil blowing away or washing away in the rain.

In the jargon of professional economists, this situation would suck. Unfortunately, there is a tendency for many of us to underestimate the obstacles that would hamper the recovery of any communal resource—whether it be pastures or an overfished lake or a depleted drinking water reservoir. Some of the more optimistic among us would think that so long as there was a single blade of grass in the pasture, that complete rejuvenation and recovery of the land would be just around the corner. But things are not so simple in nature. Not every blade of grass is created equal and the likelihood that you would have such a muscular blade of grass that it could spawn an entire pasture is probably very remote.

The same analysis applies when you are dealing with an overfished lake. Because everyone taking fish out of the lake can do so without any restrictions, then their catches are limited only by the ambitions of the individual fishermen and their abilities to carry their prizes home. So as with the pastures, there is no inherent quota or cap on what each person can remove from the pond. At some point, the remaining fish in the lake, even though there may be one or more breeding pairs that are really hot for each, will simply not be numerous enough to replenish the fish population. "Why not?" you might ask, remembering that literally billions and billions of people descended from Adam and Eve, according to respected evolutionists such as Charles Darwin. Well, there are a number of conditions and factors that could make any significant recovery of the fish population very unlikely. The fish could be wiped out by disease or parasites, or the weather could become very cold or very hot and create temperatures in the water not conducive to mating. Another problem might be that many of these fish could be sterile or find that the water had become polluted by fertilizer runoff from nearby farms or industrial wastes from factories. Indeed, it is hard enough to replenish an entire species from almost scratch when everything is perfect, but it is far more difficult to do so when the quality of the water or the food supply has been compromised. This is why any regeneration of a communal resource cannot wait until we are down to our last two fish or our last patch of grass. There needs to be a significant number of fish or an ample supply of grass so that the slings and arrows tossed by nature (or humanity) can be overcome.

A communal resource can be a small pond or a large forest or even an entire ocean. The common theme is that each is susceptible to being depleted due to the absence of an effective policing authority. You cannot really fence off an entire ocean, but you can try to deter unlawful fishing, for example, by sinking the fishing boats of a few stubborn captains and hoping that words gets around about your "no-nonsense" approach when the survivors get picked up. If you are more inclined to pursue diplomatic remedies, then you can negotiate an agreement with other countries setting specific limits on what each country can take as is the case with various fishing and whaling agreements. Not surprisingly, neither the fish nor the whales in question have ever been reliably polled as to their opinions about these harvesting agreements so we cannot be sure that they are at all enthusiastic about these compacts.

The problem that invariably arises with any attempt to curtail the use of a communal resource through international treaties is two-fold: Not every nation is a signatory to these agreements and even some of the nations who do approve of these agreements cannot necessarily prevent their fishing fleets from violating the limits or outright bans contained in these agreements. Certain countries such as Japan point to a demand (admittedly declining) at home for whale products to justify continuing some level of whaling activities. However, the growing worldwide awareness of the brutality of whaling as well as changing dietary habits in many countries where people have decided that chewing whale blubber is not as tasty as eating fine chocolate are also helping to limit whale harvesting by greatly reducing the demand for whale meat and blubber.

EXTERNALITIES

People voluntarily exchange goods and services because they each expect to derive a benefit from the completion of the deal. In many cases, these transactions involve nothing more than the exchange of money for a certain product. As a result, the benefits and costs of the exchange are confined to the parties themselves. However, there are instances in which the producer of a good may impose costs or confer benefits upon other parties who are not involved with the transaction at all and who may not even have any knowledge about the transaction. These impacts on innocent third parties—for good or bad—are called externalities because they involve costs or benefits that arise from the transaction but which are not limited merely to the actual parties involved in the deal itself.

Imagine that I own a factory that manufactures toxic chemicals used exclusively in my Real World brand of children's chemistry sets. These delightful learning products have been sold for many years around the country. The demand for these chemistry sets is strong but there are several other firms that manufacture competing youth science projects including a working electrical substation complete with transformers and a life-size Viking funeral pyre for pre-adolescents to set afire and float across backyard swimming pools and a miniature nuclear power plant boasting its own nuclear fuel pellets. Because I cannot raise my prices significantly due to the availability of so many competing youth science products, I am looking for ways to reduce my production costs to boost profits.

One day while standing outside behind my factory watching ducks paddle lazily down a nearby stream, I realize that I can dramatically cut my waste disposal costs by pumping all of the waste products generated by my factory into the waterway. After all, this stream really serves no purpose except to make annoying gurgling sounds. More importantly, it would certainly be able to whisk away my toxic wastes without my having to deal with bothersome sealed canisters or lengthy trips to the dump or the payment of hefty disposal fees. My dumping the toxic wastes into the stream would allow me to lower my costs of production and perhaps compete more aggressively in terms of price against my competitors.

Of course, my relentless pursuit of an improved bottom line would not take into account the so-called external costs caused by my dumping activities; the pollution of the stream would be a cost imposed upon all of the people whose properties bordered the stream and who now saw its formerly clear cold waters rendered a hideous blur of orange and blue. Because I had not bothered to dispose of the toxic wastes properly, I, in effect, would be passing the costs of my failure to do so onto my downstream neighbors. Moreover, my ability to sell my chemistry sets at a lower price due to my innovative disposal practices would reflect a failure of the market to account for the total costs of producing my highly desired educational products.

If government regulators who did not appreciate my efforts to provide chemistry sets at rock-bottom prices wanted me to "internalize" these external costs that I had passed onto my downstream neighbors, they could take one of two forms of action: They could impose a tax on me that would cover the costs of properly disposing of the toxic chemicals. Alternatively, they might decide that they should require me to clean up the toxic wastes myself which would probably be an extraordinarily costly endeavor. Either approach, however, would have the effect of providing a more complete tally of the costs of producing my products because they would impose most, if not all the costs of production, on the producer of the product (me).

Lost among the din of my ranting against the oppressive hand of the government leviathan that would dare to infringe upon my "Constitutional right" to dump my factory wastes in the stream would be the question of whether my chemistry sets should even be produced at all. In other words, if I cannot compete with my fellow manufacturers on price without dumping my effluents into the river, then I might have to conclude that the actual cost of production is far higher than I had originally thought. In fact, it might be so high—once I take into account the costs of disposing of my factory wastes—that it is not a competitive product at all. This leads to the additional insight that the ability to impose my costs of production onto my neighbors (even though I might not like them very much) distorts the pricing mechanism so that my chemistry sets are underpriced relative to the total costs of production. If I am required to take all of my production costs into consideration, then I would have to account for the costs of disposing of the factory wastes. That would be the only way for the pricing mechanism of the market to be restored so that the true costs of production are being borne by me and not by my undeserving neighbors.

Sadly, this conclusion might leave me no choice but to shut down my chemical production line altogether as I can no longer justify financially continuing to bring the joy of third-degree chemical burns to the fledgling chemists who would otherwise joyfully set their Bunsen burners aflame and mix explosive but colorful combinations of substances together.

PART TWO:
MONEY AND FINANCE

MONEY

There is nothing so sensuous as the feel of a newly minted bill. It has a smell that, when denominated in $50s or €50s or £50s, is of enormous appeal to essentially everyone—constituting a sort of "catnip" for human beings. And while lots of money may not buy happiness, it can usually be counted on to catch the attention of many people willing to tell you how great you are so long as they (your new-found sycophants) continue to be the willing beneficiaries of your personal philanthropy.

Aside from boosting your chances to be the center of attention at any party, money also plays a central role in the function of all modern economic systems. It serves as a medium of exchange that enables people to avoid the clumsiness of trying to exchange wildly disparate goods and services in a barter economy. We recall from our reading of Nietzsche's light-hearted *Thus Spoke Zarathrusta* (or maybe not) that the inherent difficulty of acquiring the goods you want and disposing of the goods you do not wish to keep is that you must engage in a needle-in-the-haystack search for a person who has the opposite desires of yours in wishing to dispose of something you want and acquire something you wish to sell in order to carry out a successful exchange.

An illustration devoid of such densely abstruse verbiage will help to illustrate the difficulty of commerce in a barter economy. Suppose I am a merchant in 17th century London and I have a pig that I would like to get rid of due to my newly-discovered allergy to pork. But I would be very interested in acquiring a color television set for my home–even though the absence of electricity or, for that matter, broadcast programming of any kind, in preindustrial England would suggest that such a purchase would be foolish. I must somehow surmount the issue of the double coincidence of wants: I must find another individual who wishes to obtain a porcine companion *and* dispose of his color television set. As you can imagine, this situation poses a very difficult challenge. Even if we expand our potential pool of customers to include the millions of individuals living within the length and breadth of Merrie Olde England itself—each trying to acquire and dispose of a myriad of items—my task will be a daunting one.

Enter the concept of money. Instead of my having to search for a porcine enthusiast who has a color television set they no longer wish to use as a coffee table, I can take my corpulent companion to anyone who wants to buy a pig and simply come to an agreement on the price of the pig. I would then hand over the pig and pocket my cash. I would then be free to go find a merchant who sells color televisions sets and then tender the purchase price if I so desired. Money can thus be used to enable people having an infinite variety of goods and services to buy and sell those goods and services from each other without having to exhaust themselves trying to barter anything.

In the modern economy, money represents a unit of account which is used to set the prices of all goods, regardless of whether the unit is called dollars, pounds, pesos, or very shiny pebbles. This means that both pigs and color television sets are priced in terms of the same unit of account (currency). So, if I wish to sell my pig, I would set a price of say, fifty pounds. Similarly, I would expect to find that color television sets would also be priced in pounds. My challenge would be to accumulate enough pounds to purchase the color television set; I would no longer have to worry about continuing my quixotic quest for the one porcine hobbyist wishing to get rid of a color television set.

The other advantage of money is that it is a store of value. My being able to keep my dollars or pounds or pesos in a billfold for weeks or months on end becomes evident when you consider societies in which perishable goods such as eggs or livestock are used as money. You really cannot store a dozen eggs, let alone an angry pig, in your billfold or pocketbook without risking either a mess or serious injury. Indeed, trying to use a full-grown pig as money in a fine London dining club would be considered a *faux pas* by those members who do not share your appreciation for porcine companionship. And smashed eggs, which are certainly much more portable than pigs, do not provide a convenient form of money because they start to reek after a week or so. This lack of permanence is another weakness that can come into play in a barter economy when one is dealing with items that oink or rot.

MONEY AND INTEREST RATES

We have seen that our desire for money or, alternatively expressed, our demand for money, is inversely related to the interest that the money can earn if deposited at a bank. We can look at our money as an asset that the banks wish to have because they want to loan that money out to borrowers and collect interest on that money. However, a bank must first persuade you to deposit your money and offer you something in return as an incentive for your business. Hmm. You might want to have a new sports car or a high-powered jet ski or even a charming chalet in the Swiss Alps, but most banks are not so imaginative about the measures they will take to lure you into their lobby. Instead of fancy cars or exotic homes, they will offer to pay you some amount of interest on your money; this amount is usually calculated as a percentage of the monies you keep in your account.

Whether you are persuaded by the bank officer's promise to be your best friend forever if you will only open an account, your decision will be motivated in large part by the rate of interest offered by the bank. If it is negligible, you may be more likely to say, "Why bother?" and stuff the wads of cash back under your mattress. But if the interest rates are higher, then you might find yourself intrigued, much as you were first drawn to read *Lady Chatterly's Lover* in order to appreciate its literary worthiness and better ascertain its commentaries about society as a whole.

Higher interest rates mean a greater return on your investment. When your money is under the mattress, there is no return on the investment. When your money is in a bank account, it will earn some interest. The question is whether the interest is sufficiently high to attract your attention.

How is the interest rate determined? As with much of economics, the answer is supply and demand. The interest rate reflects the supply of money created by the central banking authorities and the demand of both individuals and organizations (private and otherwise) for that money. If the central bank reduces the supply of money and the demand for that money is unchanged, then there is less money sloshing around in the economy and the interest rate will go up. Consumers will not be able to obtain the same number of dollars at the lower interest rate so the holders of those dollars will demand a higher interest rate for exchanging those dollars. Conversely, an increase in the supply of money when there is no real increase in demand will cause interest rates to fall because the holders of those dollars will have to accept less interest from borrowers if they exchange those dollars.

We all engage in various types of economic transactions in order to build our financial empires. Some of us are more prone to take a walk through the Wall Street casino and invest our money in stocks, hoping that we will discover the next big thing and make gobs of money so that we can buy enormous houses and look down upon all of our former neighbors and co-workers. Others are more geared towards real property and will seek to own real estate such as apartments or shopping centers or warehouses, hoping that they can realize both income and asset appreciation and, as an added bonus, also look down upon all of their former neighbors and co-workers. Still others would prefer less risk and will place their money in government bonds and cash accounts, realizing that they may not enjoy the gains of their colleagues who have chosen stocks or real estate, but comfortable in the knowledge that an adverse turn in either the stock market or the real estate market will not destroy their value of their accounts. Even though they may only be able to afford an average sized house, these bond and cash investors will at least have a house when some of their more risk-oriented colleagues are having their mansions foreclosed on by their banks.

People do have a demand for money, which can fluctuate from person to person, depending on the events in that particular person's life. If I am one who invests 30 percent of my after-tax money in the stock market, for example, and have continued to do so, year after year, for my entire working life, it is reasonable to suppose that I would continue doing so far into the future if the circumstances surrounding my daily routine did not change. However, if I were diagnosed with a hideous disease, then I might seek expensive medical remedies which would cut into both the amounts and frequencies of my plunges into the stock market. Indeed, I might be so upset that I would halt my stock investing altogether so that I could pursue the latest drug treatments to stop my debilitating condition in its tracks.

The demand for money can also be understood as a demand for liquidity or, alternatively, a desire to engage in monetary activities such as purchasing various goods and services. You need money to pay for groceries or your annual membership fees in the local porcine racing club. If all your wealth was tied up in illiquid assets such as a magnificent collection of dancing ceramic aardvarks, then you would find it difficult to engage in other financial transactions because of your lack of cash. You could improve your liquidity by acquiring more money—perhaps by a well-timed excursion to the local bank with a mask and firearm in hand—or you could simply sell off a few of your ceramic aardvark treasures to raise some money to pay for your purchases. If you are concerned about losing your job, then you will naturally want to reduce your expenses as much as possible and thereby stockpile your money in anticipation of your salary being cut off. Even though you may have hopes of becoming a famous foot model, these hopes may not be realized quickly so you might decide that you will have to live a much more austere lifestyle until additional funds are forthcoming. This does not mean, of course, that you will refrain from certain expenditures to assist in your job search. For example, you may hire a photographer to prepare a portfolio of enchanting photographs of both of your feet to show to prospective podiatric talent agencies.

Whether one chooses to hold more or less cash will also depend on the investment environment. In general, the lower the interest rates offered by banks on savings accounts and certificates of deposits, the less inclined you will be to stash your money at your local bank. Because the interest rates offered by most financial institutions have been historically low for much of the 21st century, bank customers have not been overwhelmed by the prospect of earning ½ percent or ¾ percent or 1 percent interest on their money. After all, there is little difference between ½ percent earned at a bank and 0 percent earned by stuffing dollar bills under your mattress—except that the resulting lumpiness in your bed may make it more difficult for you to fall asleep. The obvious point is that when there is little financial incentive to deposit your money with the bank, then you will be more inclined to spend it on important things such as sure-fire bets on your favorite porcine racers at the track. In the vernacular of economics, we would say that the lower the interest rate, the lower your demand for money. In other words, you have less incentive to keep it in your wallet or at the bank because it will not generate much of a return.

The other exogenous variable that affects your demand for money is the cost of living itself. If prices are rising, then the purchasing power of your money is being eroded. A ten percent increase in the price of pashmina for pet snakes will essentially reduce your purchasing power because it will now take more dollars to buy silk scarves for your pet python. Similarly, an increase in the price of python kibbles (as you have run out of other housepets to feed to your python) will also necessitate that you retrieve additional dollars from your pocket at the pet store check-out line. If you see many things that you consume going up in price, then you may want to get rid of your dollars because inflation has caused them to become a depreciating asset. The rising prices are steadily reducing the value of your dollars and there is nothing you can do about it except to get rid of these dollars as fast as you can. You could air your grievances about the government's incompetence in managing the economy but that may lead to other consequences such as being detained at a prison. In general, being forcibly confined for five or ten years in a prison cell will impair your ability to go shopping and spend your increasingly worthless dollars. This desire to unload money is a reflection of your lack of demand for more money because it has less and less value relative to the goods it is being used to purchase.

THE CREATION OF MONEY

The topic of money is one that attracts individuals from all walks of life because the amounts of money we possess can affect our moods, our happiness, our sense of satisfaction and, of course, our lifestyle. It is the way in which many of us measure our success relative to that of our peers whom we openly praise for their recent promotions while secretly hoping that they fall flat on their faces. For most of us, the creation of money itself, however, is not a topic that inspires much interest because most of us do not have the requisite equipment, inks, and papers to engage in full-time counterfeiting.

Unlike enterprising individuals who go to jail for counterfeiting money, banks are subject to a very different set of rules and, indeed, play an important role in the creation of money. How can that be? Banks are in the business of making money. How do they make money? Some would say that it is the quasi-usurious interest rates charged to holders of bank-issued credit cards who fail to make their payments on time. Others would argue that the primary source of revenue for banks is the interest they charge their borrowers for the use of the bank's funds. But how does a bank create money by making loans to borrowers?

Banks are subject to certain reserve requirements which means that the Federal Reserve requires banks to keep a certain percentage of their cash deposits on hand as a reserve. In other words, banks cannot lend out 100 percent of their deposits because that would leave them without a cushion to deal with unexpected losses such as borrowers who refuse to or are unable to pay back the monies they have borrowed from the bank. As a result, a bank that has $100,000 of deposits (it is not a very big bank) might be required by the all-knowing federal authorities to keep $15,000 as a reserve requirement, or 15 percent. This means that our hypothetical bank can engage in the creation of money by lending out $85,000 to a borrower in search of a house. The borrower in turn spends the $85,000 to acquire the house from the builder. The builder of the house in turn deposits the $85,000 into its bank account and that bank can then lend out 85 percent of the $85,000 deposited by the builder—or $72,250—to another borrowerr who is purchasing a racing ostrich. The seller of the racing ostrich deposits the $72,250 into his bank account and his bank in turn can lend out 85 percent of that, or $61,412.50 to a borrower who is planning to purchase a rare bottle of chardonnay. This process can go several more times, but it illustrates how the quantity of the money supply in the economy can be substantially increased through the autonomous actions of private actors such as banks and their customers as deposits are received from borrowers and used over and over again to fund additional purchases with those borrowed funds.

The Federal Reserve can influence the level of economic activity by raising or lowering the reserve requirement on banks. If it lowered the reserve requirement from 15 percent to 10 percent, then the banks would be able to lend out 90 percent of every dollar deposited instead of the 85 percent that we used in our prior example. This would make many bankers happy because more loans would mean more interest earned which would in turn mean more profits. All things being equal, the banks want to loan as much money as possible so that they can earn as much interest as possible and thus pay the most generous executive compensation packages as often as possible to those exalted few who get to have a corner office and fly in the company jet. But the lower the reserve requirement, the greater the risk that the bank may be caught with its proverbial pants down (and not looking very pretty) if the economy should suddenly start to deteriorate. A reserve requirement of 85 percent may seem stodgy to those of us who believe leverage is next to godliness but banks do not always make perfect decisions when they decide to issue credit cards or underwrite loans. A higher reserve requirement ensures that additional funds are on hand to help plug the gaps when borrowers default on their loans or credit card holders become overwhelmed by the hideous interest rates and stop making payments on their balances. As shocking as it may seem, one cannot assume that everything will go perfectly in the world of banking; the reserve requirement ensures that there is a cash cushion of some sort to absorb some of the financial blows that the bank will incur when things do not go so well.

MONEY SUPPLY

Despite those individuals who prefer to be in touch with their non-materialistic side, most of us believe that money can buy happiness if we are only given enough money to properly undertake the effort. But it does make sense to think that if we have a lot of money, we will be happier if only because we will not have to struggle so much to pay our bills. After all, there are very few people (other than guilt-ridden super-rich celebrities) who say they aspire to live in poverty. Indeed, there is a certain serenity and self-satisfaction that comes with having pockets full of gold coins as opposed to cabbages and loaves of bread stolen from the local grocery store.

Economists are similarly elated when they are able to corner one or two unsuspecting guests at a faculty cocktail party and tell them all about the money supply. Not everyone is so fortunate to be manhandled by a tenured professor while he drones on about the Federal Reserve or the abdication of fiscal responsibility by the U.S. Congress. But even if you enjoy being pinned against the wall by a tweed-coated academic, you will find that the concept of the money supply is not so intuitive and straightforward as you might have initially suspected.

What is the money supply? It would be very logical to suggest that the money supply is simply the grand total of currency floating around in the economy. And, indeed, this answer would be correct in certain circumstances but, as with many things in the social sciences, it is not true all the time and in all situations. Moreover, economists are very clever individuals who are not content with such a simple definition. They will point out that the money supply can be defined in a number of ways depending upon how wide a net one may wish to cast over the various types of monetary instruments that are present in our economy. If you listen carefully, you might hear an economist discussing mysterious acronyms such as M-0 or M-1 or M-2 or M-3 and explaining how each of these components of the money supply affect the broader economy. At the risk of revealing a deep secret, these ascending numbers (for example, M-0, M-1, M-2, M-3) simply refer to increasingly-broadly defined categories of money assets. The narrowest classification—M-0—includes all currency (notes and bills) in circulation. M-1, by comparison, would consist of currency and certain additional monetary assets such as traveler's checks and demand deposits. While it may not be as sensuous an experience to roll around naked in a pile of traveler's checks as compared to crisp, newly printed $100 bills, the traveler's checks are just as valuable as those alluring bills even though not every merchant will accept traveler's checks for payment.

How does the government affect the money supply? Well, it is not so much the government itself but the Federal Reserve, the benevolent overlord of all things money, that dictates the size of the United States money supply. The Fed was set up in 1913 in the wake of a series of financial panics that had caused enormous disruptions to the national economy. The Fed represented a more modern reincarnation of earlier 19th-century national banks but one with far greater powers to regulate the money supply and stabilize the national economic system. The Fed was also given a number of tools that it could use to control the growth of the money supply, and, to some extent, the growth of the economy itself.

First, it could raise or lower the discount rate, which is essentially the interest rate that banks must pay to borrow funds from the various regional banks in the Federal Reserve system. If the Board of Governors of the Fed wanted to make bankers sick to their stomachs, it could raise the discount rate as high as it wanted and thereby increase the costs that the banks would incur to borrow these funds. Increasing the discount rate would thus reduce the money supply because the bankers (who must always be careful not to wander outside during the daytime for fear of turning to dust) would borrow less money and therefore have less money to lend.

Second, the Fed could purchase and sell government bonds and thereby affect the interest rates on all sorts of financial products ranging from mortgages to credit cards. If the Fed were to sell bonds to empty out one of its vaults so that the vault could be turned into a sports bar, for example, then the effects of those sales would be to lower the bond prices and push up the yields on those bonds—which would in turn boost interest rates. Higher interest rates would not make our bankers happy because consumers would presumably cut back their purchases of everything from automobiles to xylophones.

Third, the Fed can increase or decrease the amount of capital that banks *must* keep on hand (the reserve requirement) which directly impacts the amount of money that banks may loan out to their bank customers. A higher reserve requirement will mean that less money is available to the borrowing public which, in turn, will negatively affect the size of the money supply while reducing the opportunities for consumers to drown in even more debt.

THE TIME VALUE OF MONEY

Suppose that you want to buy an ant farm for your bedroom. However, you do not want to stock it with the humdrum garden-variety black ants that are content to dig tunnels all day long and mind their manners. Being a more adventurous sort, you are convinced that fire ants would be a much more exciting kind of pet to own. But to purchase a first-rate fire ant colony where all the ants have had their shots is very expensive so you must consider whether you want to buy your ant farm now or at some point in the future—perhaps when you will be flush with cash due to the fortuitous, allegedly unexpected tumble to be taken down the stairs by your great Aunt Agatha, who was thoughtful enough to name you as her sole heir and careless enough to notify you of your good fortune. You really do not have enough money to buy the fire ant colony now because Aunt Agatha, perhaps sensing your eagerness to encourage her to engage in hazardous activities such as deep sea diving and parachuting, is suddenly being very careful around you and steering clear of stairways and kitchen knives. Of course you could open a credit card at the "Ants in Your Pants" pet store. But if the idea of paying an interest rate of 32 percent compounded monthly makes you sick to your stomach, then you can save your money until you have enough funds to purchase the fire ant colony outright.

The question you have to answer is whether you must have the fire ant farm today or whether you can wait for a few months until you can pay cash for it— whether due to your own efforts or Aunt Agatha's having slipped under the wheels of a passing city bus. Taking the ant farm home today will require you to borrow the money at a usurious interest rate from the credit card company. But your having to wait a few more months until you have earned enough money to purchase the ant farm outright will cause you to miss many hours of enjoyment staring into the glass tank at your marauding minions—as opposed to wasting your time on social media or personal interactions with family and friends. So the question is whether you want to pay more ultimately to take the fire ant farm home today or pay less but be deprived of the visceral pleasure of having a colony of flesh-eating insects living in your bedroom for the next few months until you get the funds. Your time preference—consume now and pay more or consume later and pay less—will necessarily determine your course of action.

The entire international banking industry developed in response to the widespread desire of people throughout the world to acquire ant farms as well as a variety of other goods such as automobiles and houses. Most of us simply do not have enough money stuffed in our mattresses to go out and buy a house for cash. It would take most of us a lifetime to save up enough money to buy a home for cash and, at that point, we would be so old that we would not be able to enjoy living in the house. Instead, we would probably spend our days staring out the window wondering what happened to our stash of cash and, indeed, all of our worldly possessions that our suddenly very interested relatives promised to take care of for us.

Our ability to buy a home or an automobile or even a starter kit for an intercontinental ballistic missile will, in all likelihood, depend on the good graces of our local banker. However, bankers are keenly aware of the desire of people to own things now as opposed to waiting until the distant future when they have amassed the needed cash to make their purchases. If I need to borrow $1 million for a second-hand cruise missile because I want to bully my neighbors with the threat of nuclear annihilation, the bank will not simply hand me the $1 million and then settle for a repayment of only that $1 million over time. No, the bank will want to collect interest on that $1 million loan because, in general, that $1 million is worth more today (buys more stuff today) than it will buy next year or five or ten years down the road.

This is due not only to the general tendency of prices for goods and services to rise over time but also to the fact that the bank places a certain value on having that $1 million available today and can choose to deploy it in any of a variety of way to earn profits for the bank. The most common use of the money would be as a loan to someone, perhaps an individual seeking to acquire illicit military hardware, or for some other purpose. But the point is that the bank must charge some type of premium or interest for the use of the money because it has its own expenses (salaries, rent, fancy corporate jets, embezzlement) that it must cover. Otherwise, the bank would quickly shut its doors. As the funds will be loaned out for some period of time, the bank would necessarily need to charge the borrower for the use of that money for that time because it is foregoing alternative opportunities to profit from the use of those funds.

THE ROLE OF MONEY

Many of us would not admit it but we are all consumed to varying degrees with accumulating more and more money because we all know that it means we are better than other people who have less money. For economists, money is vital to the operation of any modern economy because it provides the medium of exchange whereby countless transactions may take place on any given day without buyers and sellers having to scurry around for hours and hours trying to find someone with whom they can barter their goods. Instead money provides the uniformly accepted means by which any buyer or any seller may transact business in the most efficient way possible.

Some economists believe that the amount of the money supply in the economy has no real effect on the quantity of goods and services produced in that economy. They would argue that money is "neutral" in that it does not ultimately result in changes in the real gross domestic product but merely affects the nominal pricing of goods and services in the long term. Other economists, particularly the ones who have a picture of John Maynard Keynes in their wallet, believe that an increase in the money supply can stimulate productive activities and result in increased quantities of goods and services—at least in the short term. Due to these divergent viewpoints, this debate continues to be waged in the halls of academia and has not yet been settled definitively by a mixed martial arts slugfest.

How one views the impact or non-impact of money on the economy depends in large part on the significance that one attributes to the role of money in the workings of the economy itself. Some "bread and butter" economists view the economy as the sum total of goods and services produced and consumed with money playing little more than the role of a facilitator of transactions. They would not consider money to have any sort of significant impact on the actual quantity of goods and services produced because money is thought more of as something that merely greases the wheels of the economy as opposed to something that acts as a catalyst to boost the growth of the economy. For these economists, any increase in the money supply will inevitably result in nothing more than an increase in prices even though the increased money supply may stimulate economic activity in the short term.

Keynes and his drinking buddies would argue that the increase of the money supply will serve as a sort of amphetamine (my metaphor) to boost economic activity. They can point to the multiplier effect discussed elsewhere in this book in which a person selling a product receives cash and then turns around and spends some portion of that cash to acquire something else and the recipient of that cash then turns around and spends some portion of that cash and so on—until the effect has fully dissipated. Certainly this mindset is what encourages governments to boost the supply of money in an economy because it can result in lower interest rates which in turn may lead to increased borrowing and investment which in turn may ultimately lead to a higher standard of living. Maybe or maybe not.

The problem with the debate over whether money is merely a reflection of the economy whose primary value is that of a medium of exchange or whether money itself is a crucial component in the functioning of the modern economy is that both sides can point to evidence to support their positions. Money itself is of no inherent value as it is merely fancy paper featuring the portraits of famous people. But so long as people are willing to accept money in exchange for goods and services, it can facilitate commerce and reduce the time and expense that one would otherwise spend trying to exchange objects as would be the case in a barter economy. So one would have to at least concede—even if one liked to dangle life-sized pinatas bearing Keynes's likeness above bat-wielding urchins at childrens' birthday parties—that money arguably has a beneficial effect on the economy even though it may lack the tangible value of the goods and services for which it is used to purchase.

QUANTITY THEORY OF MONEY

Suppose that I am the benevolent ruler of the principality of Chrysanthemum and want to leave a lasting legacy of prosperity for all of my loyal citizens. Having dispatched my economics minister to a make-work program where he will break bigger rocks into smaller rocks for the next decade or so (so that he can no longer contradict my innovative economic theories), I have decided to give 1 million Chrysanthemum dollars to every citizen so that they will all be millionaires. I can only imagine how history will trumpet the glories of a regime that managed to bring such riches to every Chrysanthemumite regardless of his or her station in life. Why those genius bankers in Switzerland never thought of such a breathtaking plan is not something that I can answer. But once every citizen has received an official briefcase of cash, Chrysanthemum will be forever remembered as the most prosperous nation in the world—leaving those would-be pretenders in Switzerland and Liechtenstein in the metaphorical dirt.

What will be the ultimate effect of my sending stacks of dollar bills to everyone in Chrysanthemum? Surely everyone will want to name all their children after me. No doubt they will raise their glasses and toast my good health and pray for my very long life. Indeed, they might demand that their ruler be honored by a national holiday during which I can be praised around the clock. And why should I not enjoy a little deification? Every citizen will have the means to go out and get whatever they want and afford a lifestyle that they would never have dreamed of attaining before my masterstroke.

How well might this massive diffusion of money to my subjects work out in the end? Everyone can take a fistful of dollars and run to the local farm equipment dealer and pick up a new $100,000 tractor just in time for the fall harvest. No doubt Otto, the owner of the dealership, would be shocked to see a long line of people waiting to get into his store, ready to buy one of the three tractors he has in stock. But Otto, having received $1 million the day before like everyone else, would realize that everyone has a lot of money to spend. This, of course, would tempt Otto to jack up the prices of the three tractors into the stratosphere. Indeed, the price might be increased ten-fold or twenty-fold or even more, depending on Otto's perception of the willingness of his fellow citizens to part with their largesse. In fact, he might increase the prices so much that his prospective customers have to join together and pool their money to buy a single tractor to share. As a result, Otto would try to price discriminate and, perhaps using an auction format, extract the maximum number of dollars from each buyer for each of the tractors. The end result is that the tractor prices may increase so much due to the frenzied bidding wars that their cost—relative to the purchasing power of Otto's customers—may be no different than it was before the additional piles of money were passed out.

This tendency of prices to move upward as the amount of money sloshing around in the economy increases is predicted by the quantity theory of money. In short, proponents of this theory argue that changes in the money supply directly affect changes in the prices paid for most goods and services. Although this theory is not flawless due to the inherent messiness of trying to bring order to the everyday world, it does appear to be supported by enough historical studies so that it must be considered as a valid tool of inquiry. Certainly it is embraced by the so-called monetarists such as Milton Friedman who believed that inflation was essentially a function of increases in the money supply. Regardless of where one stands on the belief that an increased money supply leads to increased inflation, however, it does not appear that simply giving people more money to spend will cause more goods and services to appear magically out of nowhere. The reason for this flaw in my brilliant plan is that passing out wheelbarrows of money to all of my toadying subjects affects only the demand side of the economy; it does little to bring about the production of additional tractors or any other products for that matter. As a result, the prices for most goods can be expected to skyrocket just as was predicted by my economics minister who is now toiling in a quarry outside the capital city.

FIAT MONEY

Because politicians like to spend money, they are not particularly fond of having their profligate tendencies curbed by the need to have the currency backed by a tangible commodity such as gold. The obvious problem with a gold-backed currency is that the currency must be fully convertible into gold. In short, if I have a gold-backed dollar, I should be able to take that dollar to a bank and get a dollar's worth of gold. This of course means that the face value of the total amount of currency in circulation should be no greater than the total value of the gold held by the government. It is this sort of mindless affinity to disciplined currency management that greatly frustrates today's more freewheeling central bankers and politicians who find rigid fiscal responsibility to be so "old fashioned" and something better consigned to the scrapheap of history. After all, it is very hard for a central banker to be creative when he or she has to make sure the currency is actually backed by something of tangible value.

Fortunately for those of us who want to manage the nation's money supply with the reckless abandon that Jackson Pollock splashed paint onto canvas, it is not necessary for us to be slaves to the straightjacket of fiscal integrity. We thus owe a great debt of gratitude to those farsighted individuals who chaffed under the burden of the asset-backed currency and dared to ask why should such a sorry state of affairs be permitted to exist at all.

What if money could be created out of thin air—these brilliant thinkers wondered—backed by nothing more than the tacit agreement and crossed fingers by everyone in the country that the people would accept this fiat currency as having real, tangible value? This currency is valuable only because everyone agrees that it is valuable and will accept it as payment for goods and services; there is nothing in the way of actual assets bolstering its intrinsic worth. It seems bizarre to think that I could bring a suitcase of $100 bills to a motorcycle shop, for example, to purchase the newest Organ Donor Supercharger by handing over nothing more than several stacks of paper bills adorned with brightly colored inks and watermarks. Someone not familiar with the weighty principles of economics might think that I had pulled of an incredible deal, acquiring a magnificent coffin-on-wheels for something so mundane and so inherently worthless as a handful of rectangular sheets of paper. They would certainly be hard pressed to understand why these pieces of paper should be exchanged for any physical object or why any right-thinking person would engage in such a transaction.

Fortunately for the modern economic system in which any burden can always be "kicked down the road" to a future generation, the motorcycle vendor is perfectly willing to accept my handful of cash and part ways with his motorcycle. Why? Because he expects that he can take my stack of $100 bills to an automobile dealer, for example, and exchange that very same "worthless" paper as part payment for a shiny new automobile. In short, the paper bills, having no real value, will be accepted by the owner of the automobile shop and he may in turn use the monies to pay for his daughter's college education, and the college receiving the funds may use the monies to help finance a new chemistry laboratory, and so on and so forth without end. And so long as no miscreant points out that "The emperor has no clothes!"

and causes the whole financial system to collapse due to the lack of any actual assets to support the currency, this game can continue without limit.

COMMODITY MONEY

Consumers in today's modern economy do not typically spend a lot of time staring at the coins in their purses and pockets and wondering about the intrinsic value of these pennies, nickels, dimes and quarters. This lack of concern about the materials that make up our coins is probably a good thing because our coins are not made of the wholesome ingredients that we might otherwise suspect. Take the U.S. penny, for example, the coin that gets no respect because inflation over the past few decades has made it impossible to purchase anything for a penny except for $1/450^{th}$ of a gallon of milk or $1/25,000,000^{th}$ of a vintage Rolls Royce. This erosion in purchasing power has been accompanied by a debasement in the actual metals used to make those shiny pennies that we used to swallow as children. Nowadays, the penny consists almost entire of zinc with just a coating of copper to give it that familiar bronze glow that children find so tasty. Similarly, the nickel is more like a penny—consisting of three-quarters copper and only one-quarter nickel—even though it is coated in a finish that reminds us of a more elegant time when people took the trouble to pick up coins off the ground.

Dimes and quarters, however, have fallen furthest from the numismatic perches of metallurgical purity as the pre-1965 dime consisted of 90 percent silver and 10 percent copper whereas its more recent debased progeny consists of roughly 75 percent copper and 25 percent nickel. Quarters have gone down that same promiscuous path—shedding their 90 percent silver and 10 percent copper garment in 1965 for a tawdry frock of about 92 percent copper and 8 percent nickel. This post-modern currency has thus left the ranks of the precious metals and transmuted into commodities that are not so greatly prized. But why has this exodus from silver currency taken place? Do we not want to have a currency that is made of precious metals? Well, it would be nice to have solid silver dimes and quarters but the problem is that the amounts of silver that used to be in those coins have become more valuable than the face value of those very same coins. A silver dime, for example, can be melted down for its bullion content and be worth far more than the ten cents represented by the dime itself. So if everyone knows that the silver content of a dime or quarter is worth more than the face value of those coins, then they will hoard the coins or melt them down altogether. The supply of silver dimes and quarters would gradually disappear from circulation because it would be more profitable for people not to use them as currency. As a result, the central planners who run the government decided that we should use cheaper metals that would in effect discourage people from hoarding the coins but instead encourage them to continue to use these coins in their daily purchases. There may have also been some concern about the members of the jet set whose delicate sensibilities are such that their skin will burn if they touch base metals like nickel and copper. They certainly will not want to keep coins having such cheap metals in their possession. Similarly, the use of more expensive metals drives up the costs of manufacturing the coins in the first place which defeats the whole point of manufacturing coins that are worth intrinsically less than their face values and thus more likely to remain in circulation.

The trend toward the use of increasingly less expensive metals in coinage will probably continue unabated into the future. Unfortunately, the mints of the world have an economic incentive to substitute increasingly less valuable metals into new coins because it reduces the production costs of the coins themselves. This trend does prompt us to wonder whether we may reach the point in the future when coins are made of something less valuable than even the most debased metal—such as wood or plastic or even stone—the latter of which would represent a return to the type of currency that was used in the earliest human societies.

Yet debasement of the currency may be an irrelevant topic as time goes on due to the shift in many modern societies to digital currencies; a trend that could cause all coins to become extinct. After all, a plastic card is far less costly to produce than the most debased metal coin and is favored by revenue-hungry governments because all transactions completed using these cards can be recorded—thus eliminating the ability offered by cash to avoid taxes on the purchase of the goods in question. Moreover, these cards offer the additional advantage of providing the authorities (and aggrieved spouses who have retained expensive attorneys) with a complete history of the user's purchases and, ultimately, can reveal so much detail about the user's daily routine.

DERIVATIVES

Very few people would be able to describe a derivative because the term does not evoke an image that we can easily comprehend. After all, the word "derivative" itself is arguably amorphous, being defined in terms of something that is formed from other things or otherwise made of elements of other substances. But for our purposes, we can begin to peel away the shroud of mystery that causes even fancy-pants wine critics to shush each other when someone begins talking about derivatives. Simply put, a derivative is nothing more than a contract between two parties that contains the terms governing the performance (such as the future sales price) of a particular asset. So, a derivative (contract) could refer to a stock or a bond or a commodity such as wheat or silver. Other types of derivatives include futures, options, swaps and credit-default swaps. Although derivatives have been vilified as having been instrumental in the Great Recession of 2008, they do serve a variety of useful purposes when they are used properly. Because of the negative connotations surrounding derivatives, however, there have been suggestions that they should be traded on the major stock exchanges as opposed to over-the-counter exchanges to facilitate both transparency and efficiency.

A derivative can be used to hedge one's exposure to risk or allow one to engage in speculation about the future prices of an underlying asset. Suppose I buy a derivatives contract for $100 that will deliver 500 pounds of ox hair which has been carefully shaved from the bellies of the rare and foul-tempered Venutian ox. However, a worldwide shortage of Venutian ox belly hair coupled with an acute shortage of ox belly hair barbers causes the price of the hair itself to double to $200 in three months. This price increase would enable me to pocket $100 in profit by selling the prized ox hair as soon as the contract matures. Of course things do not always work out so well for titans of industry like myself and I could very easily have entered into that same derivatives contract for ox hair and seen the price plummet over the ensuing three months from $100 per 500 pounds to $20 per 500 pounds owing to a drastic shift in fashion sensibilities brought on by the growing realization that Venutian ox hair has a hideous odor. I would not have to sell the ox hair at a loss once I took delivery in three months, but I might not have a lot of time to continue searching for a buyer of what is now arguably one of the world's least popular luxury items.

So I could hold onto my prized ox hair for a few weeks or months, hoping that the price will recover. Or I could simply cut my losses and sell it to the first buyer that happened to come along.

Derivatives are as pervasive as stocks and bonds but people tend to be less aware of them even though they may be used to structure a wide variety of transactions and the conditions relating to those transactions such as the obligations of the parties, the maturity dates of the transactions, the prices of the underlying assets, and so forth. But because derivative contracts do not require one to both own and actually possess the asset at the same time, there is considerable room for one to engage in speculation and essentially vary the terms of the contract in numerous ways.

FINANCIAL BUBBLES

Financial bubbles are born when widespread "irrational exuberance" (to borrow from the words of the former chairman of the Federal Reserve, Alan Greenspan) displaces any rational analysis of the intrinsic value of an asset. More to the point, a financial bubble occurs when there is a widely-held conviction that a particular item or object is going to be increasing in value thus causing many otherwise sane individuals to pay prices often far in excess of the actual value of the asset itself for fear they will miss out on additional price increases. A financial bubble can occur in a variety of ways and with an almost unlimited variety of assets. One of the most famous financial bubbles involved tulips in the Nether-lands in the early 17th century.

Tulips originated in the Middle East and had attracted the attention of the Dutch elites who prized the flowers for their many pastel colors. As with the some of the assets in other bubble markets, the tulips began as exotic, highly sought after items that were cov-eted by the upper strata of Dutch society. Whether or not the purchaser actually liked the flowers themselves was less important than the fact that he or she could be seen with a handful of the precious blooms. In short, the ownership of the tulips and being seen by others as having these precious flowers quickly became much more important than whether the owner actually enjoyed the flowers themselves or whether the flowers actually had any significant intrinsic worth. Because anyone who was anyone did not want to be left behind and be viewed by his or her contemporaries as a socially-inept non-owner of tulips, many would-be tulip enthusiasts started furiously digging through their couches and chairs to find any spare guilders to fund their flower purchases. So nearly everyone who had some extra money hurried over to the flower markets to buy tulips, thus sending prices soaring into the atmosphere.

As this frenzy became more pronounced and people started using their grocery money and their rent payments to adorn their homes with the lovely but increasingly dear tulips, the prices for these exotic flow-ers rapidly escalated. Indeed, the prices continued to rise until they became so high that the Netherlands ran out of buyers who were both willing and able to pay the stratospheric sales prices, thus causing the demand for the flowers to become unsustainable and, soon thereafter, to plummet. Although the extent of the increase in the value of a single tulip bulb has been exaggerated by certain historians, it does appear to be true that a few individuals with very unfortunate timing did pay the equivalent of a worker's annual wages for a single bulb before the prices collapsed in early 1637—less than a year after the mania began.

The tulip bubble is often cited as an example in which the market price of the asset obviously exceeded its intrinsic value. Nothing about the flowers changed during the bubble; it was the psychological desires of the purchasers for the tulips that drastically shifted in an almost herd-like fashion thus causing the value of the tulips to shoot up to unimaginable heights. But we can thank our lucky wooden shoes (known as clogs or klompen in the Netherlands) that we are far too sophisticated to fall for such nonsense where we are paying extraordinary amounts of money for items of little tangible value. Unless, of course, you consider a couple of recent slip-ups such as the housing crash in the United States in 2009 (in which the average home lost one-third of its value) which triggered the so-called Great Recession and a massive contraction in the global economy or the dotcom stock bubble in the 1990s in which start-up companies with little more than a business plan commanded hundreds of millions or even billions of dollars in market value before most of them were financially vaporized as the technology-laden NASDAQ index lost almost four-fifths of its value in the span of a year.

Regardless of whether you dabble in tulips or houses or stocks, there is always the danger that the pricing of an asset can overwhelm its intrinsic value and develop into a bubble. Unfortunately, nearly all bubbles are accompanied by an almost willing ignorance by its participants to question the excessive valuations being attributed to that particular asset. Promoters will invariably try to point out why "it is different this time" to justify the lofty valuations that the assets in question command. Here, it is a good thing to remember the old adage that "what goes up, must come down." For those individuals who pile into frothy markets after the market prices have long since left the intrinsic values of those assets in the proverbial dust, it is almost inevitable that there will be a massive adjustment at some point when no one is left to pay the prices demanded for these assets and keep inflating the bubble.

ALL ABOUT BANKS

The banking system is dependent on the general public believing that the money they keep in their bank accounts is safe and sound. Indeed, public confidence in the banks is vital to the success of the banks themselves; the banks are extremely dependent on the interest income that they earn from loaning out their customers' deposits to prospective borrowers. It is the difference between the interest the banks pay to their depositors (less than impressive) and the interest they charge to their borrowers (more than you would like) that constitutes the profits of the bank's loan portfolio. Of course this is a very simplified view as it necessarily neglects to include the costs involved in operating the banks themselves (for example, rent, utilities, and salaries) or the corruption that can sometimes be found in the executive offices. Nor does it include other sources of income that might bolster the profits of the banks such as the fees charged for bounced checks and the arguably usurious rates of interest charged for the use of bank credit cards.

Suppose you are the president of Flea Bank, which boasts $10 million in deposits. To attract those deposits, you have to pay the owners of those funds enough money to convince them to deposit these funds with your bank. However, your bank can survive only if you are able to turn around and loan that money out to other individuals (and companies) at a higher rate of interest. Banks that try to do good deeds by paying more interest to their depositors than they in turn collect from their borrowers do not exist because the losses on their loans would always swamp the interest they would receive from those very same loans.

You are no doubt impressed by our having distilled the intricacies of the modern banking system into a single paragraph. The basic strategy of acquiring lower-cost deposits and then loaning these deposits out at a higher interest rate is straightforward and diabolically simple but it is one that can be fraught with risk. Why? It would appear that the most profitable strategy would be to lend every dollar in the bank vault out to borrowers clamoring to increase their indebtedness. Unfortunately, this is not a sound approach because every bank (even Flea Bank) must keep a certain amount of its deposits in reserve to meet the everyday needs of its customers. So if I wished to withdraw $100 from my account on Monday to purchase a stuffed moose head to complete my taxidermy collection of large North American mammals that are proudly mounted on the wall of my living room, I would be very unhappy if the bank teller told me that they did not have a single dollar in the till to give me and that I would have to come back another day. Indeed, I might respond in a loud and obnoxious manner, cursing violently at the bank manager as I was dragged off the premises by the teenaged security guard. But a lack of cash would be very bad for any bank because it would not only greatly inconvenience its customers (who, in this day and age of hair-trigger tempers and self-perceived victimization, would not think twice about taking their business elsewhere and unleashing a blistering barrage of nasty social media commentaries) but also cause unflattering rumors to swirl around about the financial wherewithal of the bank itself.

The other constraint that prevents banks from loaning out every single dollar in their vaults is their imperfect ability to evaluate the creditworthiness of their borrowers. Suppose that Captain Freddie Black-beard, one of the fiercest pirates to ever sail the Carib-bean, applies for a loan at Flea Bank to mend the sails and rigging on his ship. Although Captain Freddie has killed many men and burned down numerous island outposts, he might not be the best credit risk because most of his "collateral" to secure the repayment of the loan would consist of stolen treasure, which he swears is buried on several small islands. The bank might not feel very confident that the loan would be repaid by Captain Freddie, so they would be predisposed to turn him down. It is not a well-kept secret that banks detest borrowers who default on their loans because these defaults mean that the expected stream of reve-nue—in the form of monthly loan payments—will stop. If Captain Freddie actually sits down with a bank offi-cer, he will have to fill out a loan application and list all of his assets (e.g., leaky ship, forthcoming ransom payments, gold coins and jewels in his pockets) and lia-bilities (e.g., wages owed to disgruntled crew members, unpaid tavern charges, monies owed to seamstress who created swashbuckling outfits). The bank will also run a credit check on Captain Freddie to get a snapshot of his financial activities. All of these items will then be considered in the final decision by the bank board as to whether or not to loan Captain Freddie the money. All of this work by the bank is undertaken so that it can try to determine the likelihood that Captain Freddie will default on his loan.

But is defaulting on a loan necessarily a bad thing? After all, most bank loans are made only when the borrower can provide adequate collateral (such as the house for which a loan is sought). If the borrower defaults on the loan, then the bank can foreclose on the house and sell it to recover its loan. What could be easier? Plus, the loan documents signed by borrowers will provide for a bewildering array of fees and charges and expenses that can be charged by the bank if it must go through the foreclosure process. Indeed, it seems like banks should welcome foreclosures as a way to sell the collateral and collect all of the previously mentioned fees, charges and expenses. But the answer is not so simple. The reason banks genuinely hate to foreclose on properties that are serving as collateral for their loans is that the proceeds from the sale of the collateral may not be sufficient to cover the amount of the loan—let alone all of the other attendant charges. How could such a situation occur? Well, market conditions can change so that a house, for example, that was purchased for $200,000 with $40,000 in cash and $160,000 in borrowed funds might drop in value. We say that a property is "under water" when its net value is less than the amount of the mortgage itself. If a recession occurred and caused the value of the house to drop from $200,000 to $150,000, for example, then we would say that there was negative equity in the property in the amount of $10,000 ($160,000 (the amount of the original loan) less the home's post-recession value of $150,000). Other people who live in areas designated as "flood plains" might not appreciate our flippant use of the phrase "under water" but it is merely a descriptive way of conveying the fact that the loan obligation is now greater than value of the property itself. So we can understand why a lender would not be anxious to foreclose on a property that is under water because it will almost assuredly incur a loss on the sale of the property at the new, lower value. Although very few of us would cry boo-hoo for the plight of any bank, we can appreciate why a bank would have to hold back some of its depositors' funds in order to cover losses that it might suffer if it had to foreclose on properties having negative net worth.

THE YIELD CURVE

If I wish to lend my money for one year to the Vampire Company—which is in search of a quick infusion of cash to fund corporate perks—I will want to receive some amount of interest during the time that the bank is using my money. Once the installment of the solid gold fixtures in the executive bathroom is completed, however, then Vampire Company would presumably pay me back my original principal plus interest. But what if the world-renowned executive washroom designer Lev Swirley decides that the Vampire Company job will be the crowning glory of his creative career. He wastes no time and does not concern himself with getting the necessary authorizations to expand greatly the scope of the project to include solid gold toilets and a platinum ceiling. The solid gold toilets, for example, are painstakingly handcrafted by the famous goldsmith Olaf Engebretsen at his shop in Norway and any attempt to hurry Olaf will unleash an impressive string of Norwegian obscenities.

Not only does the original projected cost of the project increase ten-fold due to the hiring of some of the world's most talented artisans but the array of precious metals vastly inflates the costs of the finishes. As a result, the projected time of completion increases from one to three years. So the officials at Vampire Company might call me and ask if I would mind extending the loan for two additional years to coincide with the extended completion date of Lev's lavatory masterpiece. However, I would probably want to increase the interest rate I am charging them to compensate myself for the fact that I will not be able to use the money for three years which, of course, will delay the day that I can order my own solid-gold toilet.

A lender will typically charge a higher rate of interest as the term (duration) of the loan increases with time. This direct relationship between the interest rate and the term of the loan leads to what economists call the "yield curve." Although the term evokes images of a wheat field to some observers, the yield curve is really just a graphic plotting of the relationship between time and interest rates. As the interest rate increases on the vertical axis of the graph and the term of the loan increases on the horizontal axis of the graph, the plotted line generally moves upward. So all things being equal, a longer loan term will be accompanied by a higher interest rate. This higher interest rate is meant to compensate the lender for the increased risk involved in waiting for the repayment of the loan principal.

But sometimes you will hear noted economists and self-taught news broadcasters who like to use big words talk about an "inverted yield curve," which is not quite so sensuous as it sounds. The typical yield curve's upward track indicates that long-term interest rates will be higher than short-term interest rates. An inverted yield curve, however, occurs when short term interest rates exceed long term interest rates. This situation typically arises when investors suddenly perceive that there is a heightened risk of an economic downturn in the near future. Hence, the short term yield curve is inverted and the plotted line slopes negatively instead of positively, suggesting that interest rates will fall with time.

FINANCING YOUR EMPIRE: BANK LOANS OR COMPANY BONDS

Most business enterprises will require capital at one time or another to fund their operations. Many business owners who desire to become financially indentured to banks will seek loans for their businesses. However, other business owners may choose to bypass lenders and instead issue bonds which are debt obligations of the company that are sold to investors to raise money. Bonds typically promise to pay a certain interest rate for a fixed period of time (for example, five years) until the date of maturity at which time the bond is redeemed and the face value of the bond is paid. Of course, the vagaries of the real world can wreak havoc on such idyllic scenarios because there is no guarantee that the issuer of the bond will continue paying interest for the duration of its lifetime and that the debt obligation will ultimately be paid. The company issuing the bond can go bankrupt or it can suffer significant financial losses that prevent it from fulfilling its obligations to pay interest on the bond.

How are the interest rates set on bonds? In the market for bonds, the issuer of the bond will set an interest rate, usually based upon the rate being offered by similar companies of like creditworthiness. Anyone hoping to sell bonds must be cognizant of the interest rate that will be promised to investors so that they will purchase those bonds. No issuer of bonds wants to offer more interest than is absolutely necessary to attract the attention of investors and no investor wishes to purchase a bond paying any less than the maximum rate of interest that could be reasonably expected from such an investment.

Suppose our friends at the Flea Bank need to raise

$100,000,000 to fund the purchase of a new yacht not only to provide the higher-ups with outstanding recreational opportunities but also, for write-off purposes, to serve as a floating bank that can side up to other yachts and provide innovative marine "drive through" banking services. To pay for this noteworthy capital investment, Flea Bank could issue the $100,000,000 in corporate bonds bearing an interest rate of, say, 5 percent, which would mature in ten years. So you might choose to add a $1,000 bond issued by Flea Bank to your portfolio because you would like to be assured of a steady income to support your flashy lifestyle—in this case, a staggering monthly payment of $4.16 per month or $50.00 per year. Imagine what you could do with an extra $4.16 a month in your pocket! Why, you could buy two loaves of bread or a gallon of gas or even a new pair of socks. Or you could save the $4.16 each month until you had amassed $50 at the end of the year and then "go crazy"—spending a solid half hour at your favorite pub quaffing fine lagers. Nevertheless, you could expect to look forward to receiving a check for $4.16 a month until the bond matured—at which time your original $1,000 investment would be repaid to you.

From the perspective of Flea Bank, the sale of the bonds would give it access to an enormous amount of capital for a comparatively small upfront payment. Of course, if the bank were to go bankrupt in the interim, then the investors would probably get very little, if any, of their original investment back. But with a 5 percent interest rate, Flea Bank would be able to leverage its capital considerably by twenty-fold—paying $50 per year to get the use of each $1,000 sum invested. On a large scale, this massive influx of capital would make it possible to purchase a lot of fancy sports cars for the company's deserving executives.

Needless to say, all bonds are not created equal. Some bonds extend for a year or two whereas other bonds may not mature for 10, 15, or even 20 years. Of equal significance is the variations in the interest rates that one can find when sifting among different bonds. The lower the interest rate, the lower the perceived risk that the issuer of the bond will default on its payments to its investors. Suppose that Parasite Bank is able to sell its bonds with a 5 percent interest rate because it has always paid its bondholders in a timely manner and has never defaulted on its obligations. Now compare that pristine records with the somewhat tattered legacy of Vampire Company, which has perpetually flirted with bankruptcy. Not surprisingly, Vampire Company's debt offerings would be viewed with greater skepticism by the investing public; prospective investors would be rightly concerned that the bonds might not be paid off at maturity. As a result, the company would have to offer a much higher rate of interest on its bonds in order to lure the investing public to add its debt obligations to their portfolios.

SELLING YOUR COMPANY STOCK

All firms require capital at one time or another whether they need to purchase new plants and equipment, hire workers, or obtain materials. Some firms, as we have seen, raise capital by issuing bonds and, in effect, borrowing money from investors. This type of financing enables the firm to acquire the capital without having to give the bondholders a say in how the firm is managed or, indeed, a share of the ownership of the company. In other words, the bondholders are lenders—not owners. But the bonds are debt instruments and the bondholders expect to be paid recurring interest payments on a regular basis or else they will hire lawyers to send nasty letters threatening legal Armageddon against the company. But what if you as the owner of the company, Vulture Cosmetics, are concerned about the on-going burden of interest payments and how it affects your cash flow?

If you are interested in marshalling your cash for your new Falcon Blue Eye Shadow promotion, you might want to avoid the unceasing financial costs of making monthly or quarterly payments to bondholders by instead issuing stock in the company and selling it to the public. The obvious advantage is that the stock does not have to pay a dividend so that its effect on cash flow might be nil. Of course, the absence of a dividend payment might affect the desirability of the stock in the eyes of investors but that is a separate matter altogether. A separate consideration is the costs that you will incur in issuing and selling the stock itself, regardless of whether Vulture Cosmetics is a privately-held company or publicly traded on one of the major stock exchanges. Of course you are happy to enrich the lawyers that stand ready to carry out the necessary mountains of paperwork but there are substantial costs that will need to be paid if you become involved in a significant stock offering—not only to lawyers but also to investment banking companies who would help to sell the stock. If, on the other hand, Vulture Cosmetics were a start-up being operated out of a garage, then the costs of issuing stock will likely be negligible because you or your lawyer would tear out some new stock certificates from your corporate book and fill them out and issue them to the prospective shareholders in exchange for the cash. Even though Vulture Cosmetics might be an embryonic company, however, you would still have to familiarize yourself with the laws governing the sale of securities in your particular state—the so-called "blue sky laws." This will often require you to call upon the lawyers who are ready to leap into action at a moment's notice and start running the clock.

So if you are willing to incur the costs needed to complete an issuing of non-voting stock to prospective shareholders, it might provide a way to raise money for your company without losing control. The trade-off, of course, is that the sale of stock would involve the transfer of a proportionate share of the ownership interest in your company. Furthermore, the shareholders would have a right to claim a proportionate interest in the company profits (even though the lawyers of your ex-spouses might be taking care of any profit issues all by themselves). Once you do sell the stock and welcome your new shareholders aboard, however, you may find yourself receiving unsolicited advice about how to improve the profitability of the company or why you should hire their college dropout children to be executive vice presidents. Wishing to avoid such an unfortunate situation in which thick-headed advice is offered by shareholders who you believe are dimmer than a 40-watt light bulb, you would breathe a sigh of relief that you were smart enough to create voting and non-voting shares of the stock. In this way, you can control the decision-making process entirely while extending the tepid hand of friendship to your new non-voting shareholders. The issuance of non-voting stock is very common and may provide the optimal solution from the company owner's viewpoint as to the best way to generate a significant infusion of cash without having to give up any meaningful control of the company—leaving you to be solely responsible for eventually running it into the ground.

When selling company stock to the general public, you will also need to keep in mind the liquidity or lack of liquidity of the stock itself. The stocks of smaller, closely-held companies do not typically trade on a public exchange and so these stocks cannot be easily sold if the owner suddenly decides that he or she wants to dump his or her holdings in favor of cash or perhaps a vintage purple woolen overcoat with peacock feathers. As the owner of the company, you will have to convince potential investors that the promise of the company outweighs any likelihood that they would want to abandon their shares in the near future. Some may find your inspirational ramblings about the company's future to be appealing; others may find it terrifying that they have no way out unless and until your company either redeems the shares for cash or is bought out by another company.

CONSUMER AND STUDENT LOANS

Suppose that I work as the head ice cream scooper at Carl's Ice Cream Shoppe and Sushi Bar on the Atlantic City boardwalk. Although my job is glamorous and undoubtedly coveted by many of the patrons of our establishment, the pay is not significant. Indeed, a good day of scooping seldom yields more than $100 in wages and tips. Notwithstanding my limited income, however, I have always wanted to purchase a yacht. Not a monster-sized yacht exceeding the length of a football field, but merely a 40' or 50' ship that I can steer around the harbor. However, even the smallest yachts cost in excess of $1 million so it would appear at first glance that my dream of yacht ownership will never become a reality. Indeed, my income might limit me to purchasing one of the silk cushions on one of the teak chairs on the deck of the yacht.

But having taken a course in economics in college (or at least having attended a few of the classes), I decide that I should investigate whether such a purchase could be financed. Imagine my surprise when I checked with my local banker and found that I could borrow $1,000,000 at an interest rate of 6 percent and the loan would only take 100 years to pay it off with a monthly payment of $5,012,61. Unfortunately, most banks do not provide such long term loans and they are doubtless aware that neither myself nor the collateral for the loan (the yacht) will last the necessary 100 years—which greatly hinders any foreclosure remedies if I should default on the loan. The other depressing fact about such a loan is that the $5,012.61 monthly payment is almost all interest in the initial few decades (only $12.61 in principal will be paid in the first month) and that it will be many years before the loan balance begins to shrink appreciably. Indeed, my 1,200 payments of $5,012.61 each over 100 years will total $6,015,134.61. But I can take some pleasure in the fact that I (or, more accurately, my heirs) will eventually pay off that $1,000,000 loan even though it will entail paying $5,015,134.61 in interest over those 3 or 4 generations.

Of course I could arrange to pay the $1,000,000 loan off sooner. If I shortened the maturity date to 20 years, then my monthly payment at a 6 percent interest rate would increase to $7,164.31. So by adding $2,164.31 to each monthly payment, I would cut 80 years off the term of the loan and receive a "PAID IN FULL" notice from the lender before I lost all of my teeth. Under such a payment schedule, I would make 240 payments totaling $1,719,434.54 and the total interest paid on the loan would be $719,434.54. Were it not for the fact that I only make a couple of thousand dollars per month, I would definitely opt for the 20 year loan as a way to finance the purchase of my yacht.

The sad fact is that many people do not need to buy a yacht in order to bury themselves in debt that can take many years to pay off. My friend and colleague, Joe Stanton, borrowed nearly $200,000 in student loans to pay for ornithological studies at the very prestigious and expensive Sphincter College. The math seemed simple at the time: The loan of $200,000 would be paid off in 240 equal monthly payments of $1,211.96—a sum that did not seem too overwhelming, particularly when Joe knew he would not have to start paying the money back until after graduation. Of course, Joe was certain he would have already secured a high-paying job doing ornithological stuff before making any loan payments. But his dream of doing ornithological things never materialized and he was forced to take the assistant ice cream scooper job at Carl's to pay for his student loans.

The point: We can borrow money to acquire worthwhile toys such as yachts and finance important endeavors such as a venture into ornithology even though we may have very little actual cash on hand. The key to a cash-poor individual being able to acquire yachts or cars or expensive educations is to secure the financing at an affordable interest rate and stretch out the payments over a sufficiently long period of time so that the debtor is not suffocated by the monthly payment obligations. Of course, most banks will insist on collateralizing the loan when a tangible asset such as a yacht or car or house is being purchased. This is usually done when the lender files a financing statement for personal property such as yachts and cars and a mortgage for real property such as houses in the local public records. These filings give the world formal notice that that particular asset is encumbered by a loan obligation that must be repaid before the debtor can sell it to another person. In the case of student loans, the lender will have to resort to other ways to get their money back such as garnishing my wages until the loan is fully repaid.

CRYPTOCURRENCIES

National governments jealously guard their monopoly to print currency for use by their citizens. Needless to say, they take a rather dim view of those entrepreneurs who choose to print their own money—no matter how faithfully they replicate the originals—and instead punish this artistic enthusiasm with long prison sentences. Most governments also show a similar disdain for the so-called digital or cryptocurrencies which have developed over the past few years. Bitcoin, Ethereum and Dogecoin are among the top cryptocurrencies and, depending on the particular country, have either been banned outright or severely restricted in their use as an alternative form of money. In those nations where cryptocurrencies are permitted, they are eyed suspiciously by government regulators because cryptocurrencies operate in a separate private financial ecosystem that is outside the control of monetary authorities such as the Federal Reserve.

The term "cryptocurrency" arises from the fact that the ownership records of individual coins are encrypted and stored on a computerized ledger called a blockchain. The blockchain essentially acts as a digital "tattletale" and details the history of every transaction involving every individual (digital) coin in a particular cryptocurrency. As such, it resembles the electronic history maintained by a credit card company on each of its cardholders, the primary difference being that most credit card company records are confidential and associated with actual named individuals whereas the blockchain is publicly available and describes the transactions themselves from the beginning of cryptocurrency time to the present day. However, the names of the individuals on the blockchain are encrypted which ensures that their true identities are hidden from public view. Naturally, this lack of transparency in designating actual owners has caused governments pressing their proverbial noses against the glass outside of the cryptocurrency system to gnash their teeth and complain that these cryptocurrencies are nothing more than a vehicle whereby organized crime can finance its operations without fear of scrutiny by the police. Because government policymakers are all-knowing and never wrong about anything, there may be some credence to the theory that cryptocurrencies can serve as a conduit for the financing of illicit activities. But the protections afforded by encryption are not absolute as any information that is encrypted can be uncovered so long as the person seeking the information has the relevant encryption keys. Moreover, cryptocurrencies do not offer absolute anonymity but instead a mask that can be torn off by ambitious government regulators if the address or addresses that cryptocurrency owners use to transact business are ever linked to the individuals themselves. Then the fun can begin and the police can swoop in and break down the owner's front door in the early morning hours while strategically-placed news crews breathlessly report about the crushing blow being dealt to organized crime kingpins who have cleverly disguised themselves as bleary-eyed parents clad in bathrobes holding crying children in their arms.

Cryptocurrencies are also viewed suspiciously by many private investors who question whether they have any real value at all. You cannot demand that a bank in a country on the gold standard, for example, give you gold in exchange for your cryptocurrency coins because cryptocurrencies are not issued by the government. As such, they are not backed by anything of tangible value. But one could argue that cryptocurrencies are no different from the fiat currencies that have been issued by governments all over the world which rely on nothing more than the public's willingness to accept the notes as legal tender and use them to buy and sell goods and services. Unfortunately, cryptocurrencies cannot count on the coercive authority that the government heavyweights like to wield to ensure the exclusivity of their respective national currencies. As a result, cryptocurrencies necessarily operate in a decentralized, non-coercive environment in which the value of the coins themselves arise from the shared consensus of their users as to the value of those coins. Absent the lack of government authority, one could argue that cryptocurrencies are not that different from fiat currencies and no less lacking in intrinsic value.

Cryptocurrencies do differ from fiat currencies in that the rate of production of the digital currency itself is defined when the parameters of the system itself are established. Enthusiastic central bankers would feel very constrained by the inherent limitations built into these digital edifices as they cannot simply say "Abracadabra" and create $100 billion in new cryptocurrency out of thin air. Instead, new cryptocurrency is minted in the digital sense as certain conditions in the system are satisfied. One of the ways in which individuals can obtain cryptocurrencies is by mining. The term "mining" is somewhat misleading because it does not involve venturing down a mine shaft singing manly chain gang songs and risking life and limb with pungent coworkers.

Instead, cryptocurrency miners receive new coins in exchange for validating cryptocurrency transactions through the construction of computers which enhance the processing power of the cryptocurrency system. The problem for these miners is that it has become increasingly difficult to justify the reward of new cryptocurrency as more miners have joined the fray thus causing the costs of the machines and the electricity they consume to skyrocket.

AFTERWORD

Few readers would deny that the concepts of supply, demand, money, banking, and finance are dry topics that cannot be easily explained when set to the bouncy sounds of a music video. Even students who are interested in the basic tenets of economics may fall asleep during class and, in rare instances, tumble out of their chairs and slip into a coma. Despite its shortcomings as a source of entertainment for the masses, however, the study of economics is essential for understanding why people buy and sell goods and services from each other and, indeed, why markets arise in the first place.

Because the original version of *Economics and All That* was so intellectually daunting—or long, take your pick—it was split into two separate volumes to give you a break, much like an intermission in a Broadway musical. This first volume offers a survey of the various concepts that anchor modern economics such as an examination of the ways in which markets operate and the functions of banks in the national economy. The second volume veers into more specific areas such as monopolies and central planning and the terms of trade between countries to see how the principles of economics manifest in the real world.

In finishing Volume 1, you will have completed an incredible intellectual achievement: navigating a volume loaded with as many key concepts about daily living as any of William Shakespeare's plays. Given the lack of illustrations, such a journey can be exhausting, so this break in the action provides some relief to those who are laboring under the weight of Volume 1's deeply thoughtful pronouncements. This pause allows you to get up and walk around the room and clear your head before plunging back into the second volume.

Economics is the culmination of the search for patterns in the ways in which human beings conduct their affairs in exchanging goods and services with each other. For example, it offers predictions as to how people will respond to given situations in which the price of a good increases or decreases or the extent to which suppliers of a good will increase or decrease production due to changes in the marketplace. As such, it does not claim to be correct in each and every situation because there are always free-thinking (in some cases, just plain ignorant) individuals wandering around who behave in ways that simply do not make sense from any rational perspective. However, economics purports to explain the actions of most individuals in most situations and does offer predictive powers about the ways in which most people will carry out their day-to-day activities when buying and selling goods and services. As such, it provides a map that brings some order to the apparent messiness of the real world and gives us hope—however fleeting that may be—that we can devise policies in the political sphere that will ultimately contribute to the economic well-being of everyone.

ACKNOWLEDGMENTS / BIBLIOGRAPHY

When one is fortunate enough to possess the superlative literary talents needed to write a masterpiece such as *Economics and All That*, one must still give the appropriate credit to those other authors whose works have provided information and illumination as to various topics in economics that have been of value in the writing of this tome. Even though *Economics and All That* may be very much in the running to win a Nobel Prize in literature or economics or both, the author remains humbled by the contributions of the many scholars who have helped to develop the concepts and principles of economics over the past three centuries. In particular, the author would like to acknowledge the following works that were consulted in the preparation of this volume.

Wealth of Nations by Adam Smith; *The General Theory of Employment, Interest, and Money* by John Maynard Keynes; *Manias, Panics and Crashes: A History of Financial Crises* by Charles P. Kindleberger; *Capital in the Twenty First Century* by Thomas Piketty; *Freakonomics* by Steven Levitt and Stephen Dubner; *Basic Economics* by Thomas Sowell; *The Rise and Decline of Nations* by Mancur Olson; *Thinking Fast and Slow* by Daniel Kahneman; *The Undercover Economist* by Tim Harford; *Globalization and Its Discontents* by Joseph Stiglitz; *Economics in One Lesson* by Henry Hazlitt; *Naked Economics* by Charles Wheelan; *Principles of Political Economy* by John Stuart Mill; *Capitalism, Socialism, and Democracy* by Joseph Schumpeter; *Doughnut Economics* by Kate Raworth; *Small is Beautiful* by E.F. Schumacher; *The Worldly Philosophers* by Robert Heilbroner; *Why Nations Fail* by Daron Acemoglu and James A Robinson; *Too Big to Fail* by Andrew Ross Sorkin; *Capitalism and Freedom* by Milton Friedman; *The Big Short* by Michael Lewis; *Individualism and Economic Order* by Friedrich Hayek; *The Ascent of Money* by Niall Ferguson; *The Armchair Economist* by Steven Landsburg; *The Black Swan* by Nassim Talebut; *Evil Geniuses* by Kurt Andersen; *Capitalism in America* by Alan Greenspan and Adrian Wooldridge; *The Affluent Society* by John Kenneth Galbraith; *The Great Transformation: The Political and Economic Origins of Our Time* by Karl Polyani; *Economics in Minutes* by Niall Kishtainy; *Hidden Order* by David Friedman; *The Theory of the Leisure Class* by Thorstein Veblen; *Economics* by Paul Samuelson; *Capital* by Karl Marx.

And while the author would like to blame any errors in *Economics and All That* on these sources, the author has been informed by his lawyers that such conduct could form the basis for a lawsuit for defamation that could cost the author huge amounts of money. As a result, the author sincerely takes full responsibility for all mistakes and errors in *Economics and All That* even though it is very, very, very unlikely that he could have made a boo-boo in the writing of this book.

VOLUME 2:

FROM FIRMS AND INDUSTRIES TO LABOR, GOVERNMENT AND THE INTERNATIONAL ECONOMY

PART ONE:
FIRMS AND INDUSTRIES

PRICE DISCRIMINATION

For many years I have operated the Body Wax Spa which offers various types of cosmetic services to a predominantly female clientele. Business has been good, but it could be better. So, I start trying to think of ways that I can broaden the audience for body waxing procedures—particularly for the very delicate and intimate bikini wax. Then one day while scraping dried wax off the floor of the spa, I have a brilliant thought: Professional football players are notoriously underrepresented in the community of body waxing enthusiasts. Indeed, I would be hard pressed to recall a single professional football player who ever boasted about the smoothness of his skin after a good wax job. The challenge is to reach out to this untapped market and convert hundreds of players—both active and retired—into body waxing hobbyists.

But what should I charge these rough and ready men who like nothing more than to run into each other at high rates of speed? The simplest solution would be to charge the same fees that we charge our existing customers. But our existing customers do not have to be convinced of the merits of a thorough wax job. Indeed, we might have to do some promotional pricing in the form of selected discounts to get some of those wide-bodied linemen through the front door. So instead of charging $30 for a leg wax, we might offer a temporary "new customer" price of $20. Moreover, we could drop our $50 bikini wax price by a few dollars to attract the attention of those athletes who can appreciate a smooth groin area.

But we do not want to give away the store in our attempt to entice these players into our spa. Some players will respond more readily to the prospect of a body wax whereas others will be inherently hostile to such a "sissy" activity. One can imagine a retired linebacker turning down the offer of a discounted bikini wax and declaring to the attendant: "In my day they used a pair of pliers to pull all the hair out by the roots! Nobody could get any wax because of the war! They had to save it for the boys on the battlefield!" By contrast, a wide receiver might be more enthusiastic about getting a bikini wax and willing to pay the full price for the service.

The whole point of price discrimination is to determine who has what level of desire for a wax job and then charge each person accordingly. Our retired linebacker is not particularly interested in having a hairless perineum and, at best, might be willing to pay only a few dollars for the service. Our wide receiver—who is a diva—may embrace the ameliorative effects of hot wax on the skin and gladly pay more money. To maximize our revenues, we would try to charge each of these two prospective customers based upon their respective desires for the wax job. But successful price discrimination requires us to price our services based upon the intensity of the demand for these services by our customers, and that is not always easy to discern.

If we decide that we are not going to worry about trying to determine who has the greater desire for a body wax and instead set a single price for our service that is low enough to entice the linebacker into the spa, then we are going to leave a lot of money on the table. Why? Because we will in effect be under-charging the more narcissistic players like our wide receiver who would gladly pay a higher price for the body wax. By the same token, if we price our services at the full rates and skip the discounts altogether, the more reluctant prospective customers such as our linebacker will simply walk by our shop.

The trick to engaging in a successful price discrimination scheme is that you must be able to identify and segregate your customers based upon their willingness to pay for your service. Selective discounts can help to uncover the willingness of particular groups of people to spend money on such services. For example, you could offer senior citizens a discount because most of them will doubtless consider body waxing to be frivolous. Or you could hire a market research company to interview different people from all walks of life and see who appears to be more enthusiastic about having strips of dried wax ripped from their body. We might expect masochists and models, for example, to both have a lot of interest in this service. Of course one could be far more explicit and state the discounts available to various groups on the front door of the spa and see what happens. But pricing the service on willingness to pay alone may not solve the problem: Your big-bodied lineman is probably only willing to pay a few dollars for the service but you will use a lot more wax to cover his body whereas the wide receiver and quarterback (particularly those auditioning for skin care product commercials) will be willing to pay more but will presumably require less wax.

MAXIMIZING YOUR COMPANY'S PROFITS

As a would-be titan of industry who desires to live on

an estate behind a high wall and iron gate, you know that the key to being able to live a luxurious lifestyle and lord your shiny possessions over your neighbors is that you must accumulate a lot of money. Because you are operating a business, you want to maximize your profits. That seems straightforward because every business owner typically wants to make as much money as possible. But your ability to maximize profits is not simply an exercise in selling as many items as you can for as much as you can. Indeed, you must try to gain an understanding of your costs and your revenues as each additional item is sold.

We can better understand the concept of profit maximization by focusing on your firm which has been manufacturing counterfeit Girl Scout cookies called Ranger Girl Treats and peddling them to unwary shoppers in front of grocery stores around the country. Ranger Girl Treats are wafers covered with five different types of toppings: marshmallows, chocolate, caramel, vanilla fudge and fish. Your Ranger Girl Treats are sold by the mothers of young girls who have typically been kicked out of the Girl Scouts for behavioral problems and who are paid sales commissions based upon the numbers of boxes sold. Ranger Girl Treats have almost no natural ingredients so the cookies can last up to 500 years. Your use of chemicals and solvents also enables you to price Ranger Girl Treats far below the competition. But even though you are the low-cost producer in the cute little girl cookie market, you still need to have some idea as to your production costs and the incremental revenues that you will gain with the sale of each additional box of Ranger Girl Treats. Indeed, every decision you make—whether it be how many workers to hire or how many barrels of synthetic corn syrup to buy—will be affected by your desire to maximize profits. The tricky part is determining how many Ranger Girl Treats you will need to manufacture in order to maximize your profits.

How do you decide whether to make 1,000 cases or 2,000 cases or even 5,000 cases of Ranger Girl Treats? You start by calculating all of your manufacturing costs, including wages and the rental costs of the warehouse in which the Ranger Girl Treat Company operates. You also include the costs of your supplies and utilities, such as the company water and electricity bills. Once you calculate the total costs, you then try to figure out how many boxes of Ranger Girl Treats you need to manufacture. For example, if you sold each box of cookies for $2.00 and the thousandth box only cost $1.00 to make, then it would make sense for you to continue expanding production until the marginal cost of producing one additional box of cookies is equal to the marginal revenue that will be derived from the sale of the cookies. So, you would want to keep baking away until you reached the point (say, for example, 5,000 cases) at which the additional revenue to be derived from the sale of a box of cookies ($2.00) would be equal to the additional costs that would be incurred from the manufacture of that box of cookies (again, $2.00). You would not want to produce additional boxes of cookies (whether it be 5,001 or 6,000 or whatever) because each additional box would cost more than the revenue it would fetch at the time of sale. This sad state of affairs is due to the fact that marginal costs typically rise over time as production is increased whereas marginal revenues (the $2.00 price of a box of cookies) are unchanged (assuming a fixed sales price) for each additional box sold.

Of course, the goal of maximizing profits is far easier to discuss in theory than it is to accomplish in the messy, bruising world of pre-teen cookie sales. Although you can set a fixed sales price for each box and thereby know exactly what your total revenue will be at any given quantity of sales, you may find yourself having to change the prices in different markets (perhaps dropping them severely in areas populated by organic foods proponents who are wary of the 17 chemicals listed on the side of each box of Ranger Girl Treats) or perhaps having to reduce the price at certain times of year such as the Christmas holidays when overconsumption may cause your typical customers to be less interested in your fish-dipped treats. But if you assume that you can sell any number of boxes for $2.00 each, then you have to tally your production costs. The difficulty with that, of course, is that your suppliers (such as Toxic Chemicals Inc) may increase the prices of their solvents and thereby adversely impact your supply costs. Or your whiny workers might decide that they no longer wish to work in a windowless plant in which the ambient temperatures hover around those of a coal-fired pizza oven and go on a strike that results in your having to pay higher wages, thus further complicating your efforts to figure out the marginal costs of producing each additional box of delicious cookies. The point here, of course, is that the dynamic nature of the market will often complicate any efforts to get a perfect calculation of your marginal costs, and you may end up making too many or too few boxes of cookies to maximize your profits.

THE LAW OF DIMINISHING RETURNS

When we talk about laws in the world of economics, we are not usually referring to a law in the sense of a legislative edict. Instead, a "law" of economics is a conclusion that is drawn from repeated observations of a particular pattern of behavior or a series of events. It is not to be confused with the Law of Grandma's Hairbrush, which postulates that if we behave badly at Grandma's house, she will invariably retrieve her hairbrush and swat us on our bottoms. But the idea that a certain result can be predicted with reasonable accuracy from a fixed set of conditions is at the heart of any social science which must, unfortunately, grapple with the messy real world inhabited by human beings.

The law of diminishing returns (which might have been expected from a doom and gloomers like Malthus who foresaw only widespread misery and starvation as the world's food production failed to keep up with its exploding population) is a cornerstone of economic theory. It posits that an increase of one additional unit of either capital or labor will, at some point, negatively impact the quantity of goods and services being produced by those units. Note that the law of diminishing returns does not kick into gear at the starting gate but only comes into play at some point in the production process as more units of capital and/or labor are tossed into the mix.

Suppose that I have a firm of aggressive door-to-door cattle manure salespeople who have been indoctrinated over the course of years of training to *never* take "No" for an answer from a prospective purchaser. Because I have a very large supply of cattle manure on hand, I am very motivated to sell my organic "black gold" as quickly as possible. I assemble my five salespeople and inform them that they are to target the wealthy neighborhood of Rancho Dinero, which is three dozen mansions surrounded by a fifty-foot tall concrete wall. They gain entry under cover of darkness and then wait in the shadows until dawn. After all the residents have been contacted, we might find that three out of the 36 homes in Rancho Dinero have been persuaded to sign up for the Manure of the Month Club, which provides a dump truck load of manure on the lawn of the purchaser each month for the rest of their lives. But three out of 36 is not a good outcome because it means that 33 of the 36 homes declined, for whatever reason, to enroll in the Club. As a result, our salespeople go around the neighborhood of Rancho Dinero a second time and manage to convince another homeowner to sign up for the Club.

How does the law of diminishing returns come into play? Well, I am convinced that Rancho Dinero is the alpha and the omega of potential manure sales. I feel that there is much additional glory to be had in terms of sales in the neighborhood. However, I do not believe that I have enough salespeople to fully implement my sales blitzkrieg. As a result, I hire two more salespeople so that my newly augmented platoon of emissaries can blanket Rancho Dinero and take turns knocking on the remaining residents' doors a dozen times a day or more, day after day. Imagine my surprise, however, when the incessant harassment by my salespeople of the Rancho Dinero residents does not result in any additional sales but instead attacks by a pack of Dobermans. This lack of success in obtaining additional sales despite my having two additional representatives certainly illustrates that my sales force's productivity has passed the point of diminishing returns. In short, the addition of two more salespeople did not result in an increase in manure sales, but instead culminated in several felony charges. So it may be that the better approach would have been to cut back the number of salespeople altogether (that is, reduce the number of labor units) and utilize a softer, more nuanced approach toward the residents of Rancho Dinero.

We can also explore the law of diminishing returns in terms of capital inputs. Imagine that the world has suddenly fallen in love with manure patties that can be tossed like dinner plates into a garden or on a lawn. I might direct my salespeople to switch occupations and begin operating my newly acquired manure patty machines that stamp piles of manure into saucer-shaped goodies. Due to my great relief in having a possible market for a product that is not usually desired by people with even a rudimentary sense of smell, I might buy ten patty-stamping machines and order my salespeople to begin operating the machines around the clock. Because I only have seven salespeople, however, I would need to hire additional people to aid in both the operation of the machines and the shoveling of the raw materials into the feeder chutes. Even if I have all ten machines operating at top speed with full-time crews working on each machine, however, the apparently insatiable market for manure patties might be so intense that I would have to purchase another ten machines and hire enough new people to operate the new machines. But I might find, much to my chagrin, that the newer machines are not as productive as the older machines because the new crews are less skilled in the operation of these machines. Because of their inexperience, they tend to overload the feeder chutes and clog up the grinders, thereby causing mechanical malfunctions. The newer machines themselves are also more susceptible to breakdowns because they are computerized and do not last as long as my older, sturdier mechanical models on the manure farm. So even though my older mechanical patty-grinding machines might average 100 patties per hour, my super modern computerized patty grinding machines might average only 80 patties per hour due to their constant operational problems. So, the new machines would certainly illustrate the law of diminishing returns in a way that does not bode well for my attempts to become the manure patty manufacturing king because each of my newer machines is less productive than the original mechanical models.

MONOPOLIES

Every entrepreneur sings the praises of the free market with its idealized world of numerous firms selling undifferentiated products (such as crowbars) that do not dare raise their prices above those of their competitors for fear of losing all of their customers and going out of business. This is not to say that any of these entrepreneurs actually like unfettered markets of perfect competition accompanied by unending economic battles that every firm must fight if it is to remain in operation. Indeed, nearly all entrepreneurs, weary of the unending and, ultimately, futile search for profits in a market of perfect competition would probably admit that they would like to be a monopolist—or at least try it out for a few days.

And who can blame these entrepreneurs who are continually stymied from raising their prices by the prospect that any resulting profits will be vaporized in short order by their no-good price-cutting competitors.

Because a monopolist, by definition, is the only actor in a single market, it necessarily controls that market. As a result, it does not have to worry about those pesky competitors because they do not exist. Either the monopolist has already absorbed them in earlier mergers or it has driven them out of business altogether by temporarily lowering the prices of its goods to levels that simply cannot be matched by its less well-financed competitors over time. A monopolist might also enlist the aid of government actors to erect barriers to entry such as requiring prospective entrants to pay enormous licensing fees or demonstrate extraordinary financial reserves or sing the fight songs of their alma mater while sitting on a unicycle juggling live cobras.

Monopolies are not necessarily evil, though they are often criticized for using their market power to prop up the prices for their products and, in the process, produce less than optimal amounts of those products. But there are certain types of markets that may not be appropriate for multiple competitors such as the markets for utility services (electricity, water, sewer, gas). An electricity utility proposing to supply the power needs of a community, for example, must have substantial financial resources because it will have to construct an immense electrical grid capable of servicing all the households and businesses in that community. This investment will require the utility to incur substantial costs to install electrical pylons and wires and transmission substations and, most importantly, actual power plants. It will also have to hire hundreds, if not thousands, of employees to carry out all sorts of operational and maintenance tasks once the grid is constructed. No company officer in their right mind would want to undertake such a huge investment (that is, hundreds of millions or even billions of dollars) without getting a legally binding agreement from the relevant government officials that no other company shall be authorized to set up a competing utility system in the same market. But would this outcome not cause Adam Smith, the foremost advocate of perfect competition, to roll over in his grave? Smith was eminently practical and would understand the need for the government to provide incentives to convince a company to pay for an entire electrical grid. This is not to say that several competing companies could not construct a patchwork of separate mini grids in that same community but the efforts would be somewhat duplicative and wasteful. No, the author of *The Wealth of Nations* would likely accept the need for monopolies in certain situations so long as the government could be counted on to monitor such things as the prices charged by the monopoly. So, the trade-off would be geographical exclusivity and mutually agreed upon prices for the monopoly in exchange for the monopoly agreeing to construct the electrical grid at its sole cost. Indeed, most electricity utilities have agreements with public agencies that provide a rate schedule of acceptable charges. These rate schedules enable the utility to earn a profit but not an exorbitant profit (whatever that may be). It also provides the utility with a guarantee that a certain pricing schedule shall be maintained for some specified period into the future and thus enables the utility to plan its investments in its electrical grid with greater certainty.

You would think that today's would-be monopolists would pine for the good old days when huge companies dominated entire sectors of the national economy without so much as a "boo!" from the government. Nowadays, being a monopolist is much more difficult because there is always someone threatening to sue you if you become too big or too successful in your ability to block the entry of competitors into your market. The word "monopoly" is somewhat distasteful to many because economists have long argued that such concentrations of market power typically result in overpriced but under-produced goods and services. But in certain markets, such as those for utility services, it is not unreasonable to allow a so-called "natural monopoly" to operate—albeit with some type of oversight by learned people with fancy degrees and Roman numerals after their names. A firm acting as a natural monopolist is able to build the infrastructure to serve the entire market and avoid the tremendous waste of resources that would result from allowing other companies to erect competing systems. The utility can also take advantage of the declining cost in the per unit production of electricity, for example, that will typically occur as it increases its production of electrical power. In theory, this should make it possible for electrical power to be offered for a lower price per unit as the system expands in size. In theory.

OLIGOPOLIES

Monopolists are thought to be greedy narcissists who cackle maniacally and want to have unlimited control over the markets in which they operate so they can increase the prices of their products as much as possible without attracting the attention of government regulators. But not everyone has such a sociopathic focus on profits to the exclusion of all else in life. Some people are a little less rigid in their profit-maximizing orientation even though they still like money—not enough to kill a competitor, perhaps, but maybe enough to break a bone or two. These more balanced individuals might be satisfied with something less than total world domination. Indeed, you might be one of these more even-keeled individuals who does not see everything as a zero-sum game. Instead, you might actually believe that you can sometimes cooperate with your competitors in certain mutually beneficial ways.

If you enjoyed participating in games on the school playground, then you probably have the talents needed to become an oligopolist because you have already seen how you can work with others in pursuit of a common objective. The only other thing you have to do is climb up the corporate ladder and become the head of a major corporation. Once you have assumed the corporate mantle, you can consider various ways to improve the profitability of the company. You could invest a lot of money in a revolutionary product that will earn billions of dollars in revenue. Or you could take a more direct route and call up the other bigshots that run your competitors and set up a meeting to chat about pricing policies for your products.

Whether it is worth setting up a secret meeting depends on whether your company operates in a market that is dominated by two, three or four or so companies—the so-called oligopolistic market. In a monopolistic market, there is one big fat company reigning supreme and exercising total control of the amount of goods produced in that market as well as the prices charged for those goods. The oligopolistic market is somewhat more competitive because there are at least two companies eyeing each other warily while they try to anticipate each other's pricing strategies. But these companies do not need to have extrasensory perception or complicated computer algorithms to divine the prices that their competitors plan to charge. They can simply go to a store and look at the prices of their competitor's products. In the era of the Internet, the would-be oligopolist does not even have to climb out of bed to see what other companies are charging in the stores as that information will often be available on numerous websites.

But there is nothing better to drive a point home than an illustration of the way in which the players in an oligopolistic market might cooperate with each other in setting the prices of their products. Suppose you are the owner of the Tregg Animal Cosmetology Company and your company is one of four such entities that dominate the production, distribution and sale of nail polishes for dogs and cats. You are not particularly close friends with the owners of any of the other three companies, but you do cross paths with them on occasion while attending animal cosmetology trade shows to scout out new products for pet owners. Sometimes you might even bump into one of the other owners at a fancy restaurant. So, you do have occasional opportunities to chat with each other about things you really do not care about, such as the health of their families, and other things that you really do care about, such as new products being readied for market.

But as we pointed out before, you really do not have to even get together at all to see what your competitors are up to as there are so many sources of information available to see what each company is charging for its products. Needless to say, any changes in your prices will also be driven by the sales figures of your own products. Suppose your two-ounce bottle of rose red canine toenail polish, for example, is flying off the shelves and retailers around the country are begging you to send more bottles to replace their depleted stocks. If you then increase the price by $1.00 per bottle, your competitors will certainly take notice of the reaction of the buying public to the higher price. If the buying

frenzy continues anyways, then you and your competitors will both assume that the public still loves your
product and that it was originally underpriced. No
doubt the other companies will either roll out their own
versions of the polish or, if they already have their own
lines on the market, adjust the price so that it is close to
or possibly even the same as your product. The fact that
the other companies in your industry followed your lead
in setting the price for the canine toenail polish would
suggest that you are a price leader in this market.

Because of the small number of actors in an oligopolistic market, each company must necessarily consider
the possible reactions of its competitors to a change in
price or, for that matter, any other action—such as the
introduction of a new product line or service (for example, mobile canine and feline toenail polishing trucks).
Most oligopolists do not want to engage in a nasty price
cutting war to try to drive a competitor out of business because these competitors are often also big companies with deep pockets who can easily respond with
their own price-cutting volleys. Your decision to drop
the price of the rose red canine toenail polish will likely
be matched by your competitors. While oligopolists
will bring out new products and offer promotional (for
example, reduced or even below cost) pricing to increase
their market share, they will not continue such unprofitable activities indefinitely far into the future. After all,
if an action by the company is unprofitable, it defeats
the whole purpose of having market power to exact

above-normal profits from the sales of its products. So, any firm considering dropping its prices will necessarily try to anticipate whether its competitors will follow suit. If they do not, then the price-dropping company may be able to sell additional goods. However, these increased sales may be short-lived because the other companies might then decide they should jump in with their own price reductions to avoid losing too much in the way of sales. The net result is that everyone may end up selling the same amount of products as before but at a reduced price so that total revenue will fall. This is an outcome that, to borrow the language of economists, is "bad." It is also not a result that will please the board of directors at the annual meeting when your compensation and even your continued tenure as the corporate overlord are discussed. In any event, companies in oligopolistic industries will carefully monitor both how the buying public reacts to price increases and decreases for their products as well as the actions of their competitors.

PREDATORY PRICING

In the eyes of most economists, the concentration of extreme market power in the hands of a single firm—a monopoly—is bad. There are some exceptions to this blanket condemnation such as the so-called "natural monopolies" like utilities, which we discussed. The word "monopoly" generally evokes a negative connotation because monopolies typically produce less output at higher prices than their free market counterparts. But the ability to wield unfettered pricing power in a specific market can also lead to pricing practices that have nothing to do with maximizing profits in the short term. No, the entrenched monopolist has its eyes on earning long-term excessive profits and is often willing to incur short-term losses to reach that goal. It could act to deter the entry of new competitors into the market by dropping prices so low that the competing firms cannot sell their products profitably and are therefore forced to exit the market to avoid ruinous losses.

Suppose that the Apex Toothpaste Cap Company has long been the only manufacturer of toothpaste caps in the land. It sells its caps to the consumer products companies that manufacture toothpaste tubes. It also makes an occasional sale to consumers who have lost a toothpaste cap and who are compelled by their own obsessive-compulsive demons to get a new cap instead of being content to let the toothpaste in the tube form its own natural cap as it dries. Apex, having been in business for nearly a century, would do anything it could to guard its toothpaste cap market domination from would-be upstarts that would dare challenge its market preeminence. Apex would not be happy to learn that a longtime customer, Glitter Dental Company—a purveyor of sparkly toothpaste and toothbrushes aimed at children and flamboyant adults—has now begun to make its own toothpaste caps and will offer them for sale to other companies. This news would horrify the board of directors of Apex and no doubt strengthen their resolve to stop Glitter from trying to poach its customers.

But how might Apex prevent Glitter from stealing its customers away? Well, the board could call up their toothpaste cap engineers and ask them to reinvent the toothpaste cap and create a whole new line of products for the twenty-first century. And the engineers would come back with exciting prototypes such as fingerprint-specific toothpaste caps that would open only for the original purchaser and golf ball-sized toothpaste caps that can be more easily turned by today's weaker, more sedentary consumers and even electromagnetic toothpaste caps that boast a charge so powerful that the cap will always snap back in place with the velocity of a bullet and never go missing.

Unfortunately, the Apex engineers are more interested in cutting-edge technologies than budgetary considerations and are thus reluctant to let the costs of these brilliant inventions dampen their creative impulses: All these innovations, though doubtless enormously important, could cause the typical tube of toothpaste to increase in cost from $3.00 per tube to $54.00 per tube. This sort of price increase would obviously not go over well with most Apex customers.

Having determined that there is no economically viable way to redesign toothpaste caps, Apex would be left no choice but to try to deter Glitter from entering the toothpaste cap market by dropping the price of its caps. The question to be considered, however, is the amount of the drop. Should it be a price that would exist in a competitive market or should Apex act even more boldly and drop the price below the actual cost of producing the caps? This below-cost pricing or "predatory pricing" is a strategy that Apex knows will cost it profits in the near term because every cap will be manufactured at a loss. But Apex hopes that this aggressive pricing strategy will severely undercut the profitability of Glitter's operations and perhaps eventually cause Glitter to exit the toothpaste cap market altogether. Apex will also have to be cognizant of the attention that its below-cost pricing policy could attract among government officials who may not look kindly upon its blatantly anticompetitive pricing practices and might, in fact, seek legal redress against the company.

Glitter—like every other for-profit company—is in business to make money. It is not interested in incurring substantial financial losses, particularly if they persist over time. Once it realizes that its much larger competitor, Apex, is engaging in a scorched-earth pricing policy such that Glitter is losing money on every single cap it makes, then Glitter will have to decide how badly it wishes to try to enter this market. It will also have to look at its own financial situation to see if it has the wherewithal to engage in a protracted battle with Apex. Indeed, Glitter may decide that it is not worth the trouble to compete with Apex and simply abandon the toothpaste cap market and focus on its other products such as its new smear-free body paint that has been embraced by the stripper community for its many colors and its utility as a mouthwash.

Apex, for its part, can maintain its rock-bottom pricing program until it satisfies itself that Glitter has abandoned the toothpaste cap market. At that point, it can then raise its prices back to their original amounts and, once again, begin earning excessive profits.

CARTELS

It is not much fun to be a business owner operating in a market of perfect competition where companies must battle each other for every sale and every dollar of profits. It is a Hobbesian landscape in which life for the business owner can be "nasty, brutish, and short." Or to cast a Darwinian hue on this capitalistic free-for-all, it is a world of "the survival of the fittest." Although the perfectly competitive market is more fiction than fact in the modern era, many businesses are too small and lack sufficient market power to exert any control over the markets in which they operate. They risk losing sales if they try to raise their prices appreciably above those advertised by their competitors.

Given this specter of "ruinous competition," it would not be surprising if some of these firms, having become weary of the incessant economic bloodletting of the free market, decided to band together to try to magnify their influence over their product market. If they could come to some agreement amongst themselves as to the amount of products they would produce, then they could restrict their output and, if all goes well, raise their prices to a level above that found in a competitive market. This would seem to be a perfectly reasonable response by these business owners: Why keep beating your head against the wall to eke out a slim profit when a few clandestine meetings with your competitors could result in a much less taxing atmosphere in which you can look forward to going to work each day because you and your fellow owners will be making higher profits and not have to produce as much output? Unfortunately, those individuals who consume these products will be less enthusiastic about having to pay higher prices; some may even go whining to the government authorities about alleged price-gouging.

Although cartels can arise in a purely domestic market as described above, they are often dealt with quickly and firmly by government authorities who have the power to sue all the firms for engaging in anti-competitive practices and, on a good day for the district attorney's office, arrest the badly behaving business owners. But the most successful cartels have been operated by groups of countries who have joined together to try to control the market for a particular product. Indeed, one of the more famous and successful commodity cartels has been the Organization of Petroleum Exporting Countries (OPEC) which came into prominence in the 1970s when its members severely cut back on their production of oil. This cutback led to a quadrupling of prices and brought about a dramatic slowing down of economic activity throughout the world. It also resulted in a tremendous transfer of wealth from the wealthy oil-consuming countries to the OPEC members.

But maintaining the unity of a cartel is not always a walk in the park. Each member must reduce its own output to prop up the price of the cartel's product—which requires that each member exercise the self-discipline not to "cheat" by expanding production in order to collect more revenue while prices are higher than normal. The problem that typically arises is that the initial cutback in output will immediately reduce each member's revenues until the markets adjust and the prices rise accordingly. Those members who are living hand to mouth and have absolutely no financial reserves may find themselves sorely tempted to increase production to make up for the loss in revenue before the expected price increases take place.

Suppose that you and I and our mutual friend King Olaf are the heads of state of the three largest producers of fighting peacocks in the world. Indeed, peacock fighting has displaced dog fighting as the leading animal fighting sport in much of the civilized world. But we three kings are unhappy: We ship millions of fighting peacocks around the world to gangsters, gamblers, drug dealers, and elementary schools but we only make a few dollars or so per peacock—which is not very impressive, particularly when you take into account the costs of breeding, training and outfitting a first-rate ornithological pugilist. We are also keenly aware of the tremendous public interest in peacock fighting as illustrated by the recent "peacock death match" series which earned enormous ratings for PBS. Moreover, we know that our three countries are responsible for breeding nearly 90 percent of the world's fighting peacocks. These factors have all caused us to wonder if we might be able to join forces and create an organization that would sharply reduce the supply of fighting peacocks throughout the world and thus boost their prices enormously.

Indeed, we have gone so far as to hire a major advertising agency to create a name for us—the Organization of Peacock Exporting Countries or OPEC. Unfortunately, we were then threatened with legal action by lawyers working for that other OPEC so we settled on "Peacocks R Us." Regardless of the name chosen, the point is that we are ready to move into a bright new world of prosperity by cutting back our production of these colorful birds. Having to prune our flocks of several million birds in short order of course\ means trying to convince the citizens of our respective countries to eat peacocks instead of chickens and to enjoy peacocks and waffles for breakfast, cook peacock noodle soup and make peacock salad sandwiches until the supply of fighting peacocks has been dramatically reduced and the price pumped up. And once our plan is implemented and each of our respective countries has agreed to reduce the future production of peacocks by a third, we should find that the prices starts to increase as the supply of fighting peacocks shrinks.

Imagine my relief as these continued cutbacks in peacock production cause the price of peacocks to surge so that the increase in prices more than offsets the fall in production. The rest of the world is not thrilled to be paying bloated prices for their peacocks, but I am not particularly concerned as the increased revenues are causing the nation's treasury to overflow.

Unfortunately, all good things must come to an end: You and I would be shocked to learn soon afterward that King Olaf is secretly selling twice the number of fighting peacocks he was allotted under our agreement. King Olaf's breach of our agreement would be an absolute disaster for our pricing scheme because his sales would flood the global market with fighting peacocks and, ultimately, cause the prices to plummet. The fall in prices would, of course, cause the revenues being collected by all three of our respective nations to plummet. This new financial reality would force drastic changes in my royal lifestyle such as necessitating that I switch to a domestic brand of sparkling wine at the state dinners.

King Olaf's treacherous behavior would not really be surprising because all cartels must grapple with the same pressures on their members to scale back production to prop up prices while also guarding against the constant temptation to cheat. In the short term, any member's decision to increase production will be beneficial for it because it can sell more products at the higher price. But as sales increase further, the price will start to decline and eventually the revenue being received by the cheating member will fall. International cartels such as OPEC and Peacocks R Us are able to exist so long as they control both the supply of their particular commodity and the greed of each of their members. Furthermore, these cartels consist of countries and therefore are not necessarily subject to the antitrust laws of individual nations which cause so much trouble for domestic companies. But cartels are inherently unstable and most tend to fall apart over time.

DIVISION OF LABOR

In the olden days before the Internet, color television or, indeed, modern industrial factories ever existed, the manufacture of any particular item or object—such as a horseshoe or a pair of boots—was carried out by either a single individual or a small group of workers. For example, the village blacksmith would heat iron to such a high temperature that he could bend the molten metal at will and pound it into the shapes of objects such as nails and horseshoes and, if he was really ambitious, internal combustion engines. Similarly, the cobbler down the street would tan the leather and then he or his apprentice would cut it into pieces that could be stitched and nailed together to create a flattering boot suitable for everyday use or glamorous evenings in the village. The localized production of most goods was the rule—not the exception—in the pre-industrial era. Indeed, it was unusual for an item to have more than a few individuals involved in its manufacture prior to the Industrial Revolution.

Manufacturing was carried out on a small, almost fragmentary, scale until the beginning of the eighteenth century. Suppose you were a pin maker in seventeenth century England. Every day you would get up with the crowing of an annoying rooster. You would then head over to the hut behind your home and go over to your workbench to begin an exciting 12-hour day of making pins and enjoying the high-tension thrills of self-employment. As with many other manufactured products, the process by which pins are made is more complicated and involved than one would first expect—especially when you have to perform all of the tasks needed to make the pin by yourself. Well, how difficult could it be to make a pin? Ignorance about pin making is understandable because most people have little direct involvement with any type of manufacturing process. More than a few of these individuals would point out that you can get pins at a store but not give any further thought as to how the pins were produced. For those who did not attend a fancy private school offering pinmaking classes, pin making can be simplified as follows:

» stretch out the wire.
» straighten the wire.
» cut the wire.
» grind the tip of the wire until it has an extremely sharp point on it.

- » bend the dull end of the wire so that it can hold the top of the pin.
- » attach the head to the pin.
- » buff the pin.
- » insert the pin into the package.
- » ship it off to whoever is going to sell it to the public.

Adam Smith liked to sing the praises of craftsmen and shopkeepers and would no doubt have purchased pins from you if he needed to practice acupuncture on himself. But he was also someone who thought a lot about the ways in which labor could be more productive. Indeed, he would have acknowledged that the one-person factory was becoming an anachronism. In fact, he suggested that tremendous gains in productivity could be had by dividing the manufacturing process into a series of discrete steps, each of which would be performed by a separate individual. Of course, Smith's enthusiasm for this method of manufacturing goods was purely theoretical as Smith evidently never spent any time working a 16-hour day in a filthy eighteenth-century factory but was instead fortunate enough to lounge about at the University of Glasgow in Scotland. But his lack of first-hand experience did not dissuade him from his belief that fracturing all production processes into their most basic tasks, each of which could be performed dozens if not hundreds of times a day, by the same individual, was the way of the future. Each worker performing his or her specialized task over and over again could collectively produce far more pins in a given day than the same number of workers charged with carrying out every part of the production of each pin by himself or herself. So if you and nine other pin makers were each engaged in the manufacture of pins from start to finish you would likely be outproduced by another group of ten workers if each of them performed only one step in the pin making process—no matter how mind-numbing such a prospect might be to the casual observer. Their greater speed and, ultimately, output would result from the increased efficiency of each worker concentrating on only one task—over and over again. This division of labor would ultimately benefit society as a whole because a greater quantity of goods (pins, at least) would be produced and the cost of these pins would decline due to the increased supply. Lower prices would thus lead to a higher standard of living and improved general welfare and enable pin hoarders all over the world to amass even more impressive collections.

The value of Smith's ideas regarding the gains in productivity to be had from the division of labor was not limited to pin making, but could be extended to any type of production process involving almost any kind of product. Indeed, the twentieth century saw the construction of enormous factories in which automobiles and train engines and even airplanes were manufactured on long assembly lines in which workers performed specialized tasks dozens and even hundreds of times a day. Although many social commentators bemoaned the monotony of such routinized work, most of the line workers themselves probably preferred these repetitive tasks to the even more monotonous experience of unemployment.

SUNK COSTS

As a fledging tycoon, you will face a variety of investment decisions—some of which will be essentially irreversible such that the funds expended to make those investments are unrecoverable. Suppose that you are about to open the world's first humpless camel ranch after years of investing sweat, tears and personal funds. As part of your efforts to create a state-of-the-art breeding facility where aficionados can purchase the humpless camel of their dreams for a house pet, you have constructed specially-designed camel stables and formulated unique camel foodstuffs to provide that perfect mix of vitamins and minerals. You have also hired a trained animal psychologist to help some of the humpless camels deal with low self-esteem issues. Many of these costs are unique to your humpless camel farm and, if you were to close your doors tomorrow, you would probably not be able to recover all the monies you have spent—due in large part to the distinctive nature of your business and the special facilities that you have built for it.

So, you might find that the silk slippers you purchased for the humpless camels, for example, could not be sold for enough money to recover your original investment. In short, these costs would be unrecoverable and, in essence, "sunk." Now the phonetic tone of the word "sunk" is very depressing. The word itself does not typically appear in the happiest of contexts. We speak of sunken ships or sunken spirits or sunken hearts. Whatever it is that is sunk, it is perceived as being lost forever.

Not everyone is interested in humpless camel breeding so it may be easier to consider sunk costs in terms of the costs of obtaining a college education. Suppose you go to college to pursue your dream of becoming an accountant. After several years of intensive study, however, you discover that you do not really like numbers very much. Instead, you decide to become a salesclerk at a shoe store due to a long-standing foot fetish that you have only recently acknowledged after years of intense psychotherapy. This new career choice does not require a college degree or a professional license, so you begin your shoe sales career right away. Because of your changed educational objectives you might think that it would be reasonable to go to your college bursar's office and ask for a complete refund of the tens of thousands of dollars you have paid to study accounting for the past three years. Imagine your shock when the clerk at the bursar's office politely informs you that there are no "give backs" of college tuition and that you will have to start your shoe sales career without the expected boost that you would have otherwise realized from a refund. These monies would be considered sunk costs because they cannot be recovered—at least not without taking the college president hostage.

AVERAGE COST AND MARGINAL COST

Those persons who want to operate a profitable manufacturing business should become familiar with the concepts of marginal cost and average cost to understand better the costs of manufacturing a particular product. If you know the marginal cost of producing each additional item, you will be better able to determine how many units to produce to maximize your profits and make back the money you lost in your last divorce settlement.

Suppose that you have just opened a factory to manufacture shoes for aquarium fish—a hitherto untapped and potentially vast market that has for some reason been overlooked by other pet supply companies. A very important part of the production process will involve your identifying both the average costs and the marginal costs of producing each set of fish shoes. What is the difference? Well, the average cost is obtained by adding up the total costs of production (for example, materials, labor, fish stick lunches) and dividing that amount by the number of items produced. So, if you have to spend $800 in labor and materials to produce 80 pairs of fish sandals, for example, then the average cost per pair of fish sandals is $10. Determining the marginal cost of producing an additional pair of fish sandals, however, is a little more involved because you must focus on the incremental—as opposed to the aggregate—costs of production. If the eightieth pair of fish sandals, for example, costs $10 to produce, you would want to determine the incremental cost of manufacturing the eighty-first pair of fish sandals. If you find that the marginal cost of that pair is $7.90, then you can say that the marginal cost of production of that eighty-first pair of sandals is below the average cost of production of that same item. This means that the marginal cost of production of that eighty-first pair of sandals is declining—not increasing—which is very important because it tells you that you can increase your production of fish sandals for at least one additional unit without seeing an upward spike in the per unit costs.

If, on the other hand, you determine that the manufacture of that eighty-first pair of sandals would cost $12, then you would be concerned that your per unit cost of production would increase significantly. This increase could be the result of any number of factors such as having to hire additional fish shoe designers or purchase exotic waterproof dyes. Suffice it to say, your decision to increase or decrease or stop the production of fish sandals will depend in part on whether the marginal cost per unit is below the average cost per unit, above the average cost per unit, or equal to the marginal cost per unit. Whether the cost of manufacturing an additional pair of fish sandals is greater than or less than the average cost per unit will not, in and of itself, however, be determinative as to whether that additional pair of fish sandals will be produced. You also need to know how much additional revenue will be derived from the sale of that additional pair of fish sandals.

If the marginal revenue (additional funds) obtained from the sale of that last pair of fish sandals exceeds the marginal costs of producing that pair of fish sandals, then you could continue manufacturing fish sandals until the marginal cost of producing one more pair of sandals is equal to the marginal revenue to be derived from the sale of that pair. It is at this magical point at which the profits for the firm are theoretically maximized and economists become very pleased with the state of the world. As a result, the fact that you have declining or rising marginal costs of production by itself will not be the sole determinant of whether you decide to ramp up the fish sandal production—perhaps by starting up a new juvenile line of fish sandals adorned in primary colors—or cut it back. After all, you could have a situation where the marginal cost of production of each additional pair of fish sandals is declining but the marginal revenue obtained from selling that additional pair of fish sandals is falling even faster—due, perhaps, to your customers suddenly discovering *en masse* that fish sandals are stupid because fish do not have feet except in cartoons. So you might not have any choice but to bring your production to a grinding halt because your revenues for each additional pair of fish sandals sold are falling even faster than your costs so that any additional pairs produced would be sold at a greater loss.

ECONOMIES OF SCALE

If you had a choice, you would probably prefer to own a big factory instead of a small factory. Certainly, it would be more impressive to claim ownership of a building covering many acres of land than one barely larger than a telephone booth. More important than propping up your ego, however, is the fact that a larger building is more conducive to manufacturing on a larger scale with much greater production runs than a similar type of operation in a smaller building. As we know, having something bigger is often better.

A business owner who is able to increase the quantity of goods produced by their company without incurring additional production costs (such as expanding the size of the plant or hiring new workers) is able to benefit from an increased economy of scale. This greater economy of scale makes it possible to manufacture an increased number of goods and thereby realize greater revenue without a commensurate rise in the costs associated with the production of these additional goods.

Suppose I am opening a factory that will manufacture the world's first dung burning lawnmower. I hope to tap into that market of consumers who both disdain fossil fuel burning lawnmowers and have deficient olfactoric capabilities. My initial factory set-up might consist of a small building with a single assembly line that, when running at top speed, can produce 100 lawnmowers each month. If I am able to double the number of lawnmowers produced without increasing the size of my factory, then the average cost of production of each lawnmower will decline. All things being equal, if the costs of production remain unchanged in the face of a doubling of output, then the average cost per lawnmower will drop by half. This is what both economists and Martha Stewart call "a good thing." Indeed, we could try to run the production line even faster and give all the workers very sugary, super-caffeinated carbonated drinks so that they could work around the clock and not waste time on sleep or breaks. This frenzied level of activity would cause the average cost of each lawnmower to decline even more and our profits to explode accordingly—at least in the short term.

But there is only so much that I can do to create such an *uber*-efficient worker's paradise and at some point, it will become impossible to increase production any further without the onset of rising per unit production costs. My production line might break down or some of my workers may collapse from exhaustion or asphyxiation. The quality of the workmanship may suffer as well, particularly as my bleary-eyed workers start attaching lawnmower parts to the wrong places on the machines or even to each other. I will see lost production as more and more workers go to the hospital to have rivets and staples and nails removed from their bodies. Regardless of the reasons, these incidents will begin to disrupt the efficiency of the production process and, as a result, adversely affect manufacturing costs. As a result, it will no longer be possible to spread the cost of production out over an increasing number of dung-powered lawnmowers. This means that the average cost of each additional lawnmower I produce will start to rise.

But the fact that the average cost is rising due to factory floor issues does not mean that I have to curtail production because I may have tapped into a market that is both larger and more enthusiastic about my lawnmowers than I ever thought possible. It may very well be that my marginal revenues are increasing faster than my marginal costs so that even though each of my lawnmowers now costs more to produce, my profits are still increasing with the sale of each new lawnmower. The distinction to be drawn between average costs and marginal costs is an important one because average costs provide us with an overview of the aggregate costs of production at the factory whereas marginal costs force us to zero in on the incremental changes in the cost of production as each additional lawnmower rolls off the assembly line.

GOVERNING THE COMPANY

If you are fortunate to leaf through a basic economics textbook without nodding off, you might get to the section where the authors discuss the management of the modern corporation. All companies are owned by their shareholders but the shareholders themselves do not always participate in the management of the company.

This is particularly true in the case of gigantic corporations that have tens of thousands of shareholders and annual revenues of tens or even hundreds of billions of dollars. Indeed, even the most enthusiastic proponent of corporate democracy would have to admit that it would be difficult to operate a global corporation by allowing all of its thousands of shareholders—many of whom have conflicting views about almost everything—to have a say in its management. The obvious answer, of course, is to elect a board of directors who are all-knowing and all-powerful and overpaid. The board will, in turn, hire an all-knowing and all-powerful slate of overpaid officers who will bring their storied expertise to bear and, we hope, not run the company into the ground.

The obvious concern is that the officers and directors may not accurately represent the interests of the shareholders. After all, the shareholders want the company to be operated in a manner that maximizes profits whereas the officers and directors may have other objectives in mind—such as maximizing their own gold-plated compensation packages. The problem for most shareholders, however, is that they have comparatively little power to influence corporate policy. Bigger companies typically have many shareholders, most of whom have comparatively small stakes (shares of stock) in the company. The power of the shareholders, even though they are ultimately the owners of the company, is often diffuse and difficult to marshal in any meaningful way.

If you are a shareholder who has 50 shares of stock

in a company with 50,000,000 outstanding shares, then you are what statisticians call a very small fish in a very big pond. You are therefore not likely to be able to bend the will of the company bigwigs to your way of thinking—even if you have a really good idea to boost corporate profits. Suppose you send a proposal to the company that the salaries of all officers and directors of the company be slashed by 90 percent. One can only imagine how excited the officers would be to receive your proposal which would then be quickly filed away in the combination suggestion box/paper shredder. The other obstacle is that corporate bylaws are often written to make it difficult for shareholders to get a proposal before the board in the first place. So, if you were determined to pursue your "Don't Let Them Eat Cake" salary reduction proposal, you would probably have to gain the signatures of many shareholders who collectively own a significant share of the company's outstanding stock before it could be officially presented to the board of directors for consideration.

The biggest obstacle to getting the necessary approvals is that the other shareholders have to receive your proposal and then read your proposal and then sign your proposal and then insert the signed proposal into an envelope and then place the proper amount of postage on the envelope and then drive the car to the nearest mailbox. In short, most shareholders do not have the leisure time to devote their attention to affairs of corporate governance. Most shareholders really have no interest in reading corporate literature and would rather throw it in the trash and concentrate on more important things such as whether the Renaldo the gardener kidnapped Kitty the chambermaid on their favorite soap opera. So, your proposal must be something that is really appealing to overcome the apathy exhibited by most small shareholders who do not really feel that they have any ability to influence the way in which the company is governed. If you can come up with something that is truly meaningful like requiring the company to purchase a year's supply of glazed doughnuts for every shareholder, then you might have a chance to get your proposal backed by enough people to at least get it before the board of directors. After all, everyone likes glazed doughnuts, and one might expect that the board—unless most of the directors are diabetic—would vote to approve your proposal.

PATENTS

Suppose you invented a device that will remove hair from fruit. Ignoring the envious detractors who claim that your device addresses a need that does not exist, you press forward to obtain a patent from the Produce Division of the Office of Patents and Trademarks. Several months later, you receive a certificate suitable for framing announcing the government's formal recognition of your rights as the inventor of your fruit hair removal device.

Because you had to devote years of your life to

perfecting your invention, you are naturally anxious to reap the rewards of your efforts. By awarding you a patent, the government is conferring upon you an exclusive right of ownership which authorizes you to market or not market your invention as you see fit for a specific period of time. In other words, the patent grants a monopoly giving you sole control over the use of your invention for 20 years.

Yet if monopolies are bad, why would we want to award patents to inventors and give them the exclusive right to determine whether or not to share their devices with society— particularly when people might be crying out for a fruit hair removal device? How could we justify allowing a single person to withhold such a gift from humanity? Well, the idea of a patent is to reward the inventor for his or her efforts because we as a society want to encourage inventors to create useful devices that will help to make our lives easier. A patent will give its inventor a period of years to decide what to do with his or her device and, even though society may demand otherwise, whether to make it available at all. In most cases, the inventor will attempt to manufacture and market the device and, if all goes well, begin enjoying a fabulous lifestyle as a member of the *nouveau riche*.

As the inventor of a fruit hair removal device, you can readily appreciate the value of having a period of time to try to find companies willing to pay you a mountain of cash in exchange for the licensing rights to manufacture and sell your invention. The fact that you have exclusive control over your invention gives you the opportunity to monetize your invention for the duration of the patent and, in effect, pay yourself back for all the years of blood, sweat and tears that you spent working on it. But the awarding of the patent also means that the details of the patent (especially the engineering draw-ings) will be made available to the public. This means that unscrupulous individuals may take those designs and manufacture knock-off fruit hair removal devices of their own—without bothering to seek your approval or, needless to say, paying you a royalty for each device they sell. If you happen to be watching cable TV late one night and see an ad for the Samurai Coconut Hair Remover, you will realize that a copy-cat has stolen your intellectual property and is seeking to profit at your expense. This of course would constitute a violation of the patent and you would certainly be within your rights to go after the offending Samurai company, which, in this case, is headquartered in Siberia.

In simpler times, such outrageous behavior could be dealt with by hiring some bruisers from the dockyards but nowadays one must resort to the legal professionals that are always ready to see that justice is done—pro-vided you are willing to pay their hourly rates. Herein lies the problem: You are not independently wealthy and you have not yet begun to receive significant royalties from the licensed sales of your hair removal device. Yet you must now hire the nastiest lawyers you can find and unleash a legal blitzkrieg on the Samurai corporation.

But because the Samurai Company is headquartered halfway around the world and merely ships its knock-off hair removal devices directly to online buyers in this country, getting a judgment against them in Siberian courts, let alone enforcing that judgment, will be a daunting challenge. You may instead seek some type of injunction from the courts in this country blocking the importation of the Samurai hair removal products—deciding that it is money better spent than trying to litigate your patent infringement case half-way around the world.

Leaving aside the enforcement problems that often torment patent holders, the conferral of a temporary monopoly by the government in the form of a patent is viewed as an acceptable price to pay to encourage inventors to develop new products that can ultimately benefit society as a whole. A patent is admittedly anti-competitive in that it does not allow the invention to be made available to society free of charge right away (unless, of course, the inventor chooses to donate it to society). But the protection provided by a patent is regarded by nearly all reasonable people as a necessary incentive to encourage inventors to devote much of their lives (and savings) to improving the world as a whole or, at the very least, tackling the scourge of hairy fruits and vegetables.

PART TWO:
LABOR AND INCOME

THE DEMAND FOR LABOR

Every worker is acutely aware of the value of their services because they periodically receive a paycheck that declares in numerical terms what their worth is to that particular employer. No doubt their mood will darken further when they see that much of their check has already been vaporized by the insidious withholdings of revenue-hungry state and national governments. But if you believe that we live in a capitalist economy in which there is perfect information available to all and resources are allocated in the most efficient way possible and that there are faeries who sneak into our homes at night to exchange cash for teeth placed under pillows by young children, then you may conclude that the amount of your paycheck reflects your value as a human being.

Your paycheck is a reflection of the demand for your labor and what your employer is willing to pay for that labor. But you can also think of the cost of your labor as a component of the total costs needed to produce whatever goods or services are sold by your employer. Your employer, who presumably wishes to maximize (or at least generate) profits, will want to produce its products in the most economically efficient manner possible. This means that your supervisor, Paul, will not be disposed to passing out enormous bonuses to underlings such as you unless, of course, you can justify the amount of the bonus based upon your value to the company. Employers often prefer to give non-cash awards to employees such as fancy, multi-syllabic titles ("assistant second vice president of corporate strategy") or flimsy certificates of achievement celebrating your years of service to the company.

Yet sometimes the stars align and the balance of power shifts in favor of the employee with highly sought after skills. Suppose that you are a champion barefoot grape stomper who has earned numerous awards for your prowess in squishing grapes. You have been wooed by vineyard owners throughout Europe and North America because your pirouettes and spins and the special dirt between your toes infuses grapes with a certain *je ne sais quoi* that delights gourmets and casual wine drinkers alike. Because you are in such demand, the normal prattle that prospective employers like to espouse about needing to keep labor costs under control in order to stay competitive, does not tug at your heartstrings or, for that matter, affect your desirability as an employee. You have a unique skill set that cannot be easily duplicated and so you are able to name your own price and live a joyous life.

But suppose the labor market changes over time and many other people, having learned of the tremendous fortunes to be made in ballet grape stomping, have trained in classical dance and begun spinning and leaping in tubs of grapes around the world. Unfortunately for you, this influx of would-be pretenders has caused your own opportunities to dry up and the lofty salaries that you used to command to plummet.

Now that you are a mere mortal in the world of grape stomping, you must contend with the usual aggravations faced by other people seeking employment. Suppose that Lou Libation, the owner of the Bulk Winery, the world's largest producer of red, white and blue wines, is expanding the production of his ultra-prestigious Chug label and needs to hire additional grape stompers to ramp up production. Whether Lou considers adding you to his stable of stompers will depend on whether Lou believes bringing you aboard as a member of "Team Lou" will be a profitable hire. In other words, will the additional monies Lou must pay to you in salary be offset or perhaps even exceeded by the expected profits that your employment will bring to the Chug line of fine wines? Or as an economist will ask, will the marginal product of labor that you bring to the hallowed halls of the Bulk Winery be positive or negative? If positive, Lou will undoubtedly be very pleased because it means that he will profit from your gyrations in the grape vats; conversely, a negative marginal product of labor will mean that you are not a profitable addition to the company's workforce and Lou, despite his fondness for your tantalizing slithering through the grapey pulpy mire, will probably not keep you around for very long.

Lou's attempt to maximize his profits will cause him to try to determine how many classically trained grape stompers he should hire. As long as the marginal product of labor continues to exceed the prevailing wages being paid to his employees, then it will make financial sense for him to continue expanding production and adding additional stompers. Indeed, Lou will maximize his profits to the point at which the marginal product of labor is equal to the prevailing wages; the addition of any more grape stompers would then have a negative financial impact on the company's bottom line. Once the marginal product of labor falls below the prevailing wages, Lou will have reached the point at which additional hires of grape stompers become increasingly unprofitable.

WAGES

In the bucolic world of Adam Smith's *laissez-faire* economy, those individuals who did not succumb at a young age from the plague or a hundred other different diseases, were free to spend their time cavorting in the meadows and enjoying the benefits of living in "a nation of shopkeepers." In Smith's idealized eighteenth-century economy, wages and prices would constantly rise and fall as freely as an elevator in the modern era because purchasing power was widely diffused. There were few large companies or trade unions so individuals could sell their goods and services to prospective purchasers at whatever price they desired. But they were also keenly aware that in such a decentralized economy they had to be cognizant of the prices being charged by their competitors. Under Smith's reasoning, if a merchant became particularly greedy and increased his or her prices above those of his or her fellow vendors, then people would shun his or her products like two-year-old potato soup and look elsewhere. Although this paradigm assumed that people had information about the prices being charged by all the vendors in a given geographic area, it did underscore an important tenet of economics that prices should move upward and downward freely when no single participant has enough bargaining power to effect significant changes in prices.

A similar analysis would follow if one were to look at the wages paid to workers in Smith's economy. Each worker was on their own in terms of negotiating the wages a prospective employer would pay. There were no labor unions and the craft unions that existed at the time were few in number compared to the size of the general population and, as a result, were essentially irrelevant to the daily lives of most workers. We also have to remember that Smith lived in a time in which much of the population suffered from grinding poverty and their benevolent governments did not see any point in providing assistance to people in need. After all, those in charge were in favor of dramatically reducing the ranks of the poor; they reasoned, quite logically, that the least troublesome way to do so was to let the poor starve to death. Apparently, no one bothered to think that it might make more sense to try to improve the lives of the poor by providing improved employment opportunities and thereby helping them to become productive members of society. But it is not for us to judge the actions of these earlier generations of wise policymakers merely because their solutions to high levels of unemployment among the poor were somewhat unorthodox. Indeed, they would probably view our own government's payments of welfare benefits to help sustain poor families as misguided because these payments actually help poor people to survive. However, the point is that the workers in Smith's economy, were, for the most part, individuals who had no choice but to look out for themselves and, as a result, were solely responsible for negotiating the terms and conditions of their employment.

Since Smith's time, the government has become much more involved in the modern economy and taken a major interest in the welfare of workers. Minimum wage laws, for example, have been passed on both the national and state levels to help ensure that workers receive at least a certain basic income for their labor. These "price floors" for labor provide a sort of guarantee that workers will receive at least some mandated wage and hopefully be able to earn a living. Some economists believe that minimum wage laws in effect ensure increases in unemployment because these mandates prevent wages from falling low enough to encourage employers to hire all the unemployed workers. But such a view assumes that people are willing to go to work regardless of how little they will be paid. Maybe this view was more credible in Adam Smith's time, when there were no government assistance programs and poor people were forced to take the most menial jobs to avoid starvation. However, it is probably a flawed assumption in our own time, particularly if an unemployed worker can collect various benefits that will pay at least some of the bills instead of accepting a minimum wage job as the deep fryer operator at the Chicken Palace that would result in the loss of those benefits.

People typically act in their own self-interest and are acutely aware of the various revenue opportunities that may be had from working or from not working and instead receiving government benefits. In the modern era, the economy is no longer an atomistic "nation of

shopkeepers" but instead consists of enormous corporations employing tens or even hundreds of thousands of
people as well as powerful labor unions that represent
workers in both private industries as well as the public
sector. Needless to say, wages have become quite "sticky"
due to the advent of the minimum wage laws as well as
union contracts that set the wages for union workers.
In the modern era, the transformation of the economy
to the so-called information or "gig" economy has also
created a need for millions of workers who are adept
with all types of computers and who, due to their skills
and training, command salaries far in excess of any minimum wage. For our purposes, all these factors preclude
the fluctuations in wages that took place during Smith's
time when the government took no interest in the welfare of workers and the trade unions and companies that
existed at the time were extraordinarily small and essentially irrelevant to most individuals.

OWNERS AND EMPLOYEES

Those of us who have climbed the ladder of corporate
success and trampled over numerous colleagues and
fellow employees in our quest to be rich and powerful
are acutely aware that business owners and their employees see things differently when dealing with business
matters. As the business owner, you will naturally want
your employees to spend their every waking moment
thinking about how they can make you richer while
ignoring the concerns of their spouses and children.

Your employees, on the other hand, will have concerns about other matters such as providing food and clothing for their families. The difficulty of bringing the cold iron fist of authority down upon the heads of your employees, particularly in a large, bureaucratic organization, is made even more difficult by the fact that you really do not know what is going on at all levels of the company, despite your own god-like perfection. Indeed, the second assistant pastry cart pusher will know more than you do about certain—albeit rudimentary—things going on at work because the second assistant pastry cart pusher walks around the office and engages in casual banter with the other employees.

Although you may sit atop Mount Olympus surveying the expanse of your global empire, the second assistant pastry cart pusher will know far more about one employee's frustration about not being able to get a chart for a report on the sales of flammable nightgowns or another employee's concern about the bright green color of the chocolate pudding in the company cafeteria. You lack first-hand information about the goings-on at the most basic levels of your organization because, quite frankly, you would rather fly above it all in your private jet on your way to your winter chalet in Gstaad. This paucity of information about the comings and goings on the shop floor may make it more difficult for you to figure out how to motivate your employees to devote themselves to you as opposed to engaging in regrettable conduct that is more geared toward themselves and their own interests—particularly if you have already ruled out monetary compensation as a possible incentive.

The question as to how any owner can convince his or her employees to be reliable sycophants and toadies may be answered by determining what things really matter to the employees. This may entail bringing monetary compensation back to the forefront of any new plan to inspire your employees because the value of most other perks offered by businesses may be open to debate. It used to be that some of the younger, more naïve employees could be incentivized by giving them a more impressive title and calling it a promotion without providing anything new in the way of actual compensation. Unfortunately, most employees usually catch on to the "shiny label" game fairly quickly, particularly when they discover that their job responsibilities have increased, along with their workload, but they are no better off financially than before the promotion. Other perks such as health insurance coverage and stock option plans offer greater potential for encouraging employees to keep their noses to the grindstone because both are benefits that (at least in the case of health insurance coverage) would cost the employee a lot of money to obtain on his or her own.

COLLECTIVE BARGAINING

Classical economists such as Adam Smith viewed workers and their employers in a somewhat idealistic state in which they amicably came to an agreement over the terms and conditions of employment and then went out to play a round of tennis together. However, Smith wrote at a time during the end of the eighteenth century when large-scale business enterprises were almost non-existent and the Industrial Revolution was in its early stages. But with the construction of enormous factories, workers suddenly found themselves working 10- to 12-hour days in dimly-lit, poorly-ventilated buildings, often crowded together and barely earning a subsistence wage—all driven to endure these mind-numbing conditions for fear of being tossed out onto the streets if they lost their jobs.

Many historians have studied the appalling working conditions endured by these poor souls, whose plight was perhaps best brought to life by the novels of Charles Dickens. But these same so-called "scholars" have not concerned themselves as much with the toll that running a large-scale organization that systematically oppresses its workers exacts on the owners themselves. There is enormous stress involved in overseeing a business enterprise with hundreds or even thousands of laborers, particularly an operation that is immensely profitable. Not only does the owner have to worry about what to do with all of the thousands upon thousands of pounds or dollars or whatever that pour into his or her bank account with annoying regularity, but he or she must always be on the lookout for an ever-more grandiose country estate to purchase in order to humiliate his or her social peers—an enormously stressful and time-consuming undertaking.

Collective bargaining came about because workers gradually concluded that the owners of the factories—who were paying them barely enough money to stay alive—might not have their best interests at heart. These men and women feared that if they raised a stink, they would be fired and be replaced before they found their way to the exit. Their reticence was bolstered by the often harsh public laws— such as the Combination Acts of 1799 and 1800 in Great Britain, which prohibited most workers from joining together with each other to strike for higher wages and outlawed many trade unions altogether. Notwithstanding all these economic and legal obstacles, and apparently indifferent to the stress that their actions would inflict upon their obscenely rich employers, many workers began to come together to join unions so that they could tip the bargaining power of the workplace in their favor.

Although there was a great deal of hostility toward these unions in the early nineteenth century, both the public and the government gradually came to accept the idea that the general welfare of the people would be better served if workers had some way to act together jointly to bargain over the terms and conditions of their employment. Surprisingly, some of the factory owners themselves even began to see the advantages of negotiating with a union as opposed to having to work out separate employment deals with hundreds or even thousands of workers. Because the union was the representative of all of its members, it could present a single set of demands with the appropriate pay scales for different jobs, skills and seniority. In short, it offered a means whereby the owners—still reeling from the curse of having to buy ever more expensive clothes, furnishings and polo horses as well as having to attend a bewildering array of parties and social events—could simplify their work lives and save a lot of time by dealing only with a single labor union representative.

This is not to say that labor unions today are universally loved or even grudgingly liked by all companies or all economists or the spouses of the union bosses. Unions are criticized by many for propping up wages and salaries in excess of that which would otherwise exist in a free market. Some unions are also alleged to be more interested in pursuing the political agendas of their leadership instead of focusing all of their energies on improving the welfare of their members. Despite these issues, however, most people would acknowledge that unions do serve as a valuable counterweight to the virtually unlimited bargaining power that a major corporation would otherwise exercise over its workers about the terms of their employment. Surprisingly, however, the numbers of unionized employees in private companies have dropped dramatically in the past few decades; most of the recent increases in union membership have come from organizing efforts in the public sector—particularly state and federal workers. This decline in union membership has also been exacerbated by the massive shift in manufacturing activities from Europe and North

America (known by the quaint term of "globalization") to countries in South America and Asia that could offer significantly lower labor costs and, as a result, higher profits to their owners. This pervasive fear of having one's job "out-sourced" has undoubtedly weakened the collective bargaining efforts of many unions.

THE LABOR THEORY OF VALUE

Most classical economists believed that the value of a good depended primarily on the amount of labor needed to produce that good. Indeed, the idea that the amount of labor needed to make a good determines the value of that good goes back thousands of years. For many preindustrial societies, the analysis was fairly simple: One or more workers would obtain the raw materials and by dint of hard work and skill, and a bit of luck, create the desired product. There was no such thing as an assembly line or any division of labor; each worker performed numerous tasks and it was not unusual for a tradesman to fashion the item—whether it was a sword or a pair of sandals or a lava lamp—by himself. As a result, anyone who was studying these labor-intensive production techniques would naturally conclude that the labor input was the most important part of the production process.

This analysis might vary depending on the extent to which the tradesman changed the raw materials into a finished product. For example, a farmer who harvested apples from his trees would certainly expend labor tending to the trees. and picking the apples and carrying them off to market. However, the essential nature of the apple itself would not have been changed in any significant way. The labor utilized to grow and harvest the apples so that they could be given by evil witches to innocent princesses might not be so obvious. But what if we instead considered the labor of a blacksmith who heats iron ore to such a high temperature that he can bend it into the shape of a horseshoe which can be nailed onto the hoof of a horse or attached to a heavy chain and worn as a very fashionable necklace? Here, the metal ore is being completely transformed by heat and then reshaped into an object that is far different than the lump of iron ore that the blacksmith first heated in the forge. The blacksmith's labor appears to be more crucial to the creation of the horseshoe than the farmer's labor is to the harvesting of the apple even though labor must be expended to cultivate the apple trees and pick the fruit. Certainly, apples and horseshoes are not interchangeable.

Although the distinctions between manufactured goods such as horseshoes and farmed products such as apples can obscure the applicability of the labor theory of value, the important point is that the value of both goods could be established based upon the amount of labor needed to create each good. If labor is the common currency of all goods, then the amount of time needed to manufacture a given product would become the currency that determined the relative values of any two goods. If the horseshoe took five hours to make while the farmer's spouse took one hour to cut up the apple and make an apple pie, then we would have a sense of the relative values of the two goods based upon the amount of time needed to make each of them. In short, one horseshoe should be equal in value to five apple pies because an apple pie can be made in one-fifth of the time needed to complete one horseshoe. If everyone in a society begins to draw similar conclusions about the relative values of goods based upon the time needed to make each of those goods, then a pricing mechanism will essentially develop over time.

There are certainly difficulties with trying to define the relative values of all goods in terms of the amount of labor needed to manufacture them. Perhaps the biggest single problem is that we cannot always assume that each good was made in the least time-consuming, most efficient way possible. What if the blacksmith was a trainee and had only begun blacksmithing lessons earlier in the day when he was first given the task to hammer out a horseshoe? Indeed, he might be very slow and very inept at the most basic tasks associated with being a blacksmith and might turn out a variety of oddly shaped metal objects, including a heart-shaped horseshoe, a horseshoe shaped like the letter "J" and a horseshoe pounded out to look like the face of Ayn Rand. In such a case, it might take him twice as long to produce a functional horseshoe as it would take a blacksmith who had graduated from a proper university program in blacksmithing. So, the horseshoe pounded out by the blacksmith trainee would, under the labor theory of value, be priced in terms of 10 hours of labor. But people who were familiar with the regular price of horseshoes (5 hours of labor) would probably not agree to exchange the equivalent good or goods requiring 10 hours of labor because they would know that a horseshoe was essentially worth only 5 hours of labor. Hence, the horseshoe made by the blacksmith trainee would sit unsold until its owner dropped the price, presumably to the 5-hour level and exchanged it for goods requiring a total of 5 hours of labor to produce.

THE ECONOMICS OF KARL MARX

Karl Marx was one of the most influential thinkers of the modern era and developed a theory of economics that challenged the basic tenets of the *laissez-faire* capitalism espoused by Adam Smith and David Ricardo. He was also a grim and dour man, who struggled to provide the most basic necessities for his family and endured mind-numbing poverty and tragedy throughout his life. It is unlikely that he would have been a very good entertainer at children's birthday parties. Indeed, it is difficult to imagine how Marx would have held the attention of young children as he lectured them sternly about the rise of the proletariat or the surplus value of labor while making balloon animals.

Marx offered a very stark vision of the industrial economy that focused on the plight of factory workers whom he believed were consigned to a life of bare subsistence due to their exploitation by the factory owners (members of the so-called *bourgeoisie*) who owned the means of production. For Marx, the value of a good depended solely on the amount of labor needed to produce it—a sort of throwback to the labor theory of value discussed before. But the workers, having limited employment opportunities and fearing the loss of their jobs, were coerced into accepting minimal wages, thereby allowing the owners to extract the surplus value of their labor (the difference between the wages paid to the workers and the prices of the goods sold to the public) in the form of profits. For Marx, this continual exploitation of the workers was the catalyst that would undermine the capitalist system over time until the workers, cognizant of their new-found class consciousness, would unite to overthrow their despotic employers and seize control of the means of production. Once the workers were in control of the factories, Marx reasoned, then it would be possible to develop a more egalitarian (communistic) society in which class distinctions would be erased and the state would wither away.

At least that was the plan. Marx's theory depended on both the working class continuing to be exploited by its employers and those same workers developing a shared sense of the injustice of their plight and the need to take unified action against their exploiters. But this uprising never materialized in the way Marx envisioned, in part because workers around the world never shared the same set of goals at the same time—the condition necessary to spark a worldwide uprising against their capitalist overlords. Indeed, it is unlikely that most workers ever gave much thought to the political arguments that Marx offered, worrying more about putting food on the table and losing their jobs than mounting a worldwide crusade. Moreover, the economic systems of different countries developed at different rates and over different periods of time so that the citizens of some of the more advanced nations saw the stark brutality of capitalism. Some of the worst excesses of free market capitalism began to be softened due to both public legislation and the enlightened self-interest of some business owners who saw the benefits of improving the working conditions of their employees. As a result, the class consciousness that Marx viewed as central to the ultimate overthrow of the international system never really developed among most workers.

Marx's focus on the importance of controlling the means of production also marked an important departure from the more idealistic philosophical musings of Adam Smith. For Marx, the ultimate driver of human behavior is the ceaseless quest for material goods—whether it be food, clothing, shelter or whatever. The workers of the world should ultimately seek to join forces with each other to rid themselves of their oppressors and, by virtue of their seizure of the means of production, improve their own lives in terms of material well-being. As such, Marx's philosophy was far more materialistic in nature than that offered by many of his predecessors. Its predictions that the capitalistic system would ultimately sow the seeds of its own destruction also spawned the political movements and armed insurrections that eventually led to nearly a third of the world's nations calling themselves communist by the middle of the twentieth century. The ultimate irony is that the capitalistic system that Marx thought was doomed to failure outlasted much of the communist world—which collapsed in the early 1990s with the demise of the Soviet Union and its eastern European empire. Despite this apparent shortcoming in the historical determinism of Marx's theory, which preached the inevitable triumph of communism over capitalism, academics and politicians alike, many of whom are apparently oblivious to its shortcomings when applied to the real world, continue to study Marx's work to the present day..

COST OF LIVING INDEX

There are many statistical indexes that are used to track increases or decreases in the prices of goods and services over a given period. One of the best known of these indexes is the Consumer Price Index which is abbreviated somewhat mysteriously as CPI. The CPI is a tool that collects the prices for a bundle of goods and services that would be purchased or otherwise consumed by a typical consumer. The government statisticians compile these prices over time and then track the changes in the prices for these items from month to month and year to year. These price changes (net increases and decreases for each item) can be summarized so as to give a snapshot view of the trends that consumers are seeing in price movements when they buy goods and services or, if necessary, stuff them in their pockets if they are short of cash before they sneak out of the store. But the CPI, like all other indexes, is an abstraction and cannot encompass all the goods and services produced in the economy. Indeed, the CPI was designed to focus on those items that would be consumed by the typical consumer. As a result, it does skimp on some types of vitally important goods such as 5-carat diamond rings and private jets. But it does consist of weighted shares of more mundane (and useful) items such as food and beverages, housing, transportation, clothing, medical care and entertainment. These categories are broken down into further subcategories as needed to approximate the purchasing habits of the typical consumer.

Public tastes change over time and the typical bundle of goods that would have been consumed by individuals in the past will differ in varying degrees from those items consumed today. So, the bundle of goods that is the basis for today's CPI may be very different from those goods that would have been included in the CPI fifty years ago. As an example, older persons may recall that brightly colored and highly flammable polyester shirts were the choice of a generation of well-dressed young men in the 1970s who wanted to flaunt their fashion sensibilities. However, the winds of high fashion are fickle and polyester shirts have sadly fallen out of favor over the years so that they would not be included in the clothing component of today's CPI.

Although the CPI tends to move upward over time, the prices of the goods featured in the CPI can rise or fall or not even change at all from month to month or year to year. When the economy goes into a recession, the demand for many goods included in the CPI may fall—thus causing the CPI to rise at a slower rate or flatten out or even decline. Some items such as the cost of a college education and health care have tended to rise inexorably over time whereas the cost of commodities such as oil and wheat have gyrated wildly.

The fact that the goods and services that make up the CPI change in both price and composition over time reflects the efforts of its administrators to ensure the CPI's continued relevance as a measure of the costs of living in today's economy. It is, as pointed out above, an approximation of the aggregate pricing trends manifesting in the marketplace at a given time as well as a comparative gauge of the movements of prices over time. No one would claim that the CPI (or, indeed, any other index for that matter) perfectly encapsulates all the items purchased by the ordinary consumer; such an index would take so much time to construct and require so much data that it would probably be obsolete by the time it was available for review. The value of the CPI is that it provides a yardstick of price changes over time and a snapshot of the costs facing consumers at any given time.

Because the CPI offers a measure for quantifying prices changes over time, it is used in many different types of contracts. Landlords entering into long-term leases with tenants may require that rents be adjusted yearly, on the anniversary date of each lease, by the change in the CPI. Increasing the amounts of the rents collected to coincide with the upward swing of the CPI allows the landlord to try to preserve over time the original amount of purchasing power of the rental payments made by the tenants. Labor agreements such as those entered into between employers and their employees, particularly those who are represented by unions, will often tie increases in wages to changes in the CPI so that the purchasing power of a given amount of wages will at least remain constant over time.

LIFE CYCLE INCOME THEORY

Economists assume that people act in their rational self interests and that their actions are ultimately motivated by an innate survival instinct. As such, people are presumed to seek to take those actions in their daily routines that will promote the best possible standard of living—given their income and consumption needs. But this assumption is not limited to a single day or month or year; indeed, people are presumed to look forward in time and govern their spending and saving habits depending on their ages and projected life expectancies.

This tidbit suggests that a person in their 20s is going to save some amount of the income they earn in anticipation of needing to live on savings in later life once they have retired or, in the case of an unpopular dictator, been deposed by a popular uprising. Again, this is only a theory: It is debatable because it is unclear whether younger people will save for their golden years so they can avoid having to share cat food with their pets or if, in fact, they will live for the moment and careen from paycheck to paycheck that barely covers their basic living expenses. The lifecycle income theory offers an attractive explanation for the consumption patterns of individuals of all ages, but it at least requires some consideration as to the realities faced by younger productive workers at each stage of their lives. Most people in their twenties and thirties, for example, are very much oriented toward living in the moment and meeting the challenges of maintaining a household and starting a family. The idea of being able to save much money at this point will strike many of them as laughable because they feel buried by all the costs that come with the glorious early years of bill-paying adulthood.

But there are individuals who, by virtue of their career choices and talents, are able to save money systematically from an early age. These individuals—because they make enough money to cover their expenses and still put money in the bank or under the mattress or in a hole in the yard—are able to begin accumulating their savings at an early age and build up a nest-egg that can indeed be drawn down in their later years once they have retired. But even this analysis is simplistic because people will invariably encounter a wide variety of different events—the birth of a child, the onset of a sickness or disease, the loss of a job, the death of a spouse—that may disrupt or even destroy the best laid plans to accumulate funds for retirement.

Life, in short, is unpredictable and no amount of planning can necessarily guarantee a smooth voyage through your income-producing years. It is certainly the case, however, that you as a rational individual are better off starting to save money at an early age so there is at least the possibility that some of the money you have saved will be available for you once you are no longer working for "the Man." If you do not even think in terms of putting aside money for a rainy day or, alternatively, a wild retirement, then there is very little chance that you will enjoy your retirement. Instead, you may find yourself making arrangements with one of your children to move into their garage because you have not accumulated any money to fund your passage through the "golden years." As a result, you should simply head over to their house with all your belongings whenever you are ready to make your final move and marvel at the expressions of joy and wonder on their faces when you show up unannounced at their front door and announce: "Surprise! We are home!"

The life cycle income theory has a certain appeal but it is probably not borne out by the actions of all individuals over their working lives. Some people will make a good living, systematically put monies aside to fund their retirements, avoid most of the pitfalls that come with being alive and float through virtually unscathed. Many other people, however, will run into potentially life-altering situations that will necessitate drawing on—and possibly depleting—their savings over and over again. If they are in the habit of saving, they should be able to retire with some monies in hand to help offset the loss of income they will likely incur when they retire. But, of course, one has to start saving at some point to have money available down the road when the income dries up.

The other point is that older people who are no longer working will necessarily have to rely on their savings as well as any supplemental income programs provided by their technically bankrupt government in order to make ends meet. As such, they will, to a certain degree, be prisoners of the actions taken by their younger selves decades earlier. We have all heard older people say something like "If only I knew then what I know now" while they are droning on about such engrossing (and imaginary) topics such as how they had to walk through waist-high snow drifts 15 miles to attend school when they were young. But it would be helpful if the retired you could travel back in time and meet the younger you who is just starting his or her career and point out how the actions that the younger you took ultimately impacted the lifestyle being enjoyed (or suffered) by the retired you. If things are particularly bad for the retired you due to the profligate spending habits of the younger you, then the retired you can slap around (or use your cane to hit) the younger you to convince the younger you to get on a more financially responsible path so that the retired you does not have to scrounge and scrape to obtain the most basic necessities during your golden years.

HUMAN CAPITAL

To produce goods and services, you must have both capital and labor. The capital itself may consist of tools, equipment, or even entire factories. Labor refers to the individuals who utilize the capital available to them to make goods sorely needed by society such as fishnet stockings and tinted hairspray to cover bald spots. However, the term "labor" is, in and of itself, not very helpful because it offers little in the way of descriptive detail. Indeed, we need to understand that the primary reason businesses employ labor in the first place is so the employees will engage in activities that will create economic value for the employer. In short, businesses hire workers to help them make more money; they are not particularly interested in giving paychecks to people who wish to gossip at the water cooler for hours on end or poach the human resource director's parking space each day.

In trying to understand the labor component of the production process, economists have developed the concept of human capital. What is human capital? No doubt the whiff of sensuality that surrounds the phrase "human capital" suggests adventure and intrigue but the actual definition is more mundane. Human capital consists of that bundle of skills, knowledge, habits, creativity and, indeed, personality, that can be marshaled by individuals to produce goods and services having economic value. In short, it is a fancy way of referring to those positive attributes that an employee can bring to bear when he or she is called upon to work at a desk or on a production line or even on a sandy beach at the family compound in Barbados.

Human capital necessarily includes all the qualities that make it possible for a worker to contribute in a positive way to the profitability of the company. This definition probably precludes enterprising individuals who are able to bolster the company's profitability by creating a second set of books to obscure the company's financial weaknesses and thereby enable it to fetch a much higher price when it is acquired by a competing firm. For most employees, human capital is that sum total of intellectual and physical resources that an employee can summon to advance the economic interests of his or her employer.

Human capital is not a static concept. The human capital that may be brought to bear in the workplace can be enhanced by various measures such as vocational and technical classes and other forms of education designed to improve worker productivity. However, the job training programs need to be related in some way to the work being performed by the employee to enhance his or her human capital. A welder who takes courses in French cooking may be able to chat with his fellow welders about the best way to prepare a chocolate soufflé or the proper wrist action for blending egg whites with a whisk but these culinary revelations will not, in all likelihood, help the welder to improve his welding techniques. However, a course that teaches welders how to complete their work more quickly using fewer materials, for example, will be regarded as having enhanced that worker's human capital because of the increased productivity and reduced materials cost that result from having taken that course.

The concept of human capital is not new because economic thinkers going back to Adam Smith have considered the ways in which workers contribute to the production of goods and services. Until the mid-twentieth century, however, most economists tended to view workers as sort of an undifferentiated mass of interchangeable inputs in the production process. No doubt this view was prompted in part by the prevalence of assembly-line manufacturing employment in the national economy; the development of a massive service sector in the postwar era caused economists to focus more on the workers themselves and the various ways in which worker productivity could be improved. Various factors such as social skills, educational accomplishments, intelligence and physical attributes were studied to try to come to some conclusions about the best ways to bolster worker productivity.

Although it is tempting to suggest that large payments of cash will provide the surest means for improving the job performances of workers, cash alone does not guarantee that a given employee will not accidentally weld his head to the chassis of an automobile or nail his foot to the factory floor. But motivation is a powerful element in securing optimal performances or at least stirring the more somnolent workers from their midday comas. As a result, employers are keenly interested in finding out what sort of goodies will inspire their workers' greatest efforts. To that end, many employers in industries seeking workers whose talents are in great demand and short supply will focus on providing non-cash perks along with hefty compensation packages to win the favor of their intended recipients. They might toss in catered lunches and a car allowance, and so on and so forth. The age-old question, of course, is how long even the most generous compensation package will continue to prompt these coveted workers to put forth their best efforts for the greater glory of their corporate overlords.

Human capital is a concept that traffics in intangible qualities, but its proponents believe that an understanding of its most important elements can lead to tangible improvements in workplace productivity. Various forms of instruction and classes can clearly have a positive impact on a worker so that far fewer head welding incidents or nail-gun injuries occur on the shop floor. Certainly, workers can benefit from detailed presentations for operating machinery so that they are able to handle tasks with greater efficiency and improved competency—unless, of course, they are related to the company's founder and are fortunate enough to be exempt from all of these trivial considerations.

STAGFLATION

Stagflation has nothing to do with "stag parties" and is considerably less entertaining than going out and having drinks while watching bored strippers shimmy up and down shiny brass poles at the local nightclub. Indeed, stagflation is a term that was coined during the 1970s to explain the phenomenon of an economy suffering from increased inflation and increased unemployment at the same time. This was a disturbing occurrence because it called into question the assumptions underlying the Phillips Curve, discussed elsewhere, which posited that there is an inherent tradeoff between inflation and unemployment. In other words, nobody is in favor of increases in the levels of prices or unemployment (unless, of course, they are idiots) but the Phillips Curve at least offered the somewhat comforting conclusion that if we had to deal with higher prices, it would entail lower unemployment, and vice versa. Sadly, the ugliness of the real world intruded upon the pristine tradeoff underlying the Phillips Curve in the 1970s when soaring commodity prices and contracting economic activity (and rising unemployment) left policymakers fumbling for a way to respond to this new paradigm in which inflation and unemployment seemed to rocket upward in tandem.

The uncomfortable reality that the economy might be locked in a permanent upward rachet of galloping inflation and increasing pools of disgruntled former workers (with a lot of time of their hands to think about who they would be voting for in future elections) was terrifying to government officials. Needless to say, they consulted with their economic advisers to see who might be able to suggest a way out of this apparent morass. Although economists offered a variety of possible ways to escape the chokehold of inflation and unemployment, it fell to the Federal Reserve to take steps in the late 1970s and early 1980s to raise interest rates to unprecedented heights by severely reducing the money supply. If you did not mind paying credit card interest rates as high as 18 percent to obtain a mortgage for a house or a loan for a car, then it was a glorious time to be alive. Most people, however, found their daily lives dramatically impacted by these stratospheric interest rates and put off major purchases because they simply could not afford to pay the finance charges. Not surprisingly, these unprecedented interest rates led to a huge slowdown in economic activity and brought about one of the most severe recessions of the post-war era. The positive side of this suffering, however, was that this slowdown in economic activity convinced consumers that the government was serious about stopping inflation and, over time, changed the popular expectations that prices would continue to increase higher and higher as far as they could imagine into the future.

The extent to which the Phillips Curve or stagflation is applicable in the twenty-first century is, of course, open to debate by economists. Indeed, there is often something of an "after the fact" odor to these discussions because we have to look in the rear-view mirror and see where the inflation and unemployment statistics were at any given time to see if we can discern the tradeoffs of the Phillips Curve. Indeed, the opposite phenomena of stagflation—falling levels of unemployment and prices—manifested in the twenty-first century. This phenomenon, while suggesting that the citizenry could have the best of both worlds with near full employment and stable or even declining prices, may have resulted from things outside the control of policymakers—such as falling worldwide commodity prices—as well as persistent government deficit spending that fueled increases in domestic employment. Or we may have just been very lucky in recent years and things may have magically improved through no concerted actions by our esteemed policymakers-for-life merely because we were overdue for a new spin of the karmic wheel.

As far as stagflation is concerned, it seems to have vanished for the time being but it certainly could reappear in the future. Many conservative economists who tried to determine whether stagflation had indeed demolished the Phillips Curve as a useful theoretical tool, suggested that government policies such as increased spending could push down the unemployment rate in the short term. However, the increased dollars introduced into the economy could ultimately contribute to a higher rate of inflation. Over time, workers would perceive that the prices for the goods and services they consumed were increasing due to the bloating of the money supply so that their purchasing power would be eroded over time. They would, in turn, demand higher wages to be able to pay these increased prices, which, of course, would fuel the inflationary pressures in the economy. Higher labor prices would cause employers to cut back their workforces. At the end of the day, the prices of goods and services would be higher and the level of employment would, in all likelihood, be unchanged. Assuming that this analysis is correct, then we would expect that the Phillips Curve has some validity but that it, like all theoretical constructs, does not apply in all situations.

THE PHILLIPS CURVE

Suppose that I have just elected myself to be dictator-for-life of the principality of Marigold, having won the election by sending my last serious political rival on an excursion to the firing squad. I now rule this mountainous nation of flatulent sheep and swarthy peasants with an iron fist. But I see potential enemies everywhere due to my keen sense of anticipation as well as my well-documented paranoia and several other mental disorders that my now imprisoned psychiatrist felt emboldened to point out. Despite—or perhaps because of—my concern about my own well-being, I am deeply aware of the need to keep the citizenry happy—or, at least preoccupied enough so that they do not blame me for their grinding poverty and try to storm the presidential palace. Not surprisingly, I am very interested in trying to employ as many of Marigold's citizens as possible because busy hands are less likely to try to hang their beloved leader.

My desire to find jobs for my loyal constituents leads me to summon my one remaining advisor who had not already been tossed into the dungeon to ask him what I should do to boost the stumbling labor market. After some hesitation, perhaps due to the fates that had befallen all of his fellow advisors, my minister tells me it may not be a good idea to pump up the size of the labor force. In short, increasing government spending to boost the number of workers in the labor force—though an attractive prospect at first glance—might cause other problems such as a rise in food prices. He then calls my attention to the so-called Phillips Curve, which is a graphical depiction of the presumably inverse relationship between the rate of inflation and the level of unemployment in an economy. As such, it declares that there is a link between increases in prices and declines in unemployment or, alternatively stated, decreases in prices and increases in unemployment. Now I might want to refute the conclusion offered by the Phillips Curve—perhaps by having my palace guards track down Professor William Phillips, for whom the Phillips Curve was named, and tossing him in the dungeon as well. But the fact that Professor Phillips died many years ago would put a severe crimp in the execution of that plan. My inability to subject Professor Phillips to a show trial or perhaps torture him until he confesses that the Phillips Curve is bunk is particularly troubling because the banks from whom I would have to borrow money to fund the wages of new workers are run by bankers who believe in the Phillips Curve as well.

So let us assume that I am able to obtain a loan to fund a vast public works project that will employ all the disgruntled peasants in Marigold in the construction of various monuments to the glory of my regime. My minister might warn me that this enormous expenditure will, per the Phillips Curve, boost employment, at least in the short term, but that it will also have an inflationary effect on the prices of goods and services. My attempt to buy social peace might ultimately be frustrated by rapid escalations in the prices of bread and milk and lead to violent demonstrations in front of the presidential palace (thus marring my view of the beautiful gardens by the front gates which are also boo-by-trapped with explosives to prevent unlawful entry by some of my less loyal subjects). As a result, I may have to reduce the scope of my public works program to mute possible upswings in the prices of staple goods—even though this will mean not being able to employ as many citizens as I had originally hoped. This dilemma underscores the difficulty of being a despot—a challenge that is not typically appreciated by the general public. One has to walk such a fine line between reducing unemployment and dampening inflationary pressures in the economy and this problem cannot be avoided no matter how many people you throw in jail.

Although the tradeoff between inflation and employment embedded in the Phillips Curve appears to be borne out by empirical data, there are certainly qualifications to its underlying assumptions. After all, the Phillips Curve is a theoretical abstraction that came to prominence in the 1970s when policymakers were trying to deal with high inflation and unemployment at the same time. In countries such as Marigold where there are a lot of unemployed laborers sitting around playing checkers and dominos, it may be the case that we can put many of them to work before their increased participation in the economy begins to result in significant price increases. This employment "slack" in the Marigold economy might have to be absorbed before I really need to worry about spiraling bread prices sending the peasants running toward the presidential palace with their torches and pitchforks in hand. Indeed, the Marigold economy may have to reach what passes for full employment before I have to start watching out my bedroom window for unruly ruffians. Unfortunately, there is no way to know in advance when significant increases in the labor force will unleash inflationary pressures in the economy. However, the fact that we have multitudes of would-be laborers who are not particularly busy with income-earning activities may allow us to hire a lot of people before prices begin to increase significantly in the economy.

RATIONAL EXPECTATIONS

Economics is ultimately a social science even though some economists will insist that its mathematical underpinnings should cause it to be considered a close cousin to the physical sciences. But economists are saddled with the unfortunate task of having to form many of their theories based upon underlying assumptions about how human beings behave and the motivations that affect the economic decisions that they choose to make. After all, physicists, for example, get to study the movements of atoms which follow fairly predictable patterns as they careen about in the microcosmic world while economists must try to model the actions of humans who often engage in patently idiotic behavior that defies any predictions based upon straightforward cost-benefit analyses. Some economists will also point out the unique disadvantages to having to construct theoretical models based upon the not-always predictable behavior of their human subjects who sometimes act in ways that seem to contradict their obvious self-interests.

So the question arises as to whether people can

usually be counted upon to pursue their own betterment and thus engage in predictable patterns of behavior. Certainly a fundamental tenet of economics is that the lower the price of a good, the greater the demand for that good. Of course this rule does not always hold true because we know that we cannot always expect people to increase their purchases of hazardous wastes no matter how big a discount we offer them. But for those goods that are actually desired by consumers, it is reasonable to assume that a drop in the price of a valued good will typically result in increased demand for that good.

Economists posit that people act in a rational manner because it makes it easier to model their behavior and draw conclusions. Indeed, there would not be much left to the field of economics if we could not count on people to behave in certain predictable ways. In short, we could expect that farmers, for example, would plant more corn if the prices consumers were willing to pay for that corn increased with each successive bushel of corn grown. But it is unclear to what degree we can assume that humans are meticulous fact-gatherers who do a detailed analysis of a proposed action before engaging in that action. Instead, the decision-making process may be more intuitive or, to be less charitable, more impulsive. Suppose that you are in the market for a new car and have found a sporty little ride called the Hamlet, Which boasts inexpensive but substandard automotive technology. You have gazed longingly at the car on several occasions while visiting the dealership in the past but have hesitated to pull the trigger because its $25,000 price tag seems a bit high for a car that ranked dead last in reliability for subcompacts in all the major consumer product magazines. Our economists would posit that your decision to purchase the Hamlet might be made easier if the dealer were to drop the price by several thousand dollars. But they would be extremely puzzled if the dealer jacked the sticker price up by $5,000 and you decided at that point that it was time to get a Hamlet for your very own. Now allowing for the possibility that you might be incredibly stupid, it is, nevertheless, very unusual that a significant increase in price would be the catalyst that would cause you to jump off the fence and rush over to the dealer to sign a contract. Economic theory is premised on the fact that even though there might be an occasional idiot who purchases an overpriced, horrible car that leaves a trail of parts on the road whenever it is driven out of the garage, most people in the market for a car that can virtually guarantee numerous trips to the mechanic and perhaps a "lemon law" lawsuit, will not move ahead with a purchase solely because the price has been increased significantly.

Whether people are rational actors who engage in systematic analyses in making decisions such as whether to buy a car or a house or even a trained tabby cat is open for debate, particularly if you have ever watched people giving each other the "middle finger salute" while racing each other on the highway. Economists believe that how we act is dependent on our generalized expectations as to the probable outcomes of these actions. For example, we pony up tens of thousands of dollars each year to send our children off to distant colleges because we expect that attending college will enable us to move our children out of the house without having to resort to brute force. Not only does college free up a room or two for more useful purposes such as billiards or big screen home theaters, but the children may actually learn something and become productive citizens on their own.

KEYNES AND THE MULTIPLIER EFFECT

When you are as esteemed an economist as John Maynard Keynes, you can offer all sorts of insights about the workings of the economy and scholars around the world will study your every word. Indeed, a sneeze or a bout of flatulence might be interpreted by some as Keynes offering a unique perspective on the world of economics. Or not. But one of Keynes' most inspired breakthroughs came about when he sat in his garden at around 3:15 p.m. on August 7, 1925 (give or take) and wondered about how a single act of spending money can have a ripple effect through the economy and ultimately effect a financial impact several times greater than the original expenditure.

Suppose that you need to purchase a bouquet of flowers because you forgot your spouse's birthday. You know that you need to bring your "A game" to the florist to avoid spending the rest of your life on the couch so you squelch the desire to purchase a single long stem rose and instead opt for the "forest of flowers" display consisting of 100 roses in a massive ceramic tub adorned with bright red block letters saying "I Love You" for a mere $500. Once you tender your $500 to the florist and wheel the enormous floral spectacle home to your beloved, your money begins to take a trip through the economy.

The florist, having received your money, will probably put part of it ($200) in the bank because it is always a good idea to stash away some cash. But the florist might spend the remaining $300 on the rent for the store, sending the monthly payment to the landlord. The fact that the florist kept $200 out of the original payment would show that the florist had a marginal propensity to consume (MPC) of 0.6 which, for those who are not familiar with higher arithmetic, means that the florist spent 60 percent of the $500 payment. Conversely, the florist would have also demonstrated a marginal propensity to save (MPS) of 0.4, because the florist managed to squirrel away the remaining $200 that was not handed over to the landlord.

We would not be surprised if the landlord also likes to hide money from his family members so, continuing with the same MPC and MPS, he would stash 20 percent of $300 or $60 in an offshore bank account and then use the remaining $240 to buy a pair of tickets to see the rock group Flaming Garbage in concert. As with other concepts in economics, the analysis behind the multiplier effect is purely quantitative; no judgment is implied as to the worthiness or lack of worthiness of a particular act of consumption or savings. So even though the creative output of the members of Flaming Garbage spiraled downward into the abyss years ago, after they kicked their drug habits, economists are interested only in calculating the flow of money through the economy.

ECONOMIC CYCLES

We all have our good days and our bad days. Our economy is no different, but the good days are referred to as "booms" and the bad days are called "busts" and both will play out over a period of many months or even years. As much as we would like to have a stable economy that does not overheat too much or drop off a cliff, rising and falling cycles of economic activity are very typical in the modern era. Nevertheless, we find ourselves riveted to headline news about whether the government is printing too much money or whether the Consumer Price Index is truly an accurate representation of changes in the cost of living.

What does an economic cycle really look like? In a metaphoric sense, it can be as glorious as a sunset or as sinister as a stormy sky but the actual story is far less dramatic because it is narrated by economists who are not typically known for their lofty prose. In a nutshell, the activity in an economy will fluctuate but it will tend to shift upward over time due to both a growing population and increased productivity. At least, that is how it should be if the government is run with just a modest amount of competence. Ah, therein lies the rub! Running a country—let alone its economy—is not a task for nitwits even though some would suggest that there are nitwits running amok through the halls of power in many capitals. But there are others who argue that the modern economy is so massive and has so many actors and variables that it is impossible for anyone— no matter how brilliant they may be—to manage it and that the economy more or less runs on autopilot like a massive oil tanker floating around on the high seas. This conclusion is, of course, more reassuring to those of us who worry each day about the very real danger that nitwits could be piloting the ship of state. We may also try to console ourselves with the possibility that it takes so long for legislative acts or executive orders to have a tangible impact that the desired effects may have already been obtained or perhaps even washed out by intervening changes in the economy itself.

No government official wants to be at the helm of the ship of state when economic activity is falling and unemployment is rising. You can be the smartest president or prime minister who ever lived but if the ship of state sinks while you are standing on the bridge, then history will associate your name with this economic debacle. Instead, you want to be associated with the good times when everyone had money and was employed and was happy, or at least were convinced they were happy by the state propagandists. To that end, you may not find it shocking to learn that government officials worry about their jobs and will take all sorts of steps to pump up the economy, particularly in an election year.

So how does one go about jumpstarting an economy, particularly when it looks like it has seen better days and appears to be sliding into a recession or even a depression? Well, there are several tactics that can be followed. First, the government can print more money. Flooding the economy may offer very little in the way of any tangible benefits in the long term (except higher prices) but it can have a positive short-term impact by encouraging people to take their new-found cash and go out and buy things, thereby boosting economic activity. Second, the government can cut taxes, which will also have a similar expansionary effect as it, too, will encourage people to increase their consumption of trinkets and goodies. Third, the government can increase existing assistance programs which, like the previous two actions, will put more money in the hands of the people and prompt more shopping sprees. Whether any of these actions will actually affect the longer-term expansionary and contractionary phases of a given economic cycle, however, is debatable because they may not lead to an actual and permanent increase in the production of goods and services.

Mathematicians who study economic cycles have pointed out that no two cycles are the same and that their differences may be depicted graphically. Economists speak of V-shaped recoveries and U-shaped recoveries and even W-shaped recoveries when they are trying to predict the way in which an economy will come out of an economic downturn.

> » A V-shaped recovery is one in which economic activity suddenly plummets and then quickly recovers.
> » A U-shaped recovery, by contrast, is more gradual (more chill) and manifests over a longer period of time.
> » A W-shaped recovery is one in which the economy rises from the ashes of a recession like a phoenix but then tumbles back into the depths and then comes back to the surface again, almost taunting the hapless economists who are trying to predict its next move.

LIQUIDITY TRAPS

One of the disadvantages of running a despotic regime and maintaining iron-fisted control over its peasants is that the dictator gets blamed when the economy gets stuck in a rut. Unfortunately, even the smartest leaders can find their countries mired in a liquidity trap, which occurs when the government is unable to boost the level of economic activity regardless of the steps it takes (for example, lowered interest rates, increased social welfare payments). To better understand the concept of the liquidity trap, we must return to our discussion of the demand for money.

If I want to build a museum that will glorify my 20-year reign as the ruler of Marigold, I will probably need to borrow funds from the banks to pay for its construction. In general, my willingness to borrow money is inversely related to the interest rate that the treasurer must pay for the use of that money. The costs of servicing the loan (that is, mortgage interest) could prove to be crucial in determining the ultimate size of my museum. A low interest rate may enable me to build an edifice that will dwarf the Coliseum in Rome whereas a very high interest rate will force me to scale back my ambitions and settle for something more modest.

The tradeoff between the rate of interest charged by the First National Bank of Marigold and the amount of money that I can borrow to fund my museum is evident. It underscores the tendency of borrowers to seek smaller loans as the interest rates increase. Conversely, it follows that a decline in the interest rate will lead to increased borrowing and, ultimately, even more grandiose monuments glorifying my regime.

My discussions with the bankers and my few remaining advisors may raise a troubling issue. Even though Marigold has seen extremely low interest rates over the past decade, investment in plants and equipment has dropped off to almost nothing. Innovation has ground to a halt and there are very few new products being manufactured in the nation's factories. Also of concern are the empty shopping centers which have been likened to ghost towns in recent years because very few people venture into the stores. This sclerotic state of affairs has persisted even though my government has decreed that unprecedented amounts of money be given to everyone who voted for me in the prior election.

The Marigold economy may have reached the point that it cannot be stimulated any further regardless of how low the interest rates are dropped by the central bank or how much money the government gives to my supporters. This liquidity trap may result from the fact that the expected returns for investors are simply not high enough—in spite of the rock-bottom interest rates—to offset the costs of building new factories. But why should that be the case? Well, the political landscape could be very perilous due to heavy-handed government edicts such as the requirement that all investors pay an "investment tax" equal to ten percent of their invested funds on any construction project in Marigold. If the extraneous costs of such projects become too high, then investors will be reluctant to get involved in any type of construction project—even if the interest rates are dropped to nearly zero percent. As a result, prospective investors may decide it is not worth the financial risk and instead opt to keep their cash in their pockets or to bury it in their backyards.

It can take years for a country to crawl out of a liquidity trap because politicians have a difficult time believing that lower interest rates will not ultimately cure the problem of a stagnant economy. Indeed, if a country has enjoyed extremely low interest rates for years or even decades, then the interest rates may cease to have any meaningful impact on the decisions of investors to commit their capital to construction projects. It may instead be that more dramatic reforms are needed such as revamping the legal system governing business activities to reduce the penalties or costs associated with investments in the economy. A repeal of the "investment tax" discussed above would be an example of an action that would improve the willingness of investors to fund construction projects. But there are many other types of actions that could be taken by the government to increase economic activity, such as implementing more favorable depreciation schedules for deducting the costs of plants and equipment or allowing lower-priced, non-unionized workers to work on such projects. Those smarty-pants commentators who suggest that the most constructive move would be for the leader of the country to be deposed so that a more business-friendly regime could be installed are, of course, entitled to their opinions and, as a result, can expect to enjoy the next few years of their lives considering the wisdom of their uninformed perspectives in rat-infested cells beneath the presidential palace.

INVESTMENT AND CONSUMPTION

Economists talk about the tradeoff between consumption and investment, but it is not always clear what is meant by the two terms. Consumption involves the use of a good or a service—whether it is a bicycle or a ticket to a play or a bag of groceries. Investment, by contrast, involves the purchase of such things as factories and equipment and, indeed, training programs that enable workers to be more efficient in the manufacture of those goods and services. Consumption enables us to enjoy the fruits of our labor; investment makes it possible for the fruits of our labor to exist in the first place by initially creating the means of production of those goods. Stated another way, consumption is the immediate use of a good or service; investment is the deployment of capital to productive assets that may result in the increased output of goods and services in the future.

To return to our initial query, the tradeoff is whether we decide to spend our money today so that we can a enjoy a bottle of champagne and caviar while floating around in a hot tub or whether we invest those dollars in the stock of a company building a new semiconductor plant that may generate new products and jobs in the future. So, if we wanted to increase the size of our economy massively, we could pass a law prohibiting consumption of any kind by the citizenry so that all the money in the economy would be allocated to the construction of state-of-the-art factories and machinery. Unfortunately, this total ban on consumption would mean that no one would be able to buy food or clothing or shelter. Some basic level of consumption is necessary for life, so we cannot devote every dollar to investment or we would all die.

Similarly, we cannot consume all our resources today and neglect to invest anything in the means of production. We would accomplish little more than gaining a lot of weight because no one would be building new plants or manufacturing new products. Society would start to crumble as we consumed everything in sight and, as a result, we would begin to run out of everything. Consuming everything today would leave nothing for tomorrow.

Consumption and investment are therefore the yin and yang of the world of economics. The more we consume, the less we invest, and *vice versa*.

A market economy is driven by consumer spending on a wide variety of goods and services. Over time the actions of numerous buyers and sellers ultimately affect the amount of consumption that takes place in the economy as well as the investment that is eventually made in its factors of production. As consumption is much more fun than investment, because we as consumers get to enjoy our goodies today instead of waiting until some indefinite time in the future, we are not usually worried so much about stoking the consumption of goods and services. However, we do feel differently about investment because our current level of investment in the economy will ultimately determine the future size of the economy. Not surprisingly, the government can take several actions to increase the level of investment in the economy, such as imposing taxes on the purchase of goods and services, like luxury clothing items, that it believes detract from increased investment. It can also lower interest rates to encourage borrowing to fund the construction of new plants, the purchase of equipment, and the hiring and training of additional workers.

The important point to remember is that consumption and investment are inextricably tied together and one cannot exist without the other. People consume goods and services and must—unless they are really good at larceny—pay for those goods and services. The firms that receive those payments are in turn able to use a part of their revenues to invest in new plants and equipment and, maybe, the occasional private jet in case their officers have to skip the country in a hurry. If there were no consumption, there would be no revenue available to fund the needed investment in the nation's productive capacity to continue generating those goods and services in the future. It is certainly true that we have to chart some sort of middle ground between the extreme positions of all dollars being consumed today and all dollars being invested for a better tomorrow.

GROSS DOMESTIC PRODUCT (GDP)

As the no-nonsense ruler of the kingdom of Catarrh, I have prided myself on my farsighted reforms such as doubling the capacity of the jails so that I can lock up whiny dissidents. Even though I have shut down snippy media organizations so that I can protect the citizens of Catarrh from having to hear stories about their country that might upset them or even unfounded tales of my alleged atrocities, I am aware that I must deliver a better standard of living to my devoted subjects so that they stop trying to assassinate my body-doubles with disturbing regularity.

To show my unruly subjects that I am improving their lives and thus deserve to continue my role as benevolent dictator, I would want to show how my leadership is bolstering the national economy as reflected in the figures for the gross domestic product (GDP). The GDP is a measure of all the goods and services produced in the economy in a given year. As such, it is an aggregate number and does not really tell us much about the living standards of the population. A better idea might be to calculate the per capita production of goods and services by dividing the GDP of Catarrh by the number of its citizens. If the GDP of Catarrh is $1 billion and we have 500,000 happy-go-lucky citizens who have not yet been locked up, then the per capita GDP of Catarrh would be equal to $2,000.

The neighboring country of Unicorn, by contrast, has a GDP of $500 million, but a population of only 50,000 people, so its per capita GDP is equal to $10,000. So even though Unicorn has a smaller aggregate GDP, its much smaller population means that its per capital GDP is $10,000—which is five times as large as that of our beloved homeland. As a result, it would be considered a far wealthier country than Catarrh. Not surprisingly, the higher standard of living in Unicorn acts as a magnet to draw thousands of Catarrhites each year to step over the two-foot-high white picket fence that separates our two nations and take up residence across the porous border.

It is useful to track both the aggregate GDP and the per capita GDP over time to see if a particular economy is expanding or contracting and, also, to gauge whether the standard of living of the citizenry is improving or deteriorating. But those who live by the sword of statistics can die by the sword of statistics or at least lose some fingers. Statisticians can provide cold, hard numbers that document how the living standards of Catarrhites have declined continuously for many years while those of our neighboring Unicornians have steadily improved during that same time.

Another important consideration when comparing GDP figures from year to year is to differentiate between nominal and real GDP before jumping to any conclusions about whether things are getting better or worse or just drifting along in no particular direction. If the increases in GDP enjoyed by Unicorn each year are due to continual increases in the production of goods and services, then the people of that country would presumably be enjoying a higher standard of living. If, however, the increase in GDP is due to increases in prices alone with no material changes in the production of goods and services, then the nominal GDP will have changed while the real GDP remained the same. To complicate the analysis further, if the real GDP remained static over time while the population increased, then the per capita GDP will have actually declined during that period. In short, price increases in Unicorn might have caused significant increases in the price of goods and services throughout their economy so that the people are worse off in real terms. In contrast, we might find that the prices of goods and services in Catarrh have declined over time because of my regime's no-nonsense policy of imprisoning anyone who dares to raise the prices for any goods or services. It might be the case that the citizens of Catarrh are doing better than the statistics regarding GDP and per capita GDP might suggest. This would not necessarily lessen the envy Catarrhites feel towards the banking oasis across the picket fence border but it might make them feel a little better about the state of their own economy.

PART THREE:
INFLATION AND UNEMPLOYMENT

INFLATION

Inflation is defined by the more learned economists who went to the better schools as a nominal increase in the price of a given unit of goods or services. Others with less impressive academic pedigrees will opine that inflation is "just awful." Regardless of which definition you prefer, inflation can be problematic for anyone living in a society beset with escalating prices. Rising prices will crode the purchasing power of our money over time and cause people such as retirees living on fixed incomes to suffer declines in their standard of living. Inflation can arise from an increase in the demand for a particular good or service or it can result from an increase in the costs of supplying those goods and services.

Suppose that I am the owner of the Frantic Candy Company, which manufactures luxurious chocolates liberally sprinkled with guarana to give that "get up and go" feeling that is so coveted by low-energy chocolate connoisseurs. Our candies spark manic energy in our customers that competing companies have been unable to duplicate. Once you have eaten a few Frantic Candies, you can complete a couple of triathlons in a day or sit through a mind-numbing conversation with an old school chum. As a result, there has been a tremendous demand for our products, making it difficult for retailers to keep them in stock.

Due to our own production constraints, however, we have not been able to increase our output appreciably because we are already operating our factory with three shifts around the clock. Moreover, the candies themselves are handcrafted by skilled artisans who are both expensive and difficult to find.

A greater problem that ties in with our discussion of inflation is that we rely on substances that are often expensive and sometimes in short supply. If one of our key ingredients doubles in price, I might search for possible substitutes that are less expensive even though they might only enable people to stay awake for 24 hours. Assuming that I am not satisfied with these other possibilities, I might have no choice but to go back to my original ingredient and increase the prices of my candies accordingly. My hope would be that I could pass the higher prices onto my customers without dampening their ardor for my products. But the costs of our products would still increase due to our higher production costs.

The same conclusion could be drawn from an increase in the cost of a widely available ingredient such as lemon flavoring—which can be acquired at any grocery store. Because it is essentially a commodity that does not command a special premium, it is very likely that other manufacturers of lemon flavoring are experiencing the same pricing pressures. As a result, there may be very little possibility of finding a substitute product that is less expensive. As with our amphetamine-like additive, the inevitable result is that the prices of the lemon-flavored candies being devoured by our customers will go up.

The flip side of higher supply costs inflating the costs of production and, ultimately, the sales prices of our chocolates is price increases caused by the enormous upswing in demand for our products as evidenced by the frenzied purchases made by consumers. Many people find our having brought together the seemingly diverse audiences of chocolate aficionados and amateur pharmacologists to be a masterstroke in marketing. Indeed, the fact that people are swarming into local candy stores or standing for hours in long lines at shops to buy our candies would make any confectionary company owner happy. But the increased demand would also be noticed by many of the retailers who are having to step over the trampled bodies in their stores to get a breath of fresh air. They would naturally seek to increase the sales price for the candies so that they could make a greater profit. Of course, these increased prices would be passed on to the consumers. But the fact that our goodies are fetching such high prices would have another effect in that potential competitors would begin manufacturing their own lines of drug-infused candies which, over time, would probably cause the lofty prices for our products to decline as more and more competing products came onto the market.

HYPERINFLATION

If you were granted three wishes, it is very unlikely that you would want to use one of those wishes to request that your country's economy be subjected to a bout of hyperinflation. Although we live in an era in which most things preceded by terms such as "hyper" and "super" are thought to be desirable, the phenomenon known as hyperinflation is not one that evokes warm memories around the family dinner table— even if yours was a family that engaged in food fights by throwing knives and forks at each other. It occurs when benevolent government officials decide that they must increase spending to carry out their grandiose visions for a more perfect and just, albeit financially disemboweled, society and thereby finance their programs to bring new meaning to the lives of the citizenry—whether the citizenry wants it or not.

But governments do not really have anything to sell to raise money so they must pay for their spending sprees with new taxes if they want to maintain some level of financial discipline. Unfortunately, very few people like to pay taxes and those people who dislike paying taxes tend to vote against politicians who argue that taxes should be increased (unless, of course, the politicians promise that tax increases will be imposed only on people other than those electing to cast their ballots). As a result, the typical government will face a choice: it can either rein in its ambitious spending programs or throw caution to the winds and fire up the printing presses and start issuing a lot of brand new bills.

The net result of this increase in paper dollars flowing into the economy is that prices start to increase dramatically because everyone suddenly has a lot of cash on hand. Unfortunately, printing lots and lots of bills does not cause more goods and services to appear magically. The economy still has the same number of houses and the same number of cars and the same number of cartons of eggs. The only thing that is different is that everyone now has more dollars in their pockets. But rest assured that it will not take very long before the sellers of goods and services realize that consumers have a lot more money in hand. Their response will be to raise prices in recognition of this new reality so that if twice as many dollars are floating around, the prices of most goods and services will increase accordingly.

This increase in prices will, of course, frustrate our illustrious central planners who will try to finance their spending programs (which now have essentially doubled in cost) by printing even more money. And they could conclude that there is no reason to be shy or demure in funding their agenda so they might cajole the central bank into running the government printing presses around the clock and increase the supply of bills ten-fold. Unfortunately, as this tidal wave of money cascades through the economy, those very same providers of goods and services will react accordingly again and boost their prices—perhaps ten-fold to match the increase in the money supply. As most government officials do not want to increase taxes ten-fold and guarantee that many of them will be spending their free time making license plates or trying to tunnel out of their jail cells, they buy more printing presses and try to flood the economy with even more cash. But the inevitable result, no matter how many times they try, is that the prices go up and offset any momentary illusion that the citizens have increased purchasing power.

One byproduct of this reckless mismanagement of the national currency is that people begin to conclude that the geniuses running the government may not really know what they are doing. They begin to view the currency itself with great suspicion because they rightly believe that it is not worth the paper it is printed on and that it will continue to decrease in value due to the profligate printing presses. No one will want to hold currency because they will see it as a dissipating asset with constantly eroding purchasing power. Instead, consumers will rush out to try to get rid of their cash by purchasing all sorts of goods which, in a hyperinflated economy, can consist of such things as a $500 box of matches. Their behavior will be shaped entirely by their refusal to hold cash; they may indeed require that payments to them be made using more tangible forms of wealth, such as gold or silver. Failing that, they may insist on swapping things—thus returning to the barter economy.

History has offered examples of societies, such as Germany in the 1920s and Zimbabwe in the 2000s, in which the money supply grew so rapidly and so massively that some people used wheelbarrows to carry enough cash to the grocery store to purchase a few staple goods. These economies were essentially destroyed as the deluge of paper currency ultimately led to even the most basic items being priced in millions and even billions of dollar equivalents. Not surprisingly, the governments overseeing these disastrous policies failed and these nations suffered greatly from this incredible mismanagement of the national money supply. Indeed, the spectacle of hyperinflation is perhaps one of the most compelling arguments that there is no such thing as a free lunch and that prosperity depends on the actual production of goods and services, not the printing of enormous quantities of dollar bills.

254 | ECONOMICS AND ALL THAT

UNEMPLOYMENT BY THE NUMBERS

In even the best of times, the economy is not so efficient that everyone has a job. Indeed, unemployment is
a fact of life even when you have factories straining at
full capacity and policymakers who make well-reasoned
decisions that suggest they *do* know their knees from
their elbows. In a dynamic modern economy in which
billions or trillions of dollars of transactions occur every
day and the demand for and the supply of countless
goods and services fluctuates constantly, new businesses
are always being created and old businesses are always
being shuttered.

With the creation and destruction of so many
businesses going on all the time, people are constantly
being hired and fired. Not surprisingly, these newly
unemployed workers react to the loss of their livelihood
in different ways: Some curl up in a fetal position in
a corner and babble incoherently whereas others seek
solace in bulk liquor. But the vast majority of the newly
unemployed will try to respond constructively and start
looking for a new job because car payments and house
payments do not go away merely because your income
has been shut off. As long as these individuals continue
to look for work, they will be counted as being unemployed by the government statisticians.

Politicians do not like to hear about rising unemployment because the jobless figures reflect on their
competency (or incompetency) in managing the

economy and may not bode well for their re-election prospects. In the more progressive totalitarian regimes, unemployment can be made a crime so that you can lock up anyone who does not have a job and thus make the more visible manifestations of joblessness disappear. Plus, the likelihood of a popular uprising is greatly reduced when all the would-be uprisers are already locked up. But the problem of unemployment cannot be so easily dismissed in a democratic society where displaced workers have legal rights and cannot be tossed into a dungeon on a whim. Governments have tried to alter the definition of what constitutes "unemployment" in order to reduce the number of people who can be officially counted as being without a job. In the United States, for example, you must not only be without a job but must also be actively searching for work in order to be counted as being unemployed. So, if you are perfectly happy sitting at home and watching reality shows and do not bother trying to schedule job interviews, the government does not consider you unemployed.

Yet this syntactical winnowing of the definition of "unemployment" by government statisticians was not the end of the efforts to recast the jobless figures in the best possible light. The official unemployment statistics were further softened by excluding so-called "discouraged workers" from being considered as unemployed. These are individuals who have become so frustrated with their futile searches for work that they have given up and dropped out of the labor force altogether. Some may try to start their own businesses while others may be content to file for unemployment benefits. In either case, they are no longer of concern to the government bean counters because their enforced idleness will not be tabulated in the official unemployment numbers.

It seems almost illogical to consider workers who have been unable to find work and essentially "tossed in the towel" as not being "unemployed" but that is the alternative universe of government record-keeping. It also obscures the more serious impact of prolonged unemployment in terms of the costs both on society as a whole (for example, unemployment benefits, loss of taxable income) which is deprived of the labors of these displaced workers and the costs—economic and psychological—that prolonged joblessness imposes on both the workers and their families. Many people view their jobs as the source of their sense of self-worth. Losing a job can be a crushing blow to one's self-esteem and cause tremendous financial hardship to both the worker and his or her family. Unemployment benefits are available for those who qualify but such benefits do not typically replace the lost income. They are merely intended to provide a temporary "bridge" to help cover some of the bills while the worker searches for a new job.

GOOD AND BAD UNEMPLOYMENT

Unemployment is an unfortunate byproduct of even the most vibrant economies because people typically move from one job to another throughout their working careers. Although there are individuals who spend their entire career with the same company, most of us will work for several different companies in our lifetime or even choose the wild world of self-employment. As a result, we should view movements from one job to another as being perfectly normal and not as some sign of failure. Indeed, most workers leave their jobs voluntarily to take more desirable jobs elsewhere that typically involve promotions and better pay.

Suppose I decide to leave my job as a point tester for a knitting needle factory in favor of a job as a food-taster for a widely-despised South American dictator Don Quixote—who boasts a world-renowned collection of pictures of dogs playing poker. There may be a period between the last day that I walk out of the knitting needle factory with my heavily bandaged hands and the first day that I stand next to Presidente Quixote in his dining room, warily sniffing a cup of tea that smells suspiciously like a mix of bleach and gasoline. During this time between jobs, economists would characterize me as being frictionally unemployed. Frictional unemployment is a term that describes that transitional period of time when a worker is moving from one job to another. Whether or not the worker has a job in hand when they leave their former job for greener pastures is not relevant; frictional unemployment is a term that describes the time period beginning with the worker's departure from the old job and ending with their commencement of the new job.

Structural unemployment, by contrast, refers to a prolonged state of unemployment in which workers are subjected to an extended period of idleness. It is a longer, more pronounced form of joblessness that can result from factors such as the obsolescence of entire factories, a drastic decline in the demand for products produced by those factories, or even changes in the marketplace that cause worker skills to become superfluous. Structural unemployment is a long-term phenomenon in which economic factors may not only prevent workers from finding new jobs quickly but, indeed, from finding jobs at all. Workers may find themselves having to seek jobs in other industries or even having to relocate to other parts of the country in search of work.

I would consider myself to be structurally unemployed if the knitting factory closed and I was unable to find a new job quickly with either another knitting needle manufacturer or even another company altogether. If I continued to search fruitlessly for a new job for months on end with no luck, then my time between jobs would certainly be characterized as one of structural unemployment. Certainly, my lack of success in catching on with a new company would indicate that the local economy was weak and that any significant improvements in the job prospects for myself and my fellow workers might be a long time in coming.

PART FOUR:
THE GOVERNMENT AND THE ECONOMY

GOVERNMENT SPENDING

In the modern era, the government has become a pervasive—indeed, dominant—presence in our economy. This news will gladden the hearts of those poor misguided souls who still cling to the fantasy that a centrally planned economy is the most efficient and equitable form of economic organization. But even the most rabid free marketer would have to concede—albeit reluctantly—that the government has over time expanded its reach into almost every sector of the economy. Nothing illustrates its preponderance as the proverbial 800-pound gorilla more succinctly than the fact that the government is responsible for nearly one-third of the budgetary expenditures of even the most market-driven nations such as Germany and the United States.

There are certain areas in which the government is inextricably bound to private sector actors. Not surprisingly, its traditional obligation to provide for a common defense ensures that it has a very close relationship with defenses contractors—many of whom are dependent on government contracts for their very existence. The government also provides enormous funding for education as well as numerous research and development projects with various colleges and universities. However, the single largest role played by the government nowadays involves the administration of the gargantuan health and welfare programs that consume the biggest share of the federal budget each year.

Modern governments have grappled with the unfortunate reality that their citizens have an infinite appetite for government services (known by the technical term as "free stuff") but comparatively little willingness to pay for those services in the form of higher taxes. However, policy makers have also discovered over time that nobody really cares very much about such virtuous actions as balancing the budget (which is really a quaint notion that has quietly passed into history without so much as a whimper), let alone beginning to pay down the national debt. After all, a reduction in government expenditures might have a contractionary effect on the economy, which would in turn negatively impact the gross domestic product (GDP) of the nation and, quite possibly, the electoral prospects and financial fortunes of our leading politicians. Because government spending has become such an integral feature of the economy, with entire industries such as national defense and healthcare vitally dependent on the continued flow of government funds, there is a natural bias across the political spectrum in favor of the continuous expansion of government programs—whether they pay for military bases or highways or bridges or any of an almost infinite variety of other projects. So it is not the case that government spending is inherently bad. After all, it would be very difficult to imagine a privately funded national postal service that served every resident of the country or a military paid for by private donations that could project its power to almost every region of the world. Even the most vocal critics of government spending acknowledge that a national government is necessary for certain basic functions. What many of them criticize, however, is the fact that the government has become more entangled in the private sector and has asserted greater regulatory power over areas that were formerly left to private actors to manage. They also argue that the government is typically less efficient than private sector actors who are compelled to minimize their costs and consumption of resources to compete effectively against other businesses. This argument, while attractive on its face, ignores the fact that both private businesses and government agencies are run by fallible people. As a result, one cannot say that a private firm will invariably perform a certain function with greater competency and efficiency than a public agency. However, the private firm will typically have a greater incentive to watch its pennies because it cannot count on its monies being doled out to it by a benevolent legislature that is quite comfortable with bloated social welfare programs.

QUANTITATIVE EASING

If you like spending lots of money and shopping for all sorts of things such as glamorous new clothes and glittery jewelry and luxurious furnishings, then you have what it takes to engage in quantitative easing. All you are missing is the appropriate position of power in the national bureaucracy that will enable you to vastly expand the money supply as you see fit and hit the big red button that kicks the quantitative easing machinery into high gear at the appropriate time.

But we should probably talk a little bit about what is meant by quantitative easing because it is a term that is bandied about by commentators and academics alike even though very few of us mere mortals really know much about it. Quantitative easing is a process by which the money supply is increased substantially through purchases of both government and corporate bonds by the Federal Reserve Bank. This approach has historically been used as a back-up tool when interest rates have already been reduced to very low levels but have still failed to improve economic activity. Proponents of quantitative easing appear to embrace the long-cherished American philosophy of "throwing money at problems in the hopes they will go away." However, the point of quantitative easing is to increase the money supply so much that the interest rates available to retail borrowers will be pushed down so far that investment will invariably increase and the performance of the economy will improve.

One obvious concern is that the cash used to purchase these assets is essentially created by the Federal Reserve Bank out of thin air and is not really backed by tangible physical assets. As with money in general in the modern era, the viability of any quantitative easing program depends on the public belief that the cash being tendered for government or corporate assets is accepted both as a medium of exchange and as a store of value. As we have seen elsewhere, money itself has no inherent value; it is the willingness of people to exchange assets for money and money for assets that gives money its utility. It is probably good for our mental health, therefore, that we really do not look too closely at the balance sheet of the Federal Reserve and try to figure out what is actually backing up the cash that it chooses to deploy in its quantitative easing programs.

But the underlying concept of quantitative easing is not new as the Federal Reserve has been engaged in these so-called "open market operations" for most of its century-long existence. Quantitative easing is merely open market operations on steroids. The Federal Reserve can, for example, purchase bonds through its open market operations which will cause the prices of those bonds to increase. This increase in bond prices will cause the interest rates to fall. As a result, the Federal Reserve can affect the interest rates available to borrowers simply by increasing its purchases of bonds which, if significant enough, will lower the costs of borrowing money for investors who presumably will be more willing to invest money in plants and equipment.

The problem with the use of quantitative easing is that it has involved trillions of dollars of purchases of financial assets by the Federal Reserve in recent years. It is not so clear how easily the Federal Reserve will be able to unwind this portfolio because it will have to engage in the sale of these assets and the accompanying withdrawal of cash from the US economy. After all, quantitative easing is a lot more fun when the wizards at the Federal Reserve can wave their magic wands and create money out of thin air to fund the acquisition of government and corporate financial assets. The resulting lower interest rates excite investors and supposedly stimulate new investment in the economy. When the money supply is tightened, however, all these presumably beneficial effects of quantitative easing (for example, lower interest rates, increased investment, higher standard of living) may not continue.

How does the quantitative easing story end?

Reversing a multi-trillion-dollar program of quantitative easing could feel like the hangover to end all hangovers. It will involve siphoning trillions of dollars of cash out of the economy as the financial assets being carried on the Federal Reserve's balance sheet are sold off. This process will cause the money supply to contract enormously, which could in turn cause interest rates to rise—perhaps to double digit levels. The end result may be vastly reduced investment in new plants and equipment and, perhaps, a significant decline in our standard of living and, even more troubling, the widespread cancellation of all company holiday parties. For those of us who are involved in the purchase and sale of bonds, however, the effects may not be of any concern at all. Unfortunately, no one really knows what the actual impact of a complete shutdown of or at least a significant reduction in the quantitative easing program will be but it seems to be a foregone conclusion that it could cause the level of activity—or at least the amount of investment—in the national economy to decline swiftly.

MONETARISM

If you do not believe that fiscal policy—with its focus on changes in tax rates and government expenditures to either heat up or cool down the economy as appropriate—is ideal, then you may find the super-secret monetarist camp to be more to your liking. Monetarists focus on the size of the aggregate money supply in the economy and believe that changes in the money supply can affect the nation's economic output—at least in the short term. Many monetarists view fiscal policy as being a misguided—or at the very least an ineffective—approach to managing the economy. However, these very same monetarists are not overly optimistic about the Federal Reserve Bank's ability to manipulate the money supply with enough precision to increase the growth of the economy without igniting new bouts of inflation.

One of the most famous monetarists, Milton Friedman, famously declared in his book, *A Monetary History of the United States 1867-1960*, that "inflation is always and everywhere a monetary phenomenon." Friedman's book argued that variations in the money supply can have significant—but temporary—impacts on the production of goods and services. In the longer term, however, monetarists believe that increases in the money supply typically lead to increases in prices with little lasting effect on the growth of the economy itself.

Part of the difficulty of trying to adjust the money supply to promote economic growth arises from the fact that the economy has many different actors (for example, public agencies, private corporations, individuals) whose own policies and actions may interfere with or even offset in part the expected effects of changing the size of the money supply. Moreover, the sheer size of the economy and the fact that millions upon millions of economic decisions are made every day by individuals and business enterprises alike suggest that there is not a clear causal chain between increasing the money supply and expanding the production of goods and services. The economy simply has too many moving parts for us to be confident that the money supply can be wielded as we see fit to promote greater economic growth and prosperity.

For monetarists, the focus should be on determining the growth rate of the money supply itself rather than resorting to the Keynesian bag of tricks such as changing the tax rates and increasing or decreasing the amount of government spending in the economy. Indeed, Friedman went so far to propose that the government should decide how much it will allow the money supply to increase in a given period of time and actually stick to that goal. Such an approach would require the government to ignore the inevitable whining that would occur among the vested interests who might see their own fortunes adversely impacted by such a rigid limitation. Policymakers would also have to resist the temptation to speed up the printing presses if the economy started to totter into a recession.

Because the monetarists are so focused on keeping the growth of the money supply limited to increases in the size of the economy, one might think that they would be in favor of tying the money supply to gold or some other tangible asset—such as apple pies. But most monetarists regard linking the money supply of a dynamic economy with gold or silver or even apple pies as a fool's errand because there simply is not enough gold or silver or apple pie to back the billions upon billions of dollars of currency that are circulating throughout the economy. If the economy continued to outgrow the supply of gold or silver or apple pies, then the money supply would necessarily be constricted and the economy itself would ultimately succumb to deflationary pressures. Although one could get around that problem if one could increase the supply of gold or silver or apple pies commensurate with increases in the size of the economy, it is unlikely that this would resolve the problem for very long due to the natural constraints on the supply of these tangible assets.

For monetarists, the objective is to focus on the rate of growth in the money supply and not to use it as a means for managing the level of activity in the economy. Some might view monetarists as being pessimistic or even nihilistic about the prospects for our being able to govern our affairs to promote both price stability and full employment. Others might argue, however, that it is often as much a matter of chance or dumb luck that our policies lead to the most desirable outcomes. In other words, the economy is a very complicated, very chaotic organism that is so massive and so difficult to manipulate in the short term that it is arguably futile to try to implement policies to promote price stability and full employment because countervailing forces will naturally and inevitably arise that will dampen the impact of these policies.

FISCAL POLICY

The two primary bags of tricks used by government authorities to prod and push the economy toward a "Goldilocks" state of low inflation and full employment are monetary policy and fiscal policy. Monetary policy involves playing around with the size of the money supply in the economy whereas fiscal policy consists of both governmental tax and spending policies that are designed to promote economic growth and price stability. Most economists do not get into heated arguments as to whether monetary policy or fiscal policy is the superior tool; they would typically acknowledge that both have their place in the management or mismanagement of the economy. There are a few holdouts who would declare that monetary policy is the only way to true enlightenment or that fiscal policy is the best thing since sliced bread but most economists regard the two as being necessary for steering the economic ship of state.

Fiscal policy is more fun for politicians because it involves raising and lowering tax rates and increasing and reducing government expenditures. As such, it is far more amenable to political wrangling and deal-making than monetary policy, which is overseen by the board of governors of the Federal Reserve who sit in their palace at 20th Street and Constitution Avenue, Northwest, in Washington, D.C. In any event, the so-called Keynesian economists—who are proponents of the theoretical work of the British economist John Maynard

Keynes—have been among the foremost advocates of the government taking an active role in managing the national economy. For the Keynesians, fiscal policy offers a number of levers that can be pushed and pulled to moderate the traditional boom and bust cycles experienced by most economies. If the government believes the economy is slipping into a recession, for example, it could cut taxes and thereby allow people to keep more of their own money which they could presumably use to buy additional goods and services. In addition, the government could initiate its own spending programs such as make-work employment programs to help employ people in useful work such as moving big rocks from one side of a rock quarry to the other side or picking up trash along a highway.

The underlying theory behind increasing the money that people have available for spending is that their collective actions will increase the demand for goods and services. This increased demand, so the argument goes, will cause suppliers to boost production of those goods and services to meet that increased demand. The ultimate result should be an increase in the gross domestic product and increased employment. It will also be augmented by the so-called Keynesian multiplier effect, discussed elsewhere, in which every additional dollar of money spent has a ripple effect as each successive recipient spends a fraction of what he or she receives from the prior payor until it is fully dissipated.

Assuming that each person saves 20 cents out of every dollar they earn, we can describe the multiplier effect as follows: If a free-lance matador gets $100 and spends $80 on bandages at the local pharmacy and puts $20 in the bank, then the focus shifts to the owner of the pharmacy who spends $64 on a shipment of kale and puts $16 in the bank, and then to the kale farmer who spends $51.20 on fertilizer and puts $12.80 in the bank, and so forth and so on. So that $100 will ultimately have a more significant impact on aggregate spending in the economy than we might realize at first blush—at least in the minds of most Keynesian economists.

But not everyone agrees that fiscal policy has such a beneficial effect on the economy in the long-term. Some economists would argue that these efforts to increase aggregate demand—whether they involve tax cuts or government expenditures on social programs, which are largely transfer payments to the recipients— do not really increase the quantity of goods and services produced in the economy. These dour adherents of the "glass is half empty" philosophy would instead suggest that any increases in the demand for goods and services caused by these expansionary fiscal measures will simply drive up the rates of interest investors must pay to borrow money. These higher interest rates will thus result in fewer factories (among other productive assets) being built than would have otherwise occurred had the government simply left things alone. But as with many things in the world of economics, the debate over the effectiveness of fiscal policy shall continue into the future without any likely definitive resolution.

PROGRESSIVE TAXATION

Nothing is inevitable except death and taxes according to the proverb. And scientists are carrying out research in the cryogenics, artificial intelligence and life extension sciences to extend human life indefinitely so that taxes will be the only unavoidable pox on humanity. Whether it is really a good idea to fuse the consciousness of my great Aunt Agatha with a robot body so that she may continue offering her devastating criticisms of everyone and everything for all eternity is another question. But it does appear that taxes are here to stay and—despite the wishes of utopian thinkers throughout history—someone will always have to pay for the goods provided by the government to the population. Everyone is in favor of receiving government benefits so long as they are not the ones making the actual payments to cover the costs of those benefits.

Assuming that we do have to have a government that provides services such as a postal system, national defense and social welfare programs, then we are going to have to figure out how to pay for those services. And because most people will not willingly volunteer to send a check to the government that will cover their share of the costs, we cannot rely on the honor system for collecting taxes. Instead, we have developed the widely popular coercive tax system to facilitate tax payments from the citizenry using a variety of measures such as fines, penalties, property forfeitures and, when the revenue authorities are in a particularly bad mood, long prison sentences. Because tax evasion is a federal crime, the threat of prosecution for the failure to pay taxes is a potent one and does persuade most individuals to comply with the law. Sort of.

So, if we have a tax system, we have to decide how the burden of taxation is to be apportioned among the population. First, we have to decide who we will tax. If we want to have a fully inclusive tax system, we could tax every man, woman, and child in the country. The adults could be taxed on the income they receive from working whereas the children could be taxed on the money they receive with birthday cards from their grandparents each year or the monies they collect from operating a lemonade stand in front of their house. But the government has only so many agents that it can call upon to prosecute those dastardly young children who refuse to pay their fair share of taxes on their lemonade receipts. The difficulty for the government in these cases is figuring out how to collect the taxes on these "invisible" cash transactions—which have no records similar to those created by the use of a credit card. Certainly, most governments would like to do away with cash altogether so that every transaction in the economy would be recorded in some way and, not surprisingly, taxed.

In any event, the government has defined in excru-
ciating details the types of transactions that are taxable;
the burdens of those taxes can be imposed on adults
and children alike if desired. The next task is to determine the type of tax system we wish to use in our unrelenting efforts to bring joy and comfort to the citizenry.
We could set up a progressive tax system which would
impose higher tax brackets (higher percentiles) on
higher earning individuals such that individuals making
less than $25,000 per year would pay a 10 percent tax, for
example, but individuals making between $25,001.00
and $50,000 per year would pay a 15 percent tax, and
so on. Or we could use a flat tax system which would
impose a single percentage tax such as 20 percent across
the board on all taxpayers regardless of income. Last but
not least, we could impose a regressive tax which would
tax lower income earners at progressively higher rates;
this sort of scheme does not appear to be very popular
even though some might think that having the highest
tax rates would give the poor more incentive to work
harder and earn more money so that they could move
up to a lower tax rate. Indeed, there are certain types
of taxes such as lump sum taxes which are regressive
because they have a disproportionate impact on lower
income earners. A driver's license fee, for example, is the
same for all drivers but it imposes more of a burden on
a poor person than a billionaire. As a result, the driver's license fee could be characterized as a regressive tax

since no allowance is made for the income of the taxpayer in determining the amount of the tax.

Most countries have adopted some form of progressive taxation because of the belief that wealthier taxpayers who frolic in front of their oceanfront estates should pay a greater percentage of their income than poor persons who must struggle mightily to put food on the table every day. Less fortunate individuals will begrudgingly acknowledge that even the wealthiest citizens should be able to scour through the tax code in search of any lawful benefit that may exist while also decrying the numerous loopholes that make such tax avoidance efforts possible and, ultimately, reduce the effectiveness of our supposedly progressive tax system.

WHO PAYS THE TAXES?

If you were asked who pays the sales tax on the purchase of an item at the store, you might answer that it is the customer who is tendering the money in exchange for that item because the sales tax will be added to the purchase price. That seems simple enough. A sales tax is imposed at the time of the sale and the purchaser is the one who gets stuck with paying it. Or at least that is supposed to be how it works. But economists who study taxation and how its burdens ultimately fall would not necessarily agree that the purchaser always pays the tax. Why? Because they view the entire purchase in terms of its overall costs and whether some part of that amount is being borne by the seller, for example, as opposed to the buyer—perhaps in the form of a subsidized price. They also go to great lengths to figure out which party is bearing what portion of the tax—known as the study of tax incidence.

Suppose that the Sweaty Sporting Goods Company manufactures golf clubs with built-in lightning rods. It advertises that these unique clubs can help to divert lightning strikes away from intrepid golfers who are unwilling to let an occasional bolt of white-hot voltage dissuade them from hacking their way around the links in the middle of a tempest. Because golfers are keenly aware of the risks posed by lightning, however, they have responded warmly to these new clubs and shown up by the thousands at stores across the country to purchase a bag. In this case, the analysis of the tax incidence would be straightforward because they would tender enough money to cover the purchase price of the bag of clubs as well as the sales tax.

But what if the consumer safety bigwigs conducted an investigation of these lightning rod golf clubs and found that golfers using them were fifty times more likely to be injured or killed by a lightning strike than golfers using the other leading brands? Our first response might be that that the golfers playing with the Sweaty clubs have had a tremendous run of bad luck being in the wrong place at the wrong time. But upon further reflection we might concede that perhaps there is something about the clubs themselves that might be responsible for so many users being zapped by lightning on the links. This conclusion would likely also be shared by the consumer safety bureaucrats who might recommend that a special tax be imposed upon the company to help pay for the hospitalization costs of its injured customers. If a bag of these Sweaty golf clubs costs $500 (including sales tax), therefore, and this new special safety tax is equal to another $50, then the prospective purchaser would have to fork over $550.00 to join the ranks of the proud owners of Sweaty golf clubs.

The owners of the company would not be happy to be singled out because the golf club business is frightfully competitive and the imposition of a tax equal to 10 percent of the retail price would put their clubs at a tremendous disadvantage. On the other hand, competitors would be quite pleased to see the regulators cracking down because the new tax essentially makes their products 10 percent less expensive than those of Sweaty. Unless, of course, the company decides to do something about how it handles the burden of the tax.

If Sweaty simply increases the price of its clubs by $50 to cover the additional cost imposed by the safety tax, then it puts itself at a competitive disadvantage relative to other companies charging $500 for a similar set of clubs. Its difficulties are further compounded by the unflattering press coverage about golfers being zapped all around the country while swinging their clubs. But Sweaty could take a different approach and essentially absorb the tax to continue to sell its unique golf clubs to the public at that same $500 price per set. This is where the whole idea of tax incidence comes into play: the competitiveness of the market for golf club sets makes it virtually impossible for Sweaty to pass the additional $50 safety tax on to its customers. It is likely that many of Sweaty's prospective customers will defect to their competitors. If Sweaty continues to sell the golf club sets for $500 and essentially "eats" the safety tax, therefore, then the tax itself will fall on the company. It cannot shift the extra costs to its customers without losing sales. The safer thing for it to do is to suck it up and pay the safety tax so that the retail price of its clubs remains the same as those sold by its competitors.

The decision to not pass the tax on to customers was prompted by Sweaty's belief that the market was far too competitive and that its customers would shun its products in favor of its competitors if it tried to add the tax to the price of the clubs. What would happen if Sweaty was the only company in the country authorized to sell golf clubs to the public—despite the tendency of some of its users to burst into flames during lightning storms? This monopolistic position would cause the company to think very differently about who should pay the safety tax. If everyone who wants golf clubs has to purchase them from Sweaty, then it is quite likely that Sweaty would simply tack the additional $50 on to the price of the clubs. A possible complication might be if the consumer demand for golf equipment was very elastic so that even a modest increase in the price of the clubs would cause demand to plummet. But because golf is something of a religion to many people who spend far more time on golf courses than in churches, it is likely that the elasticity of demand is not so great that the increase in the price would cause Sweaty to lose a lot of customers.

SUPPLY SIDE ECONOMICS

For the Keynesian economists, the growth of the economy is dependent on the government increasing aggregate demand by reducing taxes and increasing government spending—even if it necessitates that the government run a deficit (perish the thought). Of course, we live in a time in which the government runs enormous deficits year after year—regardless of whether the economy is in a recession or an expansion. To be fair, Keynes himself was not in favor of governments running perpetual deficits; he expected that any deficits would be taken care of once the national economy recovered from an economic downturn and the increased tax receipts could be used to soak up the red ink. But the point remains that Keynesian economics is focused on the demand side of the economy and the supply side appears to some to be almost an afterthought.

The English physicist Isaac Newton once posited—perhaps after having been knocked on the head by an apple—that for every reaction, there is an equal and opposite reaction. To some degree, the ascendancy of the Keynesian doctrine in the post-World War II era prompted some economists to wonder if the supply side of the equation was being neglected. As a result, economists began to focus on ways in which government policies could be changed to help suppliers of goods and services to become more efficient and productive. They asked what specific actions the government could take to help factories reduce their costs and workers improve their skills? Although some might argue that getting rid of the government itself would be a good first step, others with a more practical orientation might suggest that the government should adopt policies to assist businesses and their workers.

How might our benevolent political leaders assist a corporation such as the Technicolor Bread Company, which manufactures pastries and loaves in all the colors of the rainbow? Although the Technicolor Bread Company's products have enjoyed some popularity in the past—particularly with its green loaves on St. Patrick's Day—it has seen its sales decline in recent years and has, as a result, been forced to lay off hundreds of workers. Admittedly, the Technicolor Bread Company has not seen a lot of success with recent marketing efforts, such as its jet-black "bereavement bagels" that were intended to be served at funeral receptions, so its owners are at a loss as to how they should move forward. How might this company be assisted by a government conversant with the principles of supply side economics?

Leaving aside the issue of whether it makes any sense to encourage a company that manufactures green loaves of bread to remain in business, a supply-side approach would focus on trying to increase the productivity and efficiency of the company. One thing that might be helpful would be to eliminate the colored bread tax, which was enacted a decade earlier by legislators who found the sight of purple and green loaves of bread to be repulsive. The repeal of this tax would lower the cost of the colored loaves so that consumers who eat heavily-dyed bread would be able to enjoy their guilty pleasure at a reduced cost and in presumably greater quantities.

If the government was concerned about the growing presence of foreign manufacturers of colored breads, it might try to shore up the domestic-colored bread industry. To that end, the government could impose significant tariffs on these imports thus enabling domestic producers such as the Technicolor Bread Company to sell their products to the public at a higher price without being undercut by the cheaper foreign imports. Hopefully, these domestic bread makers would use these extra profits to modernize their colored breadmaking equipment and hire back some of their former workers.

To improve the skills of the workers at the Technicolor Bread Company, the government could offer the company certain tax credits or outright payments to help reduce the costs of sending them to advanced bread-making seminars where they would learn how to dye perfect polka dot croissants or the techniques for making cakes with glow-in-the-dark frosting. The point of these subsidies would be to encourage the company to help its workers become more productive and thereby increase the efficiency of the factory.

Supply-side economics was embraced by conservative economists who were concerned about the heavy hand of government taxation. One of the foremost members of this group was the economist Arthur Laffer who proposed that tax revenues might be increased if tax rates were lowered. Now this suggestion might seem nonsensical at first glance, but Laffer argued that excessively high rates of taxation may discourage people from working at all. After all, why bother getting up in the morning and trudging off to the office if most of your pay is taken by the government? But if the tax rates are lowered so that people are able to keep more of their money, then they would have a greater incentive to work and to be productive—as opposed to lounging about in their underwear at home all day waiting for their monthly unemployment check. Laffer suggested that there is a certain ideal tax rate where tax revenues are maximized; a lesser tax rate will encourage people to work more whereas a higher tax rate will discourage people from working as much. As with most economic models that posit an optimum point, there is no clear answer as to what this perfect tax rate is, but Laffer's point was to provide a theoretical construct to consider that taxes may become so high that worker participation suffers and can only be improved by reducing those rates.

GOVERNMENT DEBT

When the government reports that expenditures exceeded revenues by hundreds of billions or even trillions of dollars in a given fiscal year, we are typically dumbstruck because it is almost impossible for us to imagine how anyone could spend such enormous amounts of money—particularly when the tax receipts themselves are on the order of several trillions of dollars per annum. If a country has a budget deficit of a trillion dollars, for example, it suggests that either the county has had to increase its spending massively to cope with a national disaster or war . . . or it could mean that the country has decided to plunge into an orgy of spending to pursue any number of programs. The fact that there is a shortfall in the government bank account is often due to the understandable reluctance of political leaders to raise taxes high enough to plug up the gaps. After all, it is very enjoyable to spend a lot of money, but it is even more pleasurable to spend it and know that it does not have to be paid back—at least for a generation or two.

Should we be concerned when a country runs persistent budgetary deficits year after year, particularly when its leaders do not appear to be concerned about paying those obligations back? This is probably not a prudent policy for any country to follow but it is not necessarily a fatal course of action. Why not? Well, we first have to step back and compare the ability of an individual to live beyond his or her means year after year with that of an actual country. For one thing, individuals do not typically have the ability to tax millions of people to pay their bills. In truth, you or I would not even need to be able to tax an entire nation of people to cover our bills; it would probably be enough to be able to tax all the people living in our neighborhood. Imagine the delight my neighbors would feel each year when they received their tax bills from me and found that, as with every prior year, their taxes had been increased even more because the costs of my decadent lifestyle had increased yet again.

A country, as we all know, does have the ability to tax its citizens and it can, if it chooses to do so, elect to raise those taxes as it sees fit. However, its ability to increase taxes is not unlimited. History is full of examples in which leaders got a little too enthusiastic about their tax collection activities and were burned at the stake or beheaded or drawn and quartered by their loyal subjects. But the nation-state has a policing apparatus which can be used to coerce even the most recalcitrant citizens into sending money to the government. Even though the government may not raise the taxes enough to cover all of its spending programs, it certainly has the ability and the legal authority to increase taxes on its citizenry. These taxes can be used to pay interest on the money the government will have to borrow to cover its budget deficits each year. Individuals, of course, have no such ability to tax an entire population.

If you are fortunate enough to have a comparatively stable government, then there is a reasonable expectation that that country will endure for a few centuries or more. Very few people, by contrast, live more than a single century. So if you are a gambler, you would probably be tempted to side with the country almost every time. In most cases, the country will last longer than most individuals and, hence, there is a perception that the country, by virtue of its longevity, is more likely to repay its debts than the individual. Of course, it is true that once a person draws his last breath, he will not be able to repay his debtors (at least in person). In many cases, that obligation will either be paid by the decedent's estate or his family members directly unless the debt is barred by law. Because countries typically "live" longer than actual human beings, however, the hope is that the country will have a longer time to get its financial house in order and pay back all of the money that it borrowed.

But those persons who lend money to countries—whether by purchasing bonds or notes—are not necessarily guaranteed that they will receive their entire investment—let alone the interest that these debt instruments are supposed to generate. Countries default on their loans more frequently than we might think. Indeed, defaults are something of a hobby for some nations that have a more cavalier view toward incessant deficit spending. Even so, few countries borrow money with the intent of going into default but both indigenous variables, such as excessive government spending, and exogenous variables, such as wars, can wreak havoc on a country's financial stability.

Deficit spending year after year may or may not be sustainable; a country's ability to shoulder an ever-increasing debt burden will depend on the rate of growth of the economy and the percent of debt as a share of the country's GDP. Some countries simply incur too much debt and lack the capability to grow out of that debt. This is particularly true of poor countries that may have little in the way of financial reserves to fall back upon in hard times and who rely on exports such as commodities that may fluctuate greatly in value. Many of us dislike the idea that any country is willing to continue incurring more debt with each passing year even though a particular country's economy may continue to grow enough to be able to shoulder the burden of additional debt without great difficulty. But others do not let the idea of ever-increasing government debt concern them very much so long as the costs of servicing the debt do not begin to crowd out government spending on social programs.

GOVERNMENT BUDGET SURPLUSES AND DEFICITS

Perhaps in no way do the theory of economics and the messy practices of the real world diverge from each other more than in discussing government budgetary practices. Economic textbooks advise us that a government seeking to pull a country out of a dark and dreary recession will increase expenditures and lower taxes and, as a result, engage in deficit spending. Similarly, in a time of sunshine and magic where everyone is working and the tax coffers are spilling over with gold coins, that government would want to decrease its expenditures and increase taxes to return to a budgetary surplus.

In the real world, however, politicians are much more interested in increasing spending than they are in increasing taxes so that the budget can be brought back into a theoretical balance. Unfortunately, there is no glory for the modern politician who is able to balance the budget. Nobody will erect a statute of you or name a school after you because you happen to bring revenues and expenditure into balance—even though such an achievement would be as miraculous as walking on water. Indeed, it is always more appealing to try to increase government spending or expand the scope of government programs and thus encourage the proletariat to cast their votes for the politicians who have brought even more largesse from the heavens above to the poor wretched masses below. Moreover, the would-be budget balancer may see his or her hard-won labors undone by the next set of leaders who are far more interested in "letting the good times roll" and kicking the proverbial balanced budget can down the road so that yet another generation can ignore it.

Another problem with trying to balance the budget is that no one really knows what the total revenues or expenditures are going to be in a given fiscal year. Certainly there are projections with every government budget but they are often merely estimates—albeit mathematically sophisticated estimates—which are not always accurate—at least on the tax revenue side. Quite frankly, we never know how much money the government will collect in a given fiscal year because people vary in both their incomes and their abilities to hide monies from the Internal Revenue Service. The expenditure side, in theory, should not be so difficult to predict if the authorities actually stick to their spending plans. But things change and spending programs typically balloon because of natural disasters or war or some other unexpected event, such as a partial eclipse of the moon. To some extent, the budget is like a moving target even though its authors try so hard to be as precise as possible. Unfortunately, they must deal with the unpredictability of both humans and the world in which they live and these uncertainties almost inevitably guarantee that the realized budget numbers will vary from those that were originally predicted.

When a budget has a deficit or a surplus, it is a short-term phenomenon that is typically defined by some arbitrary time period such as a calendar year (January 1 to December 31). Receipts and expenditures will rarely equalize at any single point during that year so if we were to tally all the taxes collected and all the money spent on any given day, we would find that we might have a hefty surplus on February 2 and an enormous deficit on April 4 and so on. But no one gets overly concerned about whether the daily budget is in surplus or deficit as it is such an inconsequential period of time. But we may get more agitated if the year has ended and we show a budgetary deficit of billions or—if we have a truly successful year of mortgaging our childrens' futures—trillions of dollars.

Regardless of the amount, this deficit is a budgetary deficit that is defined by the 12-month period of the budget itself. It is far different from the much more imposing structural deficit which is the culmination of all of the prior budgetary deficits. So if you like a trillion dollar budgetary deficit, you will be absolutely enthralled with a thirty trillion dollar structural deficit. And if red is your favorite color, the oceans of red ink that describe the structural deficit will make you giddy with joy.

Economists disagree as to the danger posed by structural deficits. Some are horrified by the prospect of an ever-growing financial shortfall that will probably never be repaid. Others are more sanguine, arguing that so long as the economy continues to grow enough to service the debt, then it does not really pose a mortal danger to the financial stability of the country. But problems can arise if no one bothers to even try to balance the budget in any given year, thus allowing the structural deficit to compound and grow at an increasing rate that may become unsustainable over time. A widespread complacency about tackling the budgetary deficit each year, year after year, decade after decade, may fuel the exponential growth of the structural deficit that will defy all attempts to tame it.

MINIMUM WAGES

When we talk about markets we are usually speaking of the unfettered interactions of sellers and buyers who negotiate with each other until they reach an agreement as to the terms of their deal. But there are many situations in which the government has chosen to intervene in a particular market in pursuit of some policy objective or social good. These actions typically involve setting certain limits as to how far the price mechanism in those markets is permitted to fluctuate. Undoubtedly, the wizards of central planning who infest most governments believe that they can direct the markets in a way that is more desirable than would otherwise be the case if they were left alone.

Most industrialized countries have adopted minimum wage legislation that, with some exceptions, requires that a certain "floor" wage be paid to hourly workers. The rationale behind these wage floors is that the market that sets the wages for these hourly workers may undervalue the labor of workers in industries that do not traditionally pay high wages such as restaurants, hotels, and retail. Apparently, government officials simply do not trust business owners to pay their low wage employees enough to afford the basic necessities of life. Minimum wage laws, while not ensuring a middle-class lifestyle, will at least provide some minimal level of financial support that might not otherwise exist.

The argument against minimum wage laws is that forcing an employer to pay an employee, say, $15 per hour, when the hourly rate would otherwise be $10 in the absence of such a wage floor, will essentially add a surcharge to the hourly wage of each employee. As every employer has a certain amount of money that it can allocate to the wages of its labor force, the obvious conclusion is that fewer employees can be hired at the higher minimum wage rate. To put it into sophisticated mathematical terms, let us assume that I own a pharmacy which caters to upscale customers who use our opioid products responsibly. Suppose that I have a weekly budget of $1,500 that I can spend on wages for on my employees. Because this is a fixed amount, I must decide the most efficient way to allocate it in terms of how many employees I keep and how many hours they work. If the free market hourly rate is $10, then I essentially can pay for 150 hours of labor by my employees. The passage of a minimum wage law (or an increase in an existing minimum wage law) that raises the rate from $10 to $15 per hour will cut my 150 hours of labor to 100 hours of labor. As my available funds have not increased, I am now forced to consider some dramatic changes to my labor force.

Fewer available labor hours necessarily force to me focus on which employees are most productive and, as a result, which employees are not. My senior employee,

292 | ECONOMICS AND ALL THAT

Naomi, is a hard worker who always shows up on time, but she constantly gets into arguments with the customers who dare to question her rants that humans are descended from extraterrestrials; by contrast, my newest hire, Ned, a painfully shy young man, spends much of his time looking at graphic messages on his phone and composing nonsensical poems featuring pharmaceutical terminology. My other employee is Aileen, who is ultimately conflicted as she must fill prescriptions all day but is opposed to taking any medications based upon religious grounds.

Because Ned is an airhead, my first thought might be to fire Ned and suggest that he go apply to work for one of my competitors. But I am not sure that all the work that needs to be done can be completed by just two employees. An additional complication is that I pay each of my employees a different hourly wage. Naomi already earns $25 an hour and has a record of showing up on time, regardless of her nonsensical rants. Ned was paid $10 per hour prior to the new minimum wage law so his hourly wage will increase 50 percent to $15. Aileen was already being paid $12 per hour so the law will result in a 25 percent increase in her hourly wage. As a result, the analysis is fairly simple: Naomi will continue to work for me at $25 per hour until she returns to the mother ship. Aileen and Ned will now both receive $15 per hour—a net increase of $8 per hour between the two of them. All three of them have always worked part-time because the $1,500 budgeted each week is simply not a large enough amount of money to employ all three of them for a full 35-hour work week. Fortunately, Naomi is training to be an anger-management counselor and so she is content to work 25 hours per week; her check is equal to $625 of the $1,500, leaving $875 for me to divide among my other two employees. Aileen is a better worker than Ned but she often "informs" customers there are alternatives to prescriptions. Still, I have to consider whether I simply split the remaining $875 between my two minimum wage employees or adjust their schedules to take advantage of their strengths. If I split the hours equally between the two, then each of them will work 29.16 hours for me each week. Before the wage was increased, in contrast, I would have been able to get 36.4 hours of work from Aileen at $12 per hour and 43.75 hours of work from Ned at $10 per hour (assuming the $875 was spent equally among the two). Together, they would have worked 80.15 hours; now I can only afford to hire them to work a total of 58.32 hours—a reduction of almost 21.83 hours of labor participation each week. This has created a predicament for me because I have essentially lost almost 23 percent of my labor force productivity because of the higher hourly rate. Now I have to operate with less and figure out how to make up this enormous loss of productivity. I will either have to come up with more money for one or both of them as needed or I may have to put in the added hours myself.

The reduced hours that I can purchase with my

$1,500 will have a significant impact on my business because it has effectively increased my labor costs substantially. Because I do not have any additional dollars that I can pay to my existing employees, the increased labor cost is reflected in fewer hours being worked by both Aileen and Ned. The other problem is that I have no ability to increase my labor force to make up for the shortened hours. The bottom line is that an increase in the minimum wage will ultimately affect the efficiency and the productivity of my business because I cannot pay any more money and, even if I could, I cannot pass the increased costs on to my customers as they are very aware of the prevailing prices Being paid for brand-name opioid products at other reputable pharmacies.

PRICE CONTROLS

Price controls are a time-honored tradition in which government officials try to cap the prices for some sort of good or service to try and make it less expensive for the consuming public. These actions are often motivated by both good intentions and political ambitions, but they can have adverse consequences. One of the most common forms of price controls is rent controls, which are very common in urban areas where the cost of housing is high. Well-meaning politicians will promise their constituents that they will limit the "excessive" rents being paid to landlords by imposing restrictions on the amount of rent that a landlord can charge his or her tenants. However, this does not always work out so well if the rent controls are significantly below the free-market rental rate.

How so? As with so many things in economics, it begins with a story about the prices that landlords wish to charge their tenants and the amounts that their tenants are willing (if not happy) to pay. Not surprisingly, landlords want to charge as much money as possible and tenants wish to pay as little money as possible. In the free market, of course, the parties will engage in negotiations and come to an agreement and a lease will be signed. When the government decides that rentals are too high and people should not have to pay as much for a necessity such as housing, then the passage of a law limiting what landlords can charge tenants disrupts the market. Unfortunately for landlords, they are not warmly regarded by many renters and have something of a public relations problem. Moreover, there are a lot more renters than landlords and so political elections usually do not favor landlords very often. You will not hear about very many candidates who campaign on a platform asserting that rents should be allowed to go up so that landlords can make more money; they will invariably be defeated by the opposition candidate who espouses a pro-tenant platform.

Suppose that I am the owner of a 50-unit apartment building. Each apartment is the same size and average rents per unit are $1,000 per month. The building is in good condition, but the roof will need to be replaced in a few years and the elevators break down periodically. In general, the revenues are enough to cover the basic maintenance expenses as well as the taxes and insurance but not quite enough to pay for needed capital improvements such as a new roof or central air conditioning. Because the rental market is very tight, I believe that I can raise the rents for each apartment by $100 per month and thus generate enough monies to pay for the roof and the air conditioning systems. With that thought in mind, I send out letters to all the tenants telling them that I will be increasing their monthly rents by an additional $100 when they renew their leases. Almost immediately, I find my photograph being splashed across the television accompanied by such phrases as "slumlord" and a litany of other terms not often mentioned in polite company. Soon afterwards, various tenants' rights groups have assembled in front of my building and are singing civil rights songs and encouraging my tenants to break their leases and, in some cases, my legs. In any event, I sit for interviews and point out that the rent increases are needed to pay for long delayed improvements to the building but I am not viewed with any great sympathy by the press or the public. Indeed, it becomes very clear that landlords rank right up there with lawyers and loan sharks in the "favorability index" and that nothing I say will cause anyone to consider my side of the story.

News of the chaos then reaches the local housing authority, which decides to get involved in the matter by passing a rule that puts a limit of $900 per month on the rents I can charge for each of these apartments. In the blink of an eye, the housing administrators have both nullified my proposed rent increases and cut my current rental income by ten percent thus leaving me unable to pay for the new roof and air conditioning. Their action has also forced me to drop my plans to make key repairs to the premises such as fixing several broken windows and repairing numerous plumbing leaks that were budgeted before the rent controls were instituted.

The $900 per month limit is an absolute cap on revenues but it does nothing to limit the costs I will incur as a landlord—such as the real estate taxes and the casualty and liability insurance. No doubt the property tax collector would not be particularly concerned about my new cash flow issues if they decided to increase my real estate taxes by 15 percent. In short, that would be my problem—not their problem. Similarly, a spike in insurance rates due to recent natural disasters in the area would also further increase my costs, leaving me little choice but to dig into my savings to make up the difference—assuming that I have any savings left. Although insurance companies are known for their warmth and concern about the less fortunate among us, they would probably not be in any rush to reduce my rates simply because I am very kind to dogs and cats. The net result may be that my building begins to slide into an inexorable decline and I cannot make enough money from my tenants to prevent its continual deterioration. Unfortunately, this may result in my having to adopt a different view of my beloved urban jewel: that of an owner who is merely trying to get whatever he can out of the building while it falls apart all around him. The end result, which has happened in many cities across the country, may be that my building sinks into such disrepair that the tenants eventually desert it and it becomes a ruin inhabited by unsavory persons such as retired late-night television hosts.

PUBLIC GOODS

If you were sitting in a college economics class and the professor asked you to define a "public good," you might fire back a perfectly logical response that "a public good is a good that is public." Although the linguistic symmetry of this response might cause some of the dullards sitting nearby to be visibly impressed, it would not be terribly helpful in explaining the nature of a public good. But all is not lost and your attempt to impress the other students would not be entirely in vain because public goods have certain characteristics which cannot be easily limited to or otherwise enjoyed by a single person.

Public goods may be tangible or intangible and can include everything from educational institutions to national defense to roads and even knowledge itself. It is difficult to prevent any single individual from enjoying the benefit of a public good because if it is provided to one person, it must be provided to everyone else. A public highway, for example, is available for use by anyone who has a truck or a car or who can run very fast because access to public roads is generally available to all persons. Restricted access highways such as toll roads would not qualify as a public good because the use of such roads is restricted to those persons who are willing to pay the tolls. National defense is another public good that all citizens benefit from unless, of course, the military forces providing the national defense are poorly trained and easily defeated—leaving all the citizens to be enslaved by barbarians. However, a well-run military that is able to keep potential enemies at bay so that the citizens can go about their business and enjoy their lives is extraordinarily valuable and is clearly a benefit that is enjoyed by all members of society. In short, it is impossible to ration or auction off the domestic tranquility that a military capable of defeating any potential aggressors brings to the nation.

Whether we are talking about roads or national defense, however, the fact that everyone enjoys the benefits provided by public goods does not mean that everyone is necessarily willing to pay for those benefits. Some people would pay a lot of money for a new highway, for example, because they wish to avoid bone-rattling drives along a pothole-laden roadway in which every bump and jolt causes pieces to drop out of their vehicles. Other, however, who are less concerned about the condition of their automobiles, may be perfectly content to bounce along the crumbling road and, hence, unwilling to pay for their fair share of the costs of repairing the road. Or they may simply be tightwads who do not wish to contribute to the common good.

The difficulty of convincing every user of a road to pay for its upkeep is complicated by the fact that one person's use of that road does not prevent another person from driving on that road. My use of the road does not typically preclude you from also using it. The impossibility of persuading every person who drives on the road to contribute to its cost becomes evident because some people are concerned about building their community whereas others are self-centered cheapskates who would not give a dime to a dying parent. This so-called "free rider problem" in which the non-exclusivity of public goods enables people to use those goods without paying for them is what gives rise to that most esteemed and revered of human institutions—taxes. These taxes are collected from all individuals—regardless of whether or not they want to pay for the use of a particular public good being funded by those taxes—and the taxes in effect compel all persons to share in the costs of those public goods.

PROPERTY RIGHTS

To generate wealth, we have to be able to persuade individuals to devote their efforts to building enterprises that will create both products and services that are useful to the citizenry. Along with the development of new businesses will, of course, come new employment opportunities which will, in turn, have a ripple effect in the community as these employees use much of their wages and salaries to purchase goods and services from other businesses. This is a version of the multiplier effect espoused by John Maynard Keynes in which a portion of each dollar received by an individual is spent on the goods and services offered by others who in turn spend a portion of each dollar they receive on the goods and services of still others, and so forth and so on.

But the key to creating the conditions that will encourage entrepreneurs to build a better mousetrap is the passage of laws that protect property rights. These laws must provide stability and predictability so that any riches people earn from their efforts will not simply be snatched from them by the authorities. The United States Constitution, for example, prohibits the taking of property by the government without the payment of just compensation. This clause restricts the ability of the government to take your house to build an important public project such as a statue of the mayor without paying you the market value of your property. This constitutional provision was seen as a sort of balance between the need of the public authority to be able to condemn real property for public purposes such as widening a road and the right of the private owner to receive the appropriate compensation for that land. The idea of the sanctity of property rights is deeply embedded in the American psyche as evidenced by its enshrinement in the Constitution.

No one who has ever tried to start a business would argue against the need to protect property rights. Autonomy is important but the biggest incentive for devoting much of your life to the creation of a new business or invention or service is the prospect that you will be rewarded for your efforts. There is also a materialistic urge that underpins the desire to create goods and services and, hopefully, amass wealth.

Suppose that you decide you are going to attempt to solve one of the most intractable problems of the modern era—the mystery of the lost sock. We have all endured the indignity of searching for a missing sock when trying to get ready for work or go out for a jog or even cover our cracked toenails so as to not scare the children. We do not know how these socks get away, but we know that they escape with annoying regularity and we are constantly forced to buy new packages of socks because we cannot find the missing socks. Moreover, we find that socks like to congregate in laundry baskets and are just different enough from each other in terms of color, pattern and size that we cannot easily match them with the other half of their pair, even if the other sock is hiding in the same basket and sticking its metaphorical tongue out at us.

You have devoted many years of your life trying to build a device to find missing socks. Finally, the day has come and you unveil your "electromagnetic sock sucker" which involves the attachment of small metal plates to every sock in your house and the installation of a powerful horse-sized electromagnet in the middle of your living room. You invite all your friends as well as many local dignitaries to the unveiling of your machine and, after a celebratory toast with a fine bottle of slightly flat champagne, you flip the switch and turn the electromagnetic dial up to "high." Almost instantly socks start flying from all parts of the house and smash into the electromagnet. But, as an added bonus, other metal objects such as several metal chairs, car keys, a pet nametag (still attached to the family cat) and an array of forks all hurtle toward the electromagnet. Aside from the wounds suffered by two of the town council members as a result of a careening butcher knife, the demonstration is a success and you are given scattered applause.

Although you may not be deeply versed in the laws regarding property rights, the fact that you gave the electromagnetic sock sucker so much time and attention for so long reflects your understanding that you will at least have the opportunity to try to market it. If you lived in a country in which any invention or product that you developed could be seized at any time without consequence by the government, it is unlikely that you would be as motivated to work so long and hard on such an important device as the electromagnetic sock sucker. No doubt such a loss would constitute an unimaginable tragedy for society.

CENTRAL PLANNING

Suppose you are the type of person who enjoys interfering in every detail of everyone's life and you believe you are the only one who can run the affairs of the world. Well, you have the sort of massively delusional personality that is perfect for running a centrally planned economy where you will exercise control over every detail and decide what goods and services are to be produced and the prices at which those goods and services are to be sold. Running a centrally-planned economy is the ultimate state of "busybody-ness" because you can insert yourself into every single decision about what is to be produced and what is not to be produced—regardless of whether anyone actually wants to purchase the goods you deem most worthy of manufacture. But the so-called Central Planning Busybody (CPB) must have an incomparable belief that he or she can do a better job figuring out what sorts of things should be manufactured than would be the case if one were to rely on the seemingly chaotic interactions of buyers and sellers in the marketplace. CPBs typically flourish in centrally-controlled economies where they can impose their wisdom on the citizenry—whether they like it or not.

Suppose I am the head of economic planning of a police state called Tetanus. I have the power to order companies to produce only those items that I believe should be available for sale. Moreover, I am able to dictate the quantities and prices for those goods and can even involve myself in the actual technical specifications of these goods. Suppose that I have long believed that socks should be made of rubber instead of cotton. As the chief central planner of Tetnaus, I can order the sock factories to stop producing cotton socks and order them to switch over to rubber socks. In a burst of hubris, I might even order the factory to run triple-shifts so that they can have enough product available to meet the expected tsunami of demand that will surely follow.

But I would be remiss if I did not tell the sock factory what price it should charge its customers for these socks and add a few mandatory design suggestions as well. So I might insist that each of the socks have separate tubes for each toe and that they be webbed so that anyone wearing these socks could engage in a competitive swimming contest at a moment's notice. As a result, I would be using my superior intellect to iron out the imperfections inherent in the modern marketplace: May decisions will avoid the inefficiencies of businesses experimenting with all sorts of possible products that never catch fire with the public by going straight to the surefire winners such as rubber socks.

No matter how brilliant one may be, it has proven very difficult, nay, impossible, for countries run by central planners to accurately predict the types and quantities of goods that should be produced because there are literally millions of different types of goods that are bought and sold in the modern economy. No individual can even hope to predict which products will sell for what price and in what quantities. As a result, most centrally planned economies have been characterized by massive misallocations of resources so that some goods that no one wants are widely available whereas other goods that people strongly desire cannot be found.

PART FIVE:
INTERNATIONAL ECONOMICS

COMPARATIVE ADVANTAGE

One of the most exciting and counterintuitive concepts in economics is that of comparative advantage. First proposed by the economist David Ricardo, it posits that countries will benefit from engaging in trade with each other even if one country is a more efficient—that is, a lower absolute cost—producer of all the items being traded.

To understand the rationale behind comparative trade, we need to begin with the police state of

Chrysanthemum, the world's leading exporter of tear gas. One of its neighbors, the nation of Dill, is known for its exports of sparkling wines. Dill is a very picturesque country of soaring snow-capped mountains and lush forests and the home to many celebrities and titans of industry. Chrysanthemum, by contrast, is a poor nation of scrubby vegetation and oppressed peasants and known as a leading producer of barbed wire and political refugees. When the ruling elites of Chrysanthemum are not hiding the nation's gold reserves in offshore accounts, they enjoy Dill's wines which are renowned throughout the world. Dill is aware that it is not thought of as a "tough" country so it has decided to beef up its military forces and has greatly increased its purchases of "peace keeping" equipment, including the tear gas produced by Chrysanthemum. Dill boasts some of the leading vineyards in the world and will sell its wine to Chrysanthemum because it has no desire to purchase the gasoline additive that passes for a pinot noir in that country. Similarly, Chrysanthemum, renowned among illicit arms dealers for its fine craftsmanship in explosive devices, will send its highest quality tear gas canisters to Dill because no one in Chrysanthemum needs any more tear gas.

But why does this exchange of goods take place between these countries in the first place? Might not either one decide to produce both tear gas and fine wine and not engage in trade at all? Well, that is possible, but it may be enormously difficult for Chrysanthemum, for example, to produce much wine at all due to the high levels of lead and other toxic metals in its soil. In contrast, Dill does not have a warrior culture and very few of its citizens have an interest in military goods such as tear gas and, as a result, would probably not be motivated armament factory workers. The theory of comparative advantage would cause us to look at the relative advantages enjoyed by both countries: It is far simpler for Chrysanthemum to buy the glorious wines of Dill and for Dill to purchase its tear gas from Chrysanthemum.

But what if Chrysanthemum could produce wine cheaper than Dill because the typical Chrysanthemum worker earns only one-tenth the income of a citizen of Dill? Well, the corrosiveness of most of Chrysanthemum's wines would squelch any possibility of these wines developing a widespread following. Moreover, the numerous incidents of blood poisoning resulting from the consumption of these wines would not be very appealing to the delicate sensibilities of most of the Dill citizenry. Given the innate ability of Dill to produce quality wines, the fact that Chrysanthemum may be a low-cost producer does not mean that it will have any commercial success in that market.

The underlying point of comparative advantage is that both countries will benefit by producing the goods in which they are most proficient: Dill wines and Chrysanthemum tear gas canisters. Even if Dill is less efficient in the production of both wines and tear gas canisters due to its high labor costs, it still makes sense for both Dill and Chrysanthemum to specialize in the production of wines and tear gas canisters, respectively. The reason for this arises from the opportunity cost that each country will incur in deciding to produce an additional unit of the good in which it lacks a comparative advantage. For Chrysanthemum, its low labor costs ensure that there are many people available to stomp grapes but its lack of vintner skills means that there will be tremendous waste and, ultimately, the product that results will not be very popular at all. Dill, by contrast, might venture into the arms business and take a stab at building its own tear gas canisters but due to the difficulty in recruiting workers—except for a few grandmothers with bad attitudes—it might find that it is simply too expensive in terms of foregone wine production for it to build a world-class tear gas canister industry. As a result, Chrysanthemum will still engage in trade with Dill even though its oppressed workers are paid so little that it could produce wine (of questionable quality) and tear gas canisters at an absolute lower price than its wealthy neighbor.

BALANCE OF PAYMENTS

If you are fortunate enough to have a checking account at a bank, you are undoubtedly aware that you must deposit funds into the account periodically so that the checks you write out of the account will be covered by the bank. You have probably also learned that banks may not want your checks to clear (at least the first time they are presented for payment) because they are able to charge massive fees for returned checks. Indeed, many banks have become very dependent on fees from overdrawn accounts. To avoid these fees, you must always take care to ensure that the deposits (credits) to your account always exceed the withdrawals (debits) out of your account. The government has not really learned this lesson very well but individual citizens have no choice because we cannot print money without being sent to prison for very long periods of time.

The individual checking account gives us a starting point to understand how the balance of payments in the international system works. No doubt we all enjoy depositing large checks into our accounts, but we do not necessarily enjoy writing even larger checks to cover our expenses. Unlike national governments, the deposits made by individual bank customers such as yourself must at least be equal to the withdrawals from that same account or else you will receive nasty letters and threatening phone calls from your creditors. Deposits make us happy because they increase our account balance and, possibly, our self-esteem. Withdrawals in the form of cash or checks are another matter; they are debits to the account that reduce our account balance and, often, our sense of self-worth. Many of us engage in a painful exercise every so often called balancing our account where we discover that our deposits were far less than we remembered and our withdrawals actually dwarfed the town budget.

The balance of payments can be thought of as a balancing of the national checkbook that contains all the transactions made by all individuals and organizations in this country with all of the individuals and organizations of every other country over a specified period of time such as a calendar year. Needless to say, this is a slightly more complicated checkbook than the one in your dresser drawer but the important point to remember is that it must always be in balance—a state of affairs that has eluded my own checking account for the past decade.

The balance of payments consists of two types of transactions: the current account and the capital account. The current account consists of transactions involving goods, services, investment income and transfer payments. The capital account tallies the flows of both capital and foreign aid in and out of the country. This is all very interesting to discuss but it does sound somewhat abstract and, dare we say, dull. We can better understand how some of these transactions are recorded in the checkbook of all check books—the balance of payments ledger— by focusing on the activities of a couple of individuals—Robert in the United States and Marie in Great Britain. Suppose that Robert stumbles across a box of fine black china that was originally used by the notorious fifth Duke of Dumbdumbshire. Such a find is quite rare. Needless to say, Robert's find attracts widespread attention and ignites a bidding war among collectors of the Duke's appalling table settings. Finally,

Marie, a resident of London, and a fifteenth-generation descendant of the Duke, tenders the winning offer of $100,000 for the china.

How would this transaction be recorded in the balance of payments? Robert would gently box up the china and send it on its way to Great Britain. This would represent an export of $100,000 to Great Britain. As Marie is not sending goods back to Robert in return, the result is a trade deficit of $100,000. This entry is not recorded in the balance of payments against Marie but is instead tallied against Great Britain. So Great Britain, through no fault of its own, now has a trade deficit of $100,000. with the United States.

But what about the $100,000 payment that Marie is sending in return for the china? Although Robert will receive the money, the balance of payments ledger will record the United States as having a capital surplus of $100,000 with respect to Great Britain. This entry on the capital account will reflect the fact that $100,000 of capital has flowed from Great Britain to the United States to pay for the china. As noted above, the transactions will balance out to $0; the fact that this china is among the ugliest of objects ever crafted does not factor into the entries that will appear on the balance of payments. But more than a few people in the United States will breathe a sigh of relief when the china is put on the plane and sent to its new home across the pond.

FREE TRADE

Free trade is as much a philosophical orientation as it is an economic concept. If you are a proponent of free trade and advocate that tariffs, quotas and other barriers to trade be dismantled to increase the flow of goods and services among nations, then you are probably inclined to be somewhat liberal in your political leanings and have a healthy distrust of governmental authority. Or you may be a diehard conservative who has a healthy distrust of governmental authority. Certainly there is at least a 50 percent chance that one of these statements is correct. What is even more likely to be correct is that most economists believe that free trade lowers the costs of goods and services for all nations. The freer movements of goods and services also force domestic industries to become more competitive or else face possible extinction.

The banner of free trade is waved by many nations, most of whom do not always practice what they preach. They are always in favor of other nations reducing their barriers to trade and increasing their imports, but they are not quite so anxious to reciprocate in kind as it can create domestic strife when workers in uncompetitive industries are idled or factories can no longer produce goods to compete with imported goods. Because economists typically prefer to see manufacturers of goods supply their products to consumers at the lowest possible prices, they will break out in hives if someone suggests that barriers to trade such as tariffs or quotas should be imposed by a country—regardless of whether policymakers are concerned about protecting the country's domestic companies or merely increasing government revenues. Free trade is thus a concept and an ideal towards which nations may strive, but it is fair to say that no nation has ever truly eliminated all impediments to trade—except in the minds of delusional policymakers.

Tariffs, which are calculated based upon the values of imported goods. and quotas, which limit the numbers of particular types of goods that can be brought into the country, are two of the more obvious means by which a nation may seek to reduce the inflow of goods across its borders. But those who sit atop the pyramids of power in the government have other ways to keep out those less expensive foreign goodies. For one thing, they can pass regulations requiring all foreign automobile manufacturers, for example, to install special pollution control equipment consisting of aerodynamic, 6-foot-tall exhaust pipes to meet domestic air pollution emission standards. Regardless of the nature of the regulations, it is easy to see how the peculiar idiosyncrasies of the bureaucrat writing the regulations that a foreign company must meet to sell its goods in this country could be arbitrary and capricious. This danger is ameliorated somewhat by the requirement that public hearings must typically take place before regulations are formally adopted so that the public is given the right to comment upon the bone-headedness of the regulation.

Free trade advocates are also frequently annoyed by so-called domestic content requirements, which require foreign manufacturers to use a certain percentage of domestically-produced materials and equipment in the construction of their products—such as automobiles. A manufacturer of tractors in the police state of Grift, for example, might be required to make sure that a fixed percentage of the parts of the tractor are actually manufactured in the United States in order for its tractors to be sold here. Domestic content legislation is very popular with local voters because it may help protect the jobs of the people who supply those materials. But economists will be less enthusiastic because they will ask whether these requirements will simply prop up more inefficient domestic producers and cause consumers to pay higher prices for the tractors.

Each nation wants total access to the markets of the world but also wants to protect its own industries from being decimated by lower-priced imported goods. These domestic considerations will always weigh heavily in the calculus of policymakers to decide how much or how little to open their own markets to foreign goods. Their actions will prompt reactions by foreign governments who seek the same open markets for their own products but also wish to protect their own industries. Because of the inherent conflict in a world in which every nation wishes to minimize imports and maximize exports, a number of treaties have been enacted in the post-World War II era which are designed to reduce barriers to trade. They have led to a massive increase in trade among the countries of the world and have contributed to improvements in the standards of living of millions of people.

PROTECTIONISM

Protection is a word that has positive connotations for most of us as it evokes images of security, safety, comfort and reliable prophylactic devices. For economists, however, protectionism is a dirty word—a term that rankles most economists because it arises in the context of a philosophy of self-interest exhibited by nations seeking to protect their own domestic industries from foreign competitors. Indeed, the word "protectionism" clearly conveys the idea of insulating homegrown factories and workers from external market forces that might otherwise be economically disruptive.

The problem with a single country going down the path of protectionism is akin to eating several pieces of heavily-frosted cake. The first step, in which you triple the tariffs on all foreign goods and thus essentially exclude them from the home market, is met with cheers by workers and shoppers alike because the workers know that they will be able to keep their jobs (at least for a while) and the shoppers can still choose from the less expensive foreign goods on the shelves of the nation's stores. This is the euphoria associated with the first slice of cake. As time goes on, however, you find that raising tariffs against the products of other countries, not unexpectedly, causes those countries to throw a tantrum and increase their tariffs on the products coming from your country. By effectively cutting off many of the foreign markets for your own country's products, you have put a huge dent in the overseas sales of many of the same businesses that you were trying to protect with the tariffs in the first place. You might feel some indigestion upon learning of this outcome, much like that experienced after wolfing down a second piece of cake. The shoppers might still be compliant but would not fail to notice that many of the less expensive foreign products that they used to buy, such as ill-fitting shoes and toys that do not always pass safety inspections, can no longer be found on the shelves. But because you are an all-knowing leader, you decide to keep the tariffs in place, raising your proverbial middle finger to the rest of the world. Unfortunately, your steely determination to continue blocking those sullied foreign goods from the pristine shores of your police state will begin to feel like that third piece of cake. At this point, many of your factories will have cut back their hours and laid off many of their workers. Also unsettling is that the nation's shoppers will have realized that all they have to choose from now are the more expensive domestically-produced ill-fitting shoes and toys. The fact that many of them may have lost their jobs due to the steep decline in foreign sales is an added problem which is causing more than a few to question your unrivalled brilliance as an economic thinker and, in many cases, to fetch their pitchforks and torches.

Although protectionism has a negative connotation, there are some arguments in favor of walling off your domestic markets from the outside world. The so-called "infant industry" argument is often raised to justify restrictions on imports when a country is trying to transition from an agrarian economy to a more advanced industrial economy. However, these restrictions are supposed to be limited to only that amount of time needed for these new companies to grow enough to be able to compete on the international stage. The problem, of course, is that these very same companies will enjoy being sheltered from their foreign nemeses and will often try to persuade the government to leave the barriers in place longer than would be economically justified. The challenge is to determine how best to weigh the tradeoff between a growing, albeit inefficient, domestic industry and increasingly closed foreign markets.

GLOBALIZATION

Globalization is the polar opposite of autarky (economic independence): the yin of global interdependence to the yang of total self-sufficiency. It is an economic concept that refers to the flattening of the costs of trade between nations so that goods made in one country can be sold for comparable prices in another country. As such, it is a phenomenon that is tied to both the reduction in the costs of transporting goods and the increase in the speed at which those goods can be moved from one country to another. Although the term globalization has become one of those words that people on television blather about, it has conceptually been with us since the rise of the railroad systems in Europe and the United States in the early nineteenth century; the applicability of the term has only expanded with the popularization of air travel and container shipping in the twentieth century.

At its very core, globalization involves the reduction of transportation costs so that the poison-tipped barbed wire made in one country can be sold at a comparable price to the hand-crafted barbed wire manufactured in a neighboring country. But the degree to which one country's poison-tipped barbed wire is going to be able to compete against the "kinder, gentler" barbed wire of another is also going to be a function of the costs of production in both countries.

Reducing transportation costs is one way, but only one way, that markets can be further integrated. The two countries could agree to reduce their tariffs on each other's barbed wire products, which would, in turn, lower the prices of the products in each country and presumably result in increased sales. The first country could also lift the quotas it had long before imposed on the second country's barbed wire products.

But transportation is not the only factor driving the trend toward the greater integration of national economies throughout the world. A growing web of communication technologies—backed up by a world-wide network of satellites and computer servers—has brought the cacophony of the Internet to most of the world's population. A shepherd in Country A can now order an inflatable sheep doll with lifelike wool from an online vender located in Country B, who can arrange to have the sheep doll shipped directly from the manufacturer in Country C to the shepherd in a matter of days. The Internet is only the most recent advance in communications among people that began with the telegraph and the telephone more than a century ago and has seen the merger of audio and visual technologies in the modern smartphone. Improved transportation and communications have also given rise to several other factors that have contributed to the economic interdependence of states in the modern era: the flow of capital and labor across borders and the worldwide reduction of transport costs.

MULTINATIONAL FIRMS

Multinational firms or MNCs, as their name implies, are corporations that operate in different countries around the world. In general, MNCs maintain a corporate headquarters in one country and then set up affiliates in other countries that engage in the production, distribution and sale of the items manufactured by the MNC. There are various ways in which the operations of an MNC can be set up, depending on how deeply it wishes to involve itself in the local economy. It can minimize its investment in foreign nations by exporting its products directly from the home country to the foreign country and selling them through local distributors. If the MNC wishes to maintain more control over the manner in which its products are sold in foreign markets, however, it may wish to set up its own wholly owned distribution networks. Alternatively, the MNC may choose to manufacture its products in the host country to take advantage of lower wage and resource costs and perhaps to evade government import restrictions. The strategies vary widely and obviously depend on an array of legal, political and economic factors.

The story of the Gargantuan Store, which sells large-scale versions of every product imaginable—ranging from golf balls that tower over small dogs to teddy bears than can barely fit through the front door of a house—can help to illustrate the various ways in which an MNC may choose to operate in foreign countries. First, one has to understand that the Gargantuan Store has an "in your face" attitude toward anyone who dares to question its corporate mission to sell oversized products of all types to every person in every country around the world. Whether there is actually a need for many of these products has not been considered because so many of them are sold to shoppers who are amazed by their sheer scale as opposed to their actual utility in the home or office. After all, how helpful can a vacuum cleaner the size of a riding lawnmower be to most people living in a one-bedroom apartment? But there is apparently an enormous demand for gag gifts and perhaps that is the audience that the Gargantuan Store has been so skillful in identifying and capturing.

So, the day has come for the Gargantuan Company to unveil its newest line of high-octane caffeine tablets under the "UP!" logo, each of which is the size of a hockey puck. But the corporate executives are unsure as to how they wish to market these super-sized tablets overseas. As a result, certain decisions need to be made, particularly with regard to the manufacturing and distribution of these tablets in foreign countries—including hitherto untapped markets such as the gulag nation of Hath. So after leaving a few briefcases of cash with representatives of the Hath embassy, the Gargantuan Company signs an agreement to export 50,000,000 UP! tablets to Hath. Although the company had originally planned to set up a factory to make the pills in Hath, the board decided that it would be more prudent to see how the demand for the UP! tablets grows over time before investing the millions of dollars needed to build a manufacturing facility. They were also undoubtedly concerned about the capricious nature of Hath politics in which governments come and go as quickly as the morning trains; today's agreement to build a factory might be torn up next week by the successor government. Indeed, they have erasable plaques on all the desks of the government ministers so that each of the incoming officers can merely rub out the names of their predecessors instead of going to the trouble to have new brass plates engraved.

If the UP! tablet is a massive success in Hath, then the wisdom of exporting the UP! tablets there will have been demonstrated. Even though none of the people of Hath who have tried the UP! Tablets have been able to sleep, any concerns about people wandering around frantically, aimlessly, bleary-eyed and babbling incoherently are soon forgotten as the monies roll in from the Hath distributors. But suppose that a month or two passes and then, true to form, the government collapses and a new government takes over and the newly appointed ministers mark up their desk plaques as per the custom there. The new prime minister gives a blistering inaugural speech attacking all foreign companies doing business in Hath and pledges to ban all imports to end the "plundering" of the country's wealth by "blood-sucking foreign vampires." The Prime Minister is not a fan of the multinational firm and does not view their activities as being purely benevolent. Moreover, his strident attacks cause great concern among the members of the Gargantuan board, several of whom suggest ceasing sales operations altogether in Hath. However, others vote to stay the course and see what happens.

The perils of doing business in unstable countries becomes apparent when the new Hath government passes a law requiring any foreign company wishing to do business to set up a joint venture with the Hath government and manufacture their goods in the country.

Now the Gargantuan board must revisit the idea of building a factory there, which, despite the $5 million price tag, is approved. So the factory is built and Gargantuan hires local workers who are finally beginning to come down from their initial UP! high as well as a few government lackeys who are there, as required by the new law, to "make sure nothing bad happens to the factory." Now the Gargantuan Company can manufacture as many tablets as the citizenry can swallow without fears of the government closing off the country to imports.

But the on-site factory has created a whole new set of issues for the company. First, it has a significant fixed investment and is more vulnerable in a financial sense to changes in the ever-fluid political landscape there. In short, the next government could toss out the law that forced Gargantuan to build the factory in the first place and, if it so chose, it could take over the factory altogether and toss the Gargantuan supervisors out of the country. Perhaps of greater concern is the potential theft of trade secrets associated with the manufacturing process of the UP! tablets. With the factory being located in Hath, it is not out of the realm of possibility that someone could steal the formula for the tablets on his own or for the government itself. The worst outcome here would be that the government of Hath takes over the factory and begins manufacturing the Up! tablets under the loosely disguised hipster name 'SUP! to sell the very same product to the citizens of Hath and, ultimately, consumers in other countries.

Even though the Gargantuan Company could try to seek legal remedies against the government of Hath in the event it nationalized the factory, such a process would take time and be very expensive. Indeed, it would probably find itself better served to try to lobby the government of the home country (the country in which Gargantuan is headquartered) to take punitive actions against Hath such as closing its markets to the import of any products from there. Or it might seek some type of resolution with the government which, in most cases, would involve the payments of cash to many of the individuals who have already participated in the bonus program that has been unwittingly set up by the Gargantuan Company for the Hath thugocracy.

THE GOLD STANDARD

Every so often a politician or even an entire political party—aghast at the trillions of dollars of government debt that has accumulated over the past few decades—will declare that the country must return to the gold standard. Indeed, some economists who worry that the government will continue to increase its spending by pressing the accelerator of the government printing presses to the floor, suggest that we could enjoy a more stable, prosperous economy by tying the dollar to a tangible asset such as gold. Because very few of us consider the government to be particularly adept at—or even interested in—balancing its books, the idea of constraining the growth of government spending by pegging changes in the money supply to changes in the value of the gold bullion stashed underneath the government's mattresses is an appealing prospect.

A worldwide gold standard would bring a certain degree of order to the global financial system because all currencies would be fixed in value relative to gold. These currencies would all have fixed values relative to each other as well. As an example, if it took $50 to purchase one ounce of gold and 100 kroner to purchase that same ounce of gold, then 1 dollar would necessarily be worth 2 kroner. Such a setup would offer predictability and stability to both traders and businesses alike. It would also greatly limit the autonomy of individual nations because they would all be tied into this very rigid international financial system.

But there are some difficulties that would arise if we were to link the national money supply to the value of the nation's gold reserves—not the least of which is the loss of the same discretion that policymakers currently exercise (and some say, abuse) in determining how much to increase or decrease the money supply at a given time in response to changes in the state of the economy. Reining in an out-of-control government that is spending far beyond its means sounds like a good idea. However, if the money supply is tied to the value of the nation's gold reserves, the government may find itself unable to act during a national emergency because it cannot increase its spending unless it is able to increase its gold reserves accordingly.

Suppose that a dam collapses and a wall of water cascades through a valley and floods several towns. We would expect the government to spring into action and send rescue workers and supplies to help the victims of this disaster accompanied, of course, by preening politicians who talk about their empathy for the victims while making sure to show their better sides to the television cameras. But we would be outraged if the government declined to send any assistance to the stricken area because it had already spent every last dollar that it could, based upon the value of its gold reserves. Indeed, the popular distress would probably not be alleviated even if the government issued a very sincere apology for its inaction.

By pegging the number of dollars that a country can print to the value of its gold reserves, the government is essentially tying its hands and limiting its ability to bring its financial resources to bear in times of trouble. Indeed, the extent to which the gold standard hobbled the ability of the US government to stimulate the economy during the Great Depression is one of the primary reasons that the government abandoned it in 1933. Once freed from the straitjacket imposed by the gold standard, the government was free to pursue expansionary fiscal policies and gradually reawaken the moribund economy. Although dollars could still be converted into gold for another four decades, this convertibility ended in 1971 and the dollar became the high-flying, free-floating, fun-loving fiat currency that it is today.

But if we are so worried about the recklessness of unending deficit spending, then should we not consider going back to the gold standard? Very few economists are in favor of such a plan because of the fact that there simply is not enough gold in the world to back the currency of the United States, let alone the currencies of the other developed nations of the world. Were a new gold standard to be imposed by a benevolent dictator such as myself, much of the money supply would have to be drained out of the economy and a massive recession—perhaps even a depression—would ensue because the money supply far exceeds the current value of the nation's gold reserves. Even if the nation decided to implement a more gradual reduction of the money supply over time, the resulting slowdown in economic activity would cause great pain to many people and perhaps lead to significant social unrest.

THE BRETTON WOODS AGREEMENT

As World War II came to a close and the true devastation to the world economy became all the more apparent, policymakers of the leading industrial nations began to plan for a new international system that would promote economic growth among nations, create a framework for the exchange of foreign currencies and stabilize the comparative values of national currencies.

Although many of the participants had hoped to meet on the sunny beaches of Florida or the French Riviera, their travel agents managed to obtain very discounted tour packages that took 730 delegates representing 44 countries to Bretton Woods, New Hampshire—which is only 92 miles from the beaches of the Atlantic coast. Once they got over their initial annoyance about not being able to wander on the "naturalist" beaches along the Mediterranean coast or to go to lavish dinner parties aboard yachts owned by Greek shipping tycoons in Monaco, they began a series of very productive meetings in which they created three institutions that have greatly influenced the global economy to the current day: (1) the International Monetary Fund (IMF) to help advise countries how best to reform their economies in order to promote economic growth; (2) the World Bank to provide low interest loans to poor countries to spur economic development; and (3) the General Agreement on Tariffs and Trade (GATT) which is now known as the World Trade Organization (WTO), which oversees a wide variety of trade agreements and implements the rules for the participating countries to abide by in their trading relationships with each other. For those who enjoy committing acronyms to memory, the Bretton Woods Agreement was a windfall discovery; it also set off an explosive expansion in world trade that has grown exponentially for the past seven decades with an average annual increase in global trade of nearly 7 percent per annum. Indeed, the WTO website itself boasts that global exports have increased nearly 250-fold since the late 1940s.

Because the United States was the only major industrialized nation that had not suffered catastrophic damage during World War II, it was able—in the paraphrased and somewhat mangled words of Theodore Roosevelt—to speak loudly and swing a big stick. It insisted that the Bretton Woods system be based upon both the US dollar and gold as the United States controlled more than half of the world's gold supply at that time. The idea was to maintain a system of fixed exchange rates among nations with the US dollar and gold providing the foundation. This system prevailed for nearly a quarter of a century but was abandoned in 1971 when the United States decided to end the convertibility of the dollar to gold. The reason for this decision was that foreign trading nations holding US dollars wished to convert them to actual gold because they liked to have shiny, beautiful gold bars more than crinkly, frayed dollar bills. The United States, for its part, realized that if everyone kept turning their tattered dollars in for lustrous gold, it would soon not have enough gold in its vaults to make a mouthful of dental fillings. As a result, the United States stopped exchanging gold bullion for dollars and ushered in a new era of freely floating currencies.

The end of the convertibility of the dollar to gold also put an end to the notion of asset-backed currencies. This was a pleasing development for most policymakers because nothing grates more than not being able to fire up the government printing presses and throw untold amounts of money at all sorts of real and imaginary problems. The dollar itself, following the end of convertibility, became a so-called fiat currency, in which its value was not tied to a tangible asset (as had been the case with gold) but instead dependent on the willingness of people to hold it and exchange it for goods and services. So long as people continued to believe in the viability of the dollar—coupled with the government's willingness to throw anyone into prison who dared to offer a competing currency that might challenge the government's seigniorage monopoly—the primacy of the dollar would be ensured.

The development of so-called crypto-currencies such as bitcoin and ripple—which are digital assets exchanged outside of the traditional banking system and distributed through an electronic ledger known as a blockchain—may pose a significant challenge to the dominance of the dollar as well as other national currencies in the future. However, these digital currencies are still in their infancy and are subject to many of the same criticisms that are lobbed at fiat currencies (e.g., no assets backing the value of the currency). They are also hindered by the fact that they can essentially be put out of business if the national governments of the world should collectively decide that they wish to continue exercising a currency monopoly within their respective borders and outlaw all other (that is, non-government issued) currencies.

EXCHANGE RATE SYSTEMS

Many people are surprised to learn that currencies are bought and sold much like everyday household products such as a pound of butter or a loaf of bread or a box of laundry detergent. Of course, there are not many supermarkets where you can go pick up 1 million Swiss francs or sell off 100 million euros but that is more an illustration of the limitations that still must be overcome before these establishments can truly claim to be "full service." But the important point is that the price of a particular currency at any given moment reflects both the demand for and the supply of that currency. If currency traders suddenly decide that they must have all the pesos that they can lay their hands on, then this spike in demand will cause the price of pesos to rise relative to that of other currencies. Conversely, if these very same traders decide that dollars are "icky" and decide to dump them in favor of more "friendly" currencies such as the Russian rouble, then the price of dollars will fall and the prices these traders are willing to pay for these other currencies will appreciate accordingly.

In a floating exchange system, the currencies of each of the nations are permitted to rise and fall as dictated by changes in the demand for and the supply of each of those currencies. For those freewheeling monetary enthusiasts, the floating exchange system can be both as exhilarating and as terrifying as riding a roller-coaster standing up while nursing a hangover. Central banks are theoretically supposed to allow the values of their respective currencies to adjust until the demand and supply for them equalize. But any decision to leave the valuations of the individual currencies to the vagaries of the market may have consequences for both their respective governments and their economies: A rapidly appreciating currency can make a country's exports much more expensive and have a detrimental impact on employment whereas a currency that drops like a rock can result in a rapid increase in the prices of products from other countries and thereby set off a nasty spat of inflation.

Regardless of whether or not there is a freely float-ing exchange system, national governments are not really able to restrain themselves from getting involved in efforts to manipulate the values of their currencies. One of the most popular tricks of the trade is to devalue the currency and thus cause it to fall in price relative to that of other currencies. Why would a country want to cause the value of its currency to decline? Would not a falling currency be considered a sign of economic weak-ness or national sloth? The answer lies in the impact of a cheaper currency on the prices of a country's imports. A devalued currency means that the country's exports are cheaper for other countries to purchase and so, if all goes well, the volume of exports should increase which should, in turn, have a positive impact on domestic employment levels. The problem, of course, is that every other country is also trying to increase its exports at the expense of its trading partners and will often devalue their own currencies to offset any temporary advantage that may have been gained by the initial perpetrator. The result may be a race down the economic rabbit hole with each nation furiously devaluing its currency in response to the actions of each of the other nations but with no real long-term advantage gained by anyone.

A fixed exchange rate system is much more structured than a floating exchange rate system and appears to offer in a metaphorical sense the calm of a croquet game on a village green. But this veneer of orderliness may be an oversimplification because a fixed exchange rate system requires an ongoing effort by any participant to maintain a fixed ratio between any two currencies. While any country in a floating system can simply go off and pout in a corner if it is unhappy with the valuation of its currency relative to those of the other countries, a country in a fixed exchange rate system must engage in actions to increase or reduce the price of its currency to maintain a set value relative to the other currencies. So if the Country A blot is worth half of a Country B bile, then the blot will be tied to the bile and will be exchanged at a 2:1 ratio. The fixed rate system is far more constraining because a country will have to manage its money supply and its interest rates in order to continue maintaining these ratios. Needless to say, government policymakers do not like having any limits on either their ability to manipulate interest rates or their power to open the spigots and flood the economy with cash. As a result, fixed rate systems, while intrinsically appealing, are far more difficult to maintain (and have largely been discarded by most countries) because they require ongoing discipline and cramp the style of today's more flamboyant policymakers.

DEPENDENCY THEORY

The international system consists of wealthy states and poor states. The ranks of the wealthy states include most of the traditional industrial democracies such as the United States, the United Kingdom, Germany, France, Japan and Italy, as well as several east Asian states such as South Korea and China. The ranks of the poor states are much more numerous and include many countries in Latin America, Africa and Asia. There are also some up-and-coming nations such as India and Brazil that are not poor by some measures but which have not quite yet managed to oppress enough other countries to be considered part of the so-called First World of wealthy states.

The fact that the wealthy, predominantly European nations, have continued to remain atop the global hierarchy for generations has prompted some scholars to try to develop models to explain this continued and arguably static hierarchy in the international system. Some scholars characterize the wealthy nations as the "core" or "lucky" members and the poor nations as the "periphery" or "unlucky" members of this system as a convenient means of differentiating the "haves" from the "have-nots" in the international hierarchy. One result of this effort to understand better the persistent gaps in wealth between these two groups of nations was the development of "dependency" theory. Although it is not so widely followed these days, dependency theory was all the rage in the 1960s and 1970s. However, it does provide a theoretical perspective that still permeates much of the relations between wealthy and poor countries to the present day.

The theory itself started with the assumption that the wealthy nations of the world enjoy enormous technological and financial advantages relative to their less fortunate brethren. This gap is allegedly due in part to the ability of the more developed nations to extract more favorable terms of trade from poor states. In short, wealthy nations sell expensive manufactured goods (automobiles, machinery) to the poor nations who, in turn, are relegated primarily to selling lower-priced raw commodities (for example, copper, coffee, iron ore) to those same wealthy states. As such, the poor states, so the argument went, would be permanently relegated to being the "hewers of wood and drawers of water" for their wealthier customers. Now there is nothing inherently wrong with honest labor that involves fetching buckets of water and chopping down trees. Indeed, there are significant cardiovascular benefits to be had

by engaging in strenuous labor and developing the tra-
pezius, deltoid, pectoral and bicep muscle groups. But
the dependency theorists did not seem to be very interested in the physical benefits of hard labor; they focused
instead on what appeared to be the obstacles in the
international order that made it almost impossible for
commodity-exporting countries to develop into export-
ers of higher-valued manufactured goods.

Dependency theory developed as a reaction to
the prevailing modernization theory whose proponents
argued that all states progress along a similar path from
agricultural and commodity-based economies to higher-valued manufacturing economies. In other words, a
country has to start with some sort of resource-based
economy and export commodities such as copper or tin
or oil or fighting peacocks to earn the foreign exchange
necessary to purchase tools and machinery needed to
build higher-valued manufactured products. The problem, of course, is that those states already at the top
of the international system building such high-valued
products as airplanes and automobiles are not anxious
to cease their manufacturing activities or to allow newer,
prospective manufacturing nations to join their exclusive club. Needless to say, the existing industrial powers
have absolutely no desire to scale back, let alone shut
down, their manufacturing sectors and return to commodity-based economies. Such a transformation would
cause their standards of living to collapse and prompt
millions of newly-displaced industrial workers to look

for high ranking government officials to toss off the tops of high buildings.

The self-interests of the industrial powers would, in most cases, compel them to take whatever steps they could to at least protect their own higher-value product turf—even if they cannot prevent other nations from trying to move up the economic food chain to challenge their manufacturing primacy. Many economists sympathetic to the plight of the poor nations concluded that there was little to be gained by waiting in a line that never seemed to move very much. So it did not require a great intellectual leap for most dependency theorists to conclude that the international system is inherently skewed against the poor states and that they have little hope of following a traditional path of development. After all, the current economic powers were, in large part, the first industrial powers and so they did not need to displace other wealthy nations on their way up the development ladder.

What do the dependency theorists suggest if the international economic system is rigged to prevent most poor countries from developing industries that can export higher-valued manufactured goods to the wealthier states? Well, there are the usual calls for wealthier countries to provide greater foreign aid and technical assistance. However, these proposals are controversial due to the uncertainty as to the value of foreign aid itself. Some people argue that these funds often disappear into the offshore bank accounts of enterprising government officials whereas others assert that foreign assistance merely props up faltering economies and does not lead to any sort of organic development of higher-valued industries. Most of these writers call for improved infrastructure and education, and improved access to the markets of the wealthier countries. Those with greater ambitions simply declare that there should be a massive redistribution of wealth from the rich states to the poor states and that such enormous capital flows will somehow enable poor states to short circuit the development process. Not surprisingly, most rich states are skeptical about the value of such large capital transfers and doubt that infusions of cash will do anything more than to enable the higher-ups in poor states to purchase palatial estates and private jets.

EXPORT GROWTH ECONOMICS

Any intrepid explorer rambling through the thickets of classical economics would probably conclude that all economic activity is a function of inputs of capital and labor. The capital can consist of factories, equipment, and raw materials, whereas the labor is, of course, the workers who rouse themselves out of bed every day (except for weekends, federal, state and local holidays and days of protest and meditation and contemplation) and they show up for work at least a few months out of the year. The goods and services produced by these workers are consumed by the citizenry and, to varying degrees, exported to other countries. According to capitalistic theologians such as Adam Smith and David Ricardo, it was this melding of capital and labor that would ultimately enable a nation to develop and its population—if it was not overwhelmed by the depressing specter of Malthusian economics—to prosper.

But what if you lived in a country that was relegated to the backwaters of the international economic system and had largely missed the Industrial Revolution? What if your country was still dependent on subsistence agriculture or extractive industries such as mining or even low-wage, labor-intensive enterprises such as sewing stuffed dolls with scary-looking faces? What if the closest thing your country could claim to a high-tech industry was several makeshift factories where obedient workers assembled alarm clock radios and plastic fish that move to the tunes of songs that were popular when your grandparents were attending high school? How might you shift the seemingly dismal future of your nation from the continued role of an impoverished commodity producer to a wealthy industrial power—particularly when there already are a number of other industrial powers ahead of you in the international hierarchy? Well, you could throw your hands up in disgust and move to a wealthy industrial country and not worry about the fate of your fellow citizens. Or you could take stock of the ways in which you could enrich your country and gradually help it to move up the ranks of the international system.

This was the problem faced by a number of countries in the mid-twentieth century, particularly those along the eastern Asian coast such as South Korea, Hong Kong, Taiwan and Singapore (now known as the "Four Asian Tigers"). Many of these countries had only recently freed themselves from the rule of their colonial overlords after having suffered enormous devastation during World War II and were, by most accounts, economically moribund. Needless to say, it is difficult to build up a stable, prosperous society when enemy soldiers are shooting at your citizens driving their tanks up and down your streets and dropping bombs on your homes and businesses. However, the leaders of these countries began implementing policies in the 1950s and 1960s that emphasized labor-intensive, low-cost manufacturing industries which targeted the domestic markets of wealthy foreign countries. At the same time, these countries also erected trade barriers to protect their own nascent industries from being overwhelmed by foreign competitors. Over time, the Four Asian Tigers—not to be confused with the technopunk quartet of the same name that sports brightly-dyed hair and offers songs that have been likened to the sounds of a truck hitting the ground after falling off the roof of a 10-story parking garage—developed sophisticated high-income economies offering products ranging from computers and cell phones to automobiles and semiconductors. This so-called "Asian miracle" was facilitated by comparatively low taxation rates, significant investments in education and infrastructure, and a fairly widespread distribution of income among the citizenry.

Although the Four Asian Tigers (the countries—not the "musical" group) followed somewhat different paths to develop world-class manufacturing sectors, they all implemented national economic strategies that focused on improving worker productivity and expanding the sales of their products in overseas markets. These countries also avoided excessive budget deficits and managed their currencies so as to keep the prices of their exports from becoming too expensive relative to the products of foreign competitors. Unlike many other countries seeking to claw their way out of the poverty swamp, the Four Asian Tigers also enjoyed the active support of the United States; it offered access to its domestic markets to bolster the economies of the Four Asian Tigers—which coincided with its own strategy to contain the spread of communism in Asia. Most economists who study the development paths followed by successful nations in the modern era believe that the Four Asian Tigers would not have become modern economic powerhouses in the absence of pervasive government efforts to grow key higher-valued manufacturing industries.

POST-INDUSTRIAL ECONOMICS

Industrialized nations such as the United States, Germany, Japan and China are fortunate because they have many factories that manufacture high-value items ranging from disposable diapers and first-rate hair grooming products to jet plane engines and lollipops that take hundreds of licks to consume. As such, their manufacturing sectors constitute significant parts of their respective economies, employing tens of millions of workers in a variety of fields, many toiling away on the factory floor, waiting for the moment (just after lunch-time)—according to Karl Marx—when they would all simultaneously decide to overthrow their oppressors—real or imaginary. Manufacturing jobs are highly desired by most policymakers because they often provide work-ers with higher pay and better benefits than even the most glamorous jobs in the service sector, such as the deep fryer operator at a local fast food restaurant or the customer service representative who "accidentally" hangs up over and over again on disgruntled callers daring to complain about their purchases.

Due to the insidious effects of globalization, how-ever, many developed nations have gradually seen much of their manufacturing sectors move off-shore in search of lower-labor costs. After all, if you can hire a worker in sub-Sahara Africa for $2.00 per hour to mix phospho-rescent hair coloring products for teen-age malcontents instead of having to pay $15.00 per hour to a worker in the United States to do the same thing, then you will probably leap at the chance to move your operations overseas. You may also feel that these foreign work-ers—who have formerly eked out a meager existence on $5.00 a day will be far more grateful to receive a crisp new $2.00 bill for every hour of mind-numbing work as opposed to their "overpaid" American counterparts who grumble and complain about everything such as the open vats of toxic wastes strewn all over the workplace. In any event, cheap labor costs have caused many companies to set up manufacturing operations all over the world and, in many instances, cut back or completely shut down their activities in their home countries. These factory closings have, of course, cost many millions of workers their jobs.

This shifting of manufacturing activity to countries with lower labor costs coupled with the increasing size of the services sector in the economies of developed countries has given rise to what some economists refer to as "post-industrial" economies. This is a nice way of saying that the services sectors in these developed countries are now generating a greater share of the national wealth than the manufacturing sector. Some commentators are perfectly fine with the idea of a shrunken manufacturing presence because they argue, with some justification, that the hydraulic toenail clippers that used to cost $20.00 in the United States can now—joy of joys—be manufactured in Upper Volta and then exported back to the United States and sold for only $5.00—which represents a huge savings in the average consumer's toenail cosmetology expenses. So consumers enjoy the lower expenses of purchasing these imported shiny new hydraulic toenail clippers but the workers who used to assemble these hydraulic toenail clippers in the United States may find themselves working reduced hours or out of a job altogether. Advocates of the benefits of free trade are fine with this outcome because they would argue that Upper Volta now has a comparative advantage in the manufacturing of hydraulic toenail clippers due to its extremely low labor costs. But the analysis is not so straightforward because it does not take into account the higher social costs that will be incurred by the unemployed workers in the United States who are suddenly no longer able to earn a living at the hydraulic toenail clipper factory. Indeed, many of these same workers may be unable to find jobs quickly and will have to rely on public assistance to help offset some or all of their living expenses. Thus society as a whole will be adversely impacted because it must now provide monies to help these displaced workers find new jobs—perhaps working as vendors at baseball games selling knick-knacks made in Upper Volta.

But the shift in post-industrial societies is not only toward services but also new knowledge-oriented industries in which ideas and creativity are a significant driver of economic activity. Many economists laud the advent of a so-called "creativity culture" in which artists, educators, managers, designers, actors, authors and other persons (who have no real ability to build homes or buildings or cars or anything with moving parts) become enormously influential because they have, in many cases, advanced degrees from fancy universities. The unfortunate byproduct of this shift is that those individuals who actually do know how to make things out of metal, wood, glass and other materials often find themselves out of work because of the declining importance of manufacturing in this new "knowledge-based" economy. Fortunately, the government is always ready to offer job training programs for newly-displaced workers so that they can learn vital skills such as writing computer code for cutting-edge video games.

Knowledge and data are considered by many to be the currency of the post-industrial age. The social media industry has exploded in the past two decades to become an enormous multi-billion dollar player in the national economy by offering free accounts to users in exchange for personal data. These companies then sell the information provided by their users to advertisers who in turn are able to more precisely target their desired audiences on those very same social media platforms. Privacy concerns do not seem to pose an enormous problem: Many people are happy to tell the world about whatever mundane things they may be doing at two o'clock in the morning, such as doing "internet research" or "shaving their backs" or posting photographs of their latest surgical procedures. Moreover, the internet search engine companies are able to collect enormous amounts of data merely by merely tracking the websites that are visited by each of their subscribers and then selling this information to advertisers. According to surveys of internet users, the most commonly visited websites are those offering religious counsel, patriotic songs and instructions as to the ways in which the user can help humanity. For some reason, however, the search engine companies themselves reveal that the most popular websites on the internet are not typically oriented toward religious or patriotic matters even though a few do show graphic videos featuring very enthusiastic actors wearing nothing more than a priest's collar or a nun's cornette or perhaps a scarf cut from the American flag.

THE DIGITAL ECONOMY

The way in which people communicate with each other and buy and sell goods and services has been transformed by the creation of the internet and the rise of e-business and e-commerce. These advances have been accompanied by the development of the smartphone—which has brought the worldwide web to every user and given people the ability to communicate not only via voice but also by using emails and text messaging (the latter of which has been a boon to teen-agers who can dash off pithy, one-word responses to the annoying queries of their parents who dare ask them such prying and inappropriate questions such as where they are at 4 o'clock in the morning). Text messaging has freed many tens of millions of young people from the burden of actually having to speak to their parents so that they have more time to devote to their studies in advanced calculus, biochemistry and English literature.

The digital economy has nothing to do with fingers

and toes but is a catch-all term that refers to the evolving internet economy which is based on digital computing technologies. It is also a catchier title than some other possible synonyms such as the automated economy, the cybernated economy, the programmed economy, or the computerized economy—all of which sound a little Big Brotherish. This new internet-based economic system has not replaced the traditional economy but has instead transformed the ways in which individuals and organizations interact with each other. The internet, computer networks and smartphones themselves have enabled billions of individuals to plug into an interconnected global network offering unlimited amounts of data and goods for sale that are available to all users at all times. It has also given rise to new industries such as internet search engines, social media companies, high tech manufacturers as well as associated service providers that operate on the worldwide web.

The fact that billions of people carry around smartphones that have their own tracking devices provides unprecedented surveillance opportunities to the smartphone companies and, possibly, government officials—which could not have ever been dreamed of by even the most authoritarian secret police services such as the now defunct East German Stasi or the Soviet Union KGB. Having people voluntarily wear and pay for their own tracking devices and, as an added bonus, taking hundreds of billions of photographs of everything around them, has made it possible for national governments to vastly expand their knowledge of the daily routines and habits of people everywhere without having to employ tens of thousands of domestic spies. Of course these very same governments routinely deny that they have even the slightest interest in the subversive activities of their populations. After all, why would anyone want to overthrow any government that provides so perfectly and completely for the needs of every individual?

The digital economy consists of a worldwide electronic network that has profoundly affected the ways in which individuals and organizations do business as well as the means by which goods and services are transported from sellers to buyers. The Porcine Clothing Company, for example, which is the largest manufacturer of porcine swimwear and formal wear in the world, has found that it has had to revamp its marketing and delivery services in order to remain competitive with other porcine clothing manufacturers. It has hired the founder's 8-year-old granddaughter to teach all the employees how to operate powerful new workstations while implementing a variety of new technologies enabling the factory managers to stay in constant touch with both the overly enthusiastic sales personnel who are prone to making ruinous business deals and the company buyers who are always on the lookout for the hottest new designs and fabrics in the porcine fashion world. It has also closed its five retail outlets—which were the only remaining stores in a string of shuttered shopping malls—and shifted almost exclusively to online marketing. Nowadays, its customers do not have to risk their lives visiting actual stores but can instead indulge in their favorite porcine fantasy purchases from the comfort of their own homes. This shift to internet marketing has also enabled the company to target its marketing efforts more precisely on social media networks by focusing on porcine fan sites and not squander digital advertising dollars needlessly by trying to market porcine products to consumers whose religious orientations prohibit them from indulging in porcine products of any kind.

AFTERWORD: WITHER SCARCITY?

The *raison d'etre* for economics has always been the ceaseless efforts by its practitioners to reconcile the infinite wants of humanity with its limited means to provide for those wants. Indeed, it is the limits of our productive capacities that force us to consider how best to utilize our resources to provide for the needs of the people. However, some individuals find economics to be depressing because it must focus on limitations and scarcity as opposed to fun and frolic. But economists are not a particularly jovial group because they are professionally charged with having to tell everyone else that you cannot always have everything you want. These are the types of individuals who you will not typically invite to a party but who would be very handy to have filling the extra seats at a lightly-attended funeral service.

But is economics still constrained by limitations? Has the internet and the rise of the digital world allowed us to circumvent the constraints that have bedeviled economic theorists since Adam Smith first decided to compile his very heavy, doorstop-worthy *Wealth of Nations* more than two centuries ago? Or do we still continue to live in the same world of finite resources that has cast such a damper over our otherwise playful personalities.

The rise of the digital world has enabled us to circumvent certain bottlenecks in the production of goods. How so? you may ask with feigned interest. Well, the Assyrian Software Company, which offers a wide variety of software programs catering to scholars specializing in the study of Assyrian languages and culture, will be able to sell, once the actual digital prototype is completed, a virtually unlimited number of its popular "Assyrian Dating Techniques" software packages online without incurring significant additional costs. The program itself can be digitally duplicated over and over again with the push of a button so that this bestselling Assyrian dating program will incur little in the way of additional manufacturing costs regardless of whether the second copy is sold or the fourteenth copy is sold or . . . well, as it turns out, only fourteen copies were sold. But the important point is that one could sell a million or ten million or a hundred million copies of the Assyrian Dating Techniques software packages online with little change in the costs of production.

Unfortunately, this ability to scale without limit and avoid additional manufacturing expenses does not extend to the physical world. We cannot duplicate houses or cars or food or clothing with the push of a button. Resources must be expended in order to create each of these items and the use of these resources necessarily precludes them from being used elsewhere to create other material objects. No one has been able to figure out how to get around this problem in the physical world even though the digital world of electronic images does offer a tantalizing glimpse into a world—albeit virtual—without limits. This digital overlay has also made possible numerous advances in the way we conduct our daily affairs in both our private and public lives but it has not enabled us to circumvent the age-old problem of satisfying infinite wants with limited means.

ABOUT THE AUTHOR

JEFFERSON HANE WEAVER is a transactional attorney who specializes in corporate law, real estate law and estate planning in Coral Springs, Florida. He received his undergraduate degree in Economics and Political Science from the University of North Carolina at Chapel Hill. He also received his J.D. and his Ph.D from Columbia University. He is the author or co-author of numerous books including The World of Physics, The Story of Physics, The Concepts of Science, The Atomic Scientists, The Story of Mathematics, The Unfolding Universe, Conquering Statistics, Conquering Mathematics, The Compact Guide to Contract Law, The Compact Guide to Tort Law, The Compact Guide to Property Law, and What are the Odds? He and his wife, Shelley, have 5 children and 3 grandchildren. He is also the co-host of the Omaha Bugle podcast.

Printed in the USA
CPSIA information can be obtained
at www.ICGtesting.com
LVHW041727291123
765083LV00002B/3